THE

Religious Beliefs

of Our Presidents

FROM WASHINGTON TO F.D.R.

THE

Religious Beliefs

of Our Presidents

FROM WASHINGTON TO F.D.R.

Franklin
Steiner

 **Prometheus Books**

59 John Glenn Drive
Amherst, NewYork 14228-2197

Published 1995 by Prometheus Books
59 John Glenn Drive, Amherst, New York 14228-2197.
716-691-0133. FAX: 716-691-0137.

Library of Congress Cataloging-in-Publication Data

Steiner, Franklin.
    The religious beliefs of our Presidents : from Washington to F.D.R. /
Franklin Steiner.
        p.   cm. — (The Freethought library)
    Originally published: Girard, Kan. : Haldeman-Julius Publications,
c 1936.
    ISBN 0-87975-975-5 (pbk. : alk. paper)
    1. Presidents—United States—Religion. I. Series.
E176.1.S72   1995
973'.099—dc20   95-10599
                                                                       CIP

Printed in the United States of America on acid-free paper.

THE FREETHOUGHT LIBRARY

Featuring Selections from the Haldeman-Julius Collection

Over a period of thirty years, publisher E. Haldeman-Julius made available to millions of readers inexpensive paperback editions of classics of literature and freethought. Prometheus is proud to be reissuing selected numbers of the renowned Blue Books, which provided a broad forum for the discussion of rationalist issues.

Additional Titles in The Freethought Library

CONTENTS

CONTENTS (Continued)

The Religious Beliefs
of Our Presidents

PREFACE

For a number of years I have promised my friends that I would produce this book. For a while other duties postponed the fulfillment of that promise. It was finished when the worst of the world-wide financial depression was upon us. This affected the book trade equally with other lines of business, which caused me to further delay publication. This, in a way, was not a disadvantage, as it enabled me to correct, revise, and make valuable additions to the book. Now, after long waiting, I take pleasure in presenting it to the public, hoping it will be an addition to reliable history and biography.

First, I wish to thank my friend Mr. Rupert Hughes, historian and dramatist, for his kindness in reading the manuscript and offering his criticisms and suggestions. This was a valuable aid, which I appreciate and am pleased to acknowledge. To Mrs. S. C. Yoemans, a surviving sister, to Mrs. Edith Roosevelt, widow of Theodore Roosevelt, to Mrs. Edith Bolling-Wilson, widow of Woodrow Wilson, thanks are due for the facts about the church membership of Presidents Cleveland, Theodore Roosevelt and Wilson. To Mr. Louis M. H. Howe, his private secretary, I owe my thanks for the facts of the religious belief of President Franklin D. Roosevelt. To Professor Roy F. Nichols, of the Department of History, University of Pennsylvania, I am indebted for knowledge of the religious views of President Franklin Pierce. Among others whose help and advice must be acknowledged are Mr. Richard J. Cooney, of Chicago, Ill., Mr. George E. Macdonald, the veteran editor of New York City, Mr. Otis G. Hammond, of the Historical Department of the State of New Hampshire, Edward Tuck, Esq., Paris, France, Mr. William Morrow, of the publishing firm of Wm. Morrow & Co., New York City; to Dr. Charles A. Beard, of Columbia University, for permission to use on the title page a quotation from his invaluable history, and other friends throughout the United States too numerous to mention. To the attendants of the Milwaukee, Wis., public library, one of the best in the United States (in which city most of this book was written), who not only placed before me the treasures of its shelves, but treated me with the highest consideration and took an interest in the progress of the work, I am deeply grateful.

Among all others, I must acknowledge the great aid I received from an old friend who died years ago, John Eleazer Remsburg (born 1848, died 1919), author, editor, lecturer, educator. For years Mr. Remsburg collected information regarding the religious views of Abraham Lincoln. He searched every book where reliable facts could be obtained. Many persons were then living, in sound health and memory, who had personally known Lincoln. Mr. Remsburg visited some of these, and wrote down their depositions. With others he corresponded. He presents the evidence of private citizens, as well as of public men who knew the great President, and were familiar with his religious views. In 1893 he published the result of his investigations in a book entitled, **Abraham Lincoln: Was He a Christian?** It is a work of 360 pages, and contains more information upon both sides of the controversy than can be found in any other book. In 1906 Mr. Remsburg incorporated this book into a larger one, entitled, **Six Historic Americans**, to which he added the facts of the religious opinions of Washington, Jefferson, Franklin, Paine and Grant. This book is still in print, and, so far as I know, no one has ever called into question any of the statements it contains. Its opponents have cautiously ignored it.

I first met Mr. Remsburg when I was a youth in high school, in 1889. I knew him until his death in 1919, knew his irreproachable integrity, and invariable accuracy, yet I have not followed him blindly. I have, when practicable, gone to the original sources and verified his quotations. Then I have added the result of my own investigations, giving evidence of which Mr. Remsburg was unaware. In one way I have followed his plan of giving the statements of both sides, of those who claimed that Lincoln was an orthodox believer, and of those who denied it; though I have been obliged to resort to condensation, giving only the testimony of the most important witnesses on both sides of the controversy.

In an appendix I have given the evidence of Lincoln's law-partner of 22 years, Mr. William H. Herndon, who, all agree, knew the real Lincoln better than anyone else. In another appendix I have dealt with the famous "Bateman Interview" of Dr. Holland, the cause of the bitter dispute which I have described. Concerning Washington, I have added, in an appendix, the conflicting statements of his private secretary, Tobias Lear, and of the Rev. Mason L. Weems, as to his deathbed scene; as well as an appendix from Sparks's **Life of Washington**, with my own comments. In the bibliography I have given an alphabetical index of the standard histories and biographies I have consulted in the general preparation of this work.

Some may say, as I have heard others say, "Well, even if all that is here said be true, it should not be published. We should be permitted to hold intact our traditions and ideals of these men." With this view I cannot agree. History and biography, if written at all, should be written truthfully.

FRANKLIN STEINER.

Milwaukee, Wis., July 30, 1936.

INTRODUCTION

A certain popular publication in a table giving information concerning the Presidents of the United States has classified them religiously as follows:

Friends (Quakers). Hoover.
Episcopalians. Washington, Madison, Monroe, General W. H. Harrison, Tyler, Taylor, Pierce, Arthur.
Presbyterians. Jackson, Polk, Buchanan, Cleveland, Benjamin Harrison, Wilson.
Methodists. Johnson, Grant, Hayes, McKinley.
Unitarians. John Adams, John Quincy Adams, Fillmore, Taft.
Reformed Dutch. Van Buren, Roosevelt.
Disciples. Garfield.
Baptists. Harding.
Congregationalists. Coolidge.

A foot-note says: "Jefferson and Lincoln did not claim membership in any Church."

While this is more accurate than most of the other tables I have seen, it contains a number of errors. If a member of the Episcopal Church is supposed to be a communicant, Washington and William Henry Harrison were not Episcopalians; and there is no evidence that Madison, Monroe, Taylor, Tyler and Arthur were. The lumping together of so many Presidents as Episcopalians is due to the fact that St. John's Church of that denomination, in Washington, is now located, as it was a hundred years ago, only 300 yards from the White House, on Lafayette Square. St. John's has always been an aristocratic, exclusive church, and required certificates of social standing from those who applied for membership. Once a young man approached President Lincoln for an office. He brought recommendations from the "best people" in Washington and elsewhere. After giving him the appointment, the President handed his references back. The young man, surprised, remarked, "Mr. President, I thought you kept recommendations and put them on file." "We generally do," said Lincoln, "but I thought yours might be of value to you in case you ever want to join St. John's Church." This church, being so near the White House, was attended by a number of Presidents, regardless of their own Church affiliations or lack of them, which is the reason some writers have classified them as Episcopalians. For instance, President Van Buren attended here, though at home, in Kinderhook, N. Y., he worshiped in the Dutch Reformed Church, the one in which he had been reared. Webster, Clay and other great statesmen of the first half of the 19th Century attended here because it was the fashionable church; though Clay was not baptized until three years before he died. and Webster while he lived in New Hampshire was a Congregationalist, and in Boston, a Unitarian.

Jackson, Polk and Buchanan all joined the Presbyterian Church after their terms in the White House had expired, as did Pierce the Episcopal Church, although none of these three Presidents had previously been members of any Church. Grant, Johnson and Hayes were not Methodists, though their wives were, which has been the excuse for counting them as members of that Church.

The religious beliefs and Church preferences of our Presidents have

8

always been a topic of public interest. Yet no writer, as far as I know, has ever investigated the subject thoroughly and given accurate information.* They have all taken certain affiliations and beliefs for granted and have given too much attention to rumor. Prejudice and self interest have, with many writers, taken the place of facts. Nearly 40 years ago I became interested in the subject, and this work is the result of what I can at least claim to be a conscientious investigation.

Two broad principles have guided me in seeking information about the religious opinions of public men. First, when such a man has in fact been religious, he has almost always made it known, either by joining some Church representing his views or by expressing them in other ways. When he has done neither, and his biographer has had little or nothing to say of his religion, it can be safely assumed that he had none that was strong or pronounced.

A man with religious convictions, particularly if they are of the orthodox, popular type, has no hesitancy in proclaiming them; in fact, such public profession is often to his advantage. If he has none, or holds some that are unpopular, it is good policy to say nothing about them. Both conditions have prevailed among public men in the past and present.

My second rule leads me to conclude that where a noted man has in fact been of a certain belief or a member of a certain Church, the fact has never been disputed. For instance, no one has ever denied that Gladstone was a communicant in the Church of England, McKinley of the Methodist Church, Benjamin Harrison, Cleveland and Wilson, of the Presbyterian Church. But in other cases, as those of Washington and Lincoln, where there have been controversies, the mass of evidence tends to prove the negative. In such cases, I intend to give the evidence, **pro** and **con** (allowing the reader to decide for himself), expressing no opinion, except where there could be no other reasonable view. That the reader may have all the information obtainable regarding the religious views of Washington, I have placed in an appendix the account of his last sickness and death, as minutely described by his secretary, Tobias Lear, who was constantly present. In the same section I have given the view of his biographer, Jared Sparks, who argues that Washington was an orthodox believer. Regarding Lincoln, I have given the statements of the friends who knew him intimately in Illinois, and who certify that while he lived in that State he was a Freethinker of the type of Thomas Paine, adding the assertions of ministers and others who claim he was converted to orthodoxy in Washington.

In speaking of these two, the greatest of our Presidents, I am aware that I shall make statements which will arouse criticism in some quarters and hostility in others. This must be expected by any writer unless he writes to be read only by a certain class of people or to sustain set popular opinions. No writer of the present day, if he professes to write truthfully, can afford to ignore the mythology that has entwined itself around the careers of great men. In fact, some of them are better known by what they were not than by what they were. Yet when a writer does paint them in their true colors in history, he runs counter to public prejudice. His consolation and his vindication lie in the great number of the myths of history which have been thoroughly exposed and are now considered fable instead of fact. William Tell, Barbara

---

*One writer, John E. Remsburg, in his **Six Historic Americans**, has given the religious views of four Presidents, Washington, Grant, Lincoln and Jefferson, which is the only attempt I know of to do justice to the subject.

Frietchie, General Lee surrendering his sword to General Grant, John Brown kissing the Negro child while on his way to the scaffold, Washington praying in the snow, Lincoln and his cabinet on their knees in prayer, are well-known instances of "The Myths of History." As in all other departments of knowledge, the scientific historical method must take the place of all those old traditions which have not met the test of truth.

Many men, and particularly public men, are assigned to membership in certain Churches because they sometimes accompany their wives to divine services. Then others, whether they attend church or not, are considered as believers and members because at the proper time they write their checks for the church budget. Every minister of standing will admit that neither of these acts is evidence of religious belief, though some ministers will claim such men as Christians as a means of advertising their Churches, if they are distinguished citizens of good repute. It must also be remembered that many men of prominence, politically, socially and commercially, give a conventional adherence to the Church for fear they might be suspected of "infidelity," which many of them regard as a most dire accusation.

I do not evaluate the church preferences of the Presidents by any of these criterions; but before I have called one of them a Methodist, a Presbyterian, an Episcopalian, or a member of any other Church, I have tried to satisfy myself by asking these questions: Was he a believer in the creed of the particular Church? Did he make a public profession? Did he observe the sacraments of the Church and conform to its rules? These methods are observed in judging the affiliations of other people, and why should it be unfair to apply them to a consideration of the religious beliefs of our Presidents?

At election time, the religious beliefs of the candidates are often considered, perhaps more so today than in the past. In the election of 1928 they were the chief issue. Yet in the face of this, it is a strange fact that prior to the election of Benjamin Harrison, in 1888, there had not been one President who was unquestionably a member of an orthodox Church at the time of his election. Those who are familiar with Ben. Perley Poor's **Reminisences of 60 Years in the National Metropolis,** published in 1886, will be impressed by the fact that our statesmen of a century ago, including our Presidents, gave more attention to the punch bowl than to the communion cup. Under the Volstead regime the chief effort of our Congressmen was to compel the people to keep sober, in which work they were backed by the ministers, who, a hundred years ago, were so busy seeking the salvation of souls from perdition that they had no time to frame political platforms or select candidates for office, to say nothing of keeping a card index telling of the opinions and doings of Congressmen. Now all is changed. The Church of today is in politics, sometimes more so than it is in religion. It is said that 90 percent of our present Congressmen are church members. It would be interesting, if it were possible, to know what the writers a century hence will say of the Congressmen of our day. It is to be hoped they will tell how we took great strides in all the other virtues, as well as in piety and sobriety; and that they will point with pride to our Websters, Clays, Calhouns and Bentons, as quite as great men as were those of the 1830's, but chastened by grace, while those of old were not.

Since this work was finished, but before its publication, a book was published in Boston which enables us to call attention to the methods of some writers who in the past have written upon this subject. It is entitled, **The Religious Background of the White House.** It is obviously more a book of religious propaganda than a work of biography and history. It munificiently camouflages the Presidents by stories of the piety of their wives, fathers, mothers, brothers, sisters, uncles and aunts. To say nothing of its minor inaccuracies, it abounds in many statements now known to be untrue, besides in many instances not giving well-known facts that would place the Presidents in an entirely different light.

Speaking of Washington and Lincoln, this writer says (p. 330): "Our first President was an habitual church attendant from his earliest years. He heads the list of Presidential communicants." Of Lincoln (p. 346): "Abraham Lincoln, long regarded by many as an Atheist [and who ever said that he was an Atheist? This writer holds the very crude notion that every one who does not believe in Christianity is an Atheist] and always cataloged with the Presidents who never united with the church, appears from evidence I herewith submit to have united with the Presbyterian Church three months before his assassination."

It is needless to say that no writer of today who places historic truth before zealotry in defense of an opinion will maintain either of these contentions.

As further proof that this writer is superficial in his knowledge of the subject, and careless in his presentation, I refer to certain statements regarding Presidents Monroe and Tyler. Of President Monroe, he says (p. 212): "The Liberalism of Paine religiously did not finally affect Monroe, however, for he continued to worship according to the Episcopal ritual. That he left the Paris mission to return to the United States may be attributed as a reason why the Paine doctrines did not 'take'." And again (p. 213): "Monroe's messages and state papers do not reflect the deep religious fervor which has actuated many of our chief executives. He has far fewer allusions to dependence on the divine creator than other executives whom we are disposed to consider less religious, and his correspondence fails to show any great religious experience."

This writer is unfortunate in his dearth of knowledge both of Paine and Monroe, and such ignorance is lamentable in one who assumes to instruct the public. It is well known that Monroe left Paris because he was **recalled**, and that neither the Liberalism of Paine nor of anyone else had anything to do with it. The supposition is that he was recalled because of his too great sympathy with the principles of the French Revolution, in which case we can scarcely say that the Liberalism did not "take."

Of two other important facts the writer seems to be unaware, and if he is aware of them he is guilty of the "sin of omission." He does not state that as soon as possible after arriving in Paris, Monroe had Paine released from the Luxembourg prison, and that the former United States minister, Gouverneur Morris, refused to use his influence to effect Paine's release. Then he does not tell, as an impartial historian should, that after Paine's release from prison Monroe took him to his own house, where he gave him a home for a year. One of the brightest chapters in the career of James Monroe was his courage in coming to the rescue of this greatly hated and persecuted man, hated and persecuted because he had dared to defy aristocracy and priestcraft.

Further, the writer of **The Religious Background of the White House** seems to be ignorant of another important fact, that Monroe was returned to France 10 years later by President Jefferson, when, in cooperation with Robert R. Livingston, he negotiated the treaty that made the Louisiana Purchase possible.

The latter part of the writer's statement, that Monroe has "fewer allusions to dependence on the divine creator than other executives," and that "his correspondence fails to show any great religious experience," seems to nullify his first assertion, for which there is no evidence, that Monroe continued to worship according to the Episcopal ritual.

In speaking of President Van Buren, the writer says (p. 360): "Martin Van Buren has always been classed as an attendant upon the services of the Dutch Reformed denomination, and such was the case most of his life. No biographer has claimed for him membership in that body or in any other. He is always included in the group of Presidents who never joined the church. The writer of this, however, browsing throughout the records and data of Columbia County, New York, has discovered evidence of Van Buren's church membership."

I have searched every book I could find that might give evidence of President Van Buren's church membership, including his **Autobiography**, published by authority of the United States government, a biography by Mr. Edward M. Shepard, and a more recent biography by Denis Tilden Lynch. I have found no such evidence. If the writer of **The Religious Background of the White House** was so fortunate as to discover it, "in the records and historical data of Columbia County, New York," he would have done searchers after truth a great service had he told them in what "document," or volume and page he found it. This he has failed to do. He admits that President Van Buren did not join any church in Washington, or in his home town of Kinderhook, N. Y., but would have us believe, without giving his authority, that he did join a church in Hudson, N.Y.

This reminds us of his other assertion, that Lincoln did not join the New York Avenue Presbyterian Church, which he attended when he attended any church, and whose pastor, Rev. Dr. Gurley, was a friend of his family; but did join another Presbyterian church in Washington "three months before his assassination." It is extremely improbable that Lincoln, "three months before his assassination," amidst the pressing cares of state, at a time when the war situation was most acute, would find time to wander among the different Washington churches to find one that he cared to join. No one has the right to ask us to believe this without the best of evidence. It is on a par with the silly yarns that Lincoln traveled in disguise to Brooklyn during the war to consult Henry Ward Beecher, for whom he had no use, and in the same manner was smuggled into Washington for the inauguration. It is like another story our writer tells of Washington begging the communion of a Presbyterian minister, when he never took it in the Episcopal churches he was in the habit of attending—which yarn he tells without the slightest thought that when an investigation was made no one would be able to find a word of evidence that it ever occurred.

But the evidence given by our writer for Lincoln joining a church "three months before his assassination," which would make it happen in January, 1865, is so curious that my readers may be pleased to inspect it, as a matter of amusement. An utterly unknown man, one Reiper, appears to have written ex-President James Buchanan that Lincoln had "joined the church." Mr. Buchanan replied in a brief letter, on February 24, 1865, in which he said he was glad to hear it and hoped he had done so in sincerity. This letter is to be found in the **Life and Letters of James Buchanan** (vol. xi, p. 380).

We need ask but three questions and this story annihilates itself. What were Mr. Reiper's means of knowing this to be a fact? If he had learned it from reliable sources, why did he impart the information solely to Mr. Buchanan? How does it happen that he knew of it, and no one else was ever informed of its occurrence? It seems to have been the secret of one man. When Calvin Coolidge, a much lesser man than

Abraham Lincoln, joined a church in Washington, we were told which church it was, and the newspapers telegraphed the fact throughout the country. Who has the temerity to assert that Abraham Lincoln joined a church in the capital to the knowledge of but one man, and he, so far as is known, told of it to but one other man? With these comments we can dismiss the story.

Of Julia Gardner Tyler, the second wife of President Tyler, and his widow, the writer of **The Religious Background of the White House** says (p. 296): "Julia Gardner Tyler died in the Exchange Hotel, Richmond, July 10, 1889, in her 70th year, in a home-like room which was opposite that in which her distinguished husband died more than **17 years before**." The writer did not appear to know that President Tyler died in the Exchange Hotel, more than **27 years before**, on January 18, 1862.

This work was not written for the purpose of upholding any Church or any religion, nor is it intended to promote irreligion. It merely endeavors to tell the truth, so far as it is to be found, regarding the views held of time and eternity, by the 31 men who, from the foundation of our government, have sat in its executive chair. It will be seen that in some cases their opinions widely differed, which is a noble tribute to the American principles of religious liberty and separation of Church and state.

CHAPTER I.

GEORGE WASHINGTON, THE VESTRYMAN WHO WAS NOT A COMMUNICANT

Born, February 22, 1732. Died, December 14, 1799. President, April 30, 1879—March 4, 1797.

FOREWORD.

That much myth and legend is to be found in most of the past biographies of George Washington is admitted by practically all conscientious and discriminating writers of today. That the "Father of His Country" has been delineated more in the character of a god or a superman than as a real human being is a fact now known to all who think as well as read. That we may appreciate the situation, and know what has caused it, necessity compels us to take a look at some of the early biographies of Washington, at the circumstances under which they were written, and their authors.

The first **Life of Washington**, and the one that has had the largest circulation, was written by the Rev. Mason L. Weems, and first published in 1800. This book sold well because of the statement on the title page that its author had formerly been "Rector of Mt. Vernon Parish." It passed through 80 editions, and more people have known Washington and known him exclusively by means of it, than through any other book. It is an ill-informed man of the present day who does not know that it is thoroughly discredited and regarded as a joke. Houghton, Mifflin & Co., the Boston publishers, have issued **The Literature of American History**, a practical anthology upon the subject. This states that if the "f" had been left out of the "life," making the title of Weems' book, **The Lie of Washington**, its real character would be aptly described. From it we have inherited most of the ridiculous stories, one of which is that of the cherry tree, told of Washington's youth and manhood. In 1927, a new edition was published as a literary curiosity. The editor, Mark Van Doren, speaks of its merits as follows:

"Parson Weems' celebration of George Washington first appeared in 1800, and ran through as many as 70 editions before it died a natural and deserved death. It died because it had done its work with complete effectiveness. Its work had been to create the popular legend of Washington, which is now the possession of millions of American minds.

"Weems was neither a 'parson,' nor 'formerly rector of Mt. Vernon parish,' but a professional writer of tracts and biographies. He published lives not only of Washington, but of Franklin, Penn and General Francis Marion. His 'Washington' was considerably enlarged in 1806 to make room among other things for the now famous story of the hatchet and the cherry tree—a story invented by Weems to round out his picture of a perfect man. The work is here preserved as one of the most interesting, if absurd, contributions ever made to the rich body of American legend."

Albert J. Beveridge, in his **Life of John Marshall** (vol. 3, pp. 231-232), describes the Rev. Mr. Weems in these words:

"Mason Locke Weems, part Whitefield, part Villon, a delightful mingling of evangelist and vagabond, lecturer and politician, writer and musician.

"Weems' **Life of Washington** still enjoys a good sale. It has been one of the most widely purchased and read books in our history, and has profoundly influenced the American conception of Washington. To it we owe the grotesque and wholly imaginary stories of the cherry tree, the planting of the lettuce by his father to prove to the boy the designs of providence and the anecdotes that make the intensely human founder of the American nation an impossible and intolerable prig."

Bishop Meade, in **Old Churches, Ministers and Families of Virginia** (vol. 2, p. 234), says of Weems: "If some may by comparison be called 'nature's noblemen,' he might surely have been pronounced one of 'nature's oddities!' . . . To suppose him to have been a kind of private chaplain to such a man as Washington, as has been the impression of some, is the greatest of incongruities." Bishop Meade admits that he was eccentric and unreliable.

Among the earliest biographies of Washington was one written by John Marshall, Chief Justice of the Supreme Court of the United States, with the approbation of Judge Bushrod Washington, a nephew of Washington and also a Judge of the Supreme Court. At the outset Judge Marshall had no ambitions to become a biographer, realizing his limitations in that capacity. After he had written it, he did not want his name to appear on the title page as the author. The book was a ponderous literary monstrosity. It tells little of the private or personal life of Washington, mentions his name but twice in the first volume, but combines with his biography a history of the United States. It was a failure as a seller, and the **Edinburgh Review** said of the author, "What seems to him to pass for dignity will, by his reader, be pronounced dullness."* (See Beveridge's **Life of Marshall** (vol. 3, pp. 223-273).

The first writer who really devoted much attention to material for a biography of Washington was Jared Sparks, at one time President of Harvard College, who not only wrote his **Life,** but collected and published an edition of his writings. In doing this, as well as in his other efforts in American history, Dr. Sparks has placed future generations under great obligation. He was a pioneer in historical investigation. Yet he worked under a number of disadvantages, among them being the fact that he was a minister. Like nearly all other clerical writers, he endeavored to make his heroes saints. He corrected Washington's spelling and grammar, well known to have been poor. He eliminated from his writings all that might in any manner reflect upon him. Instead of a man of flesh and blood, Dr. Sparks gives us a beautifully chiseled statue. More conscientious and careful than his predecessor Weems, he yet follows him in some of his errors.

Considering that both Weems and Sparks, who place Washington in such an unenviable light, were clergymen, it was with some pertinency that William Roscoe Thayer said, "Well might the Father of his Country pray to be delivered from the parsons."

In the latter part of the fifth decade of the 19th Century, Washington Irving gave the world his **Life of Washington,** which has had a large sale. Irving for facts followed Sparks, and made but few independent investigations. The real foundation for a truthful **Life of Washington** however, lay in his own letters and writings, as well as in other

---

*Judge Marshall afterwards rearranged his **Life of Washington,** a new edition of which was published in 1927.

contemporary documents. Sparks did a great service to American history in bringing some of these to light, even though he was prejudiced in his ideas, and imperfect in his method. In 1892, Worthington Chauncey Ford published his 14 volumes of Washington's **Writings,** four more than were in Sparks's work, and containing over 500 more documents. Speaking of Sparks's methods of depicting Washington, Mr. Ford says:

"In spite, however, of all that can be said in praise of Mr. Sparks's work, it must be admitted that his zeal led him into a serious error of judgment, so common to hero-worshipers, not only doing his own reputation, as an editor, an injury, but what is of greater moment, conveying a distorted idea of Washington's personal character and abilities —an idea that was rapidly developing into a **cult,** from which it is still difficult to break away, and in which it is dangerous to express unbelief. Not only did the editor omit sentences, words, proper names, and even paragraphs without notice to the reader, but he materially altered the sense and application of important portions of the letters. This has been done upon no well-defined principles, no general rules that could account for the expediency or necessity of a change so radical, and, it must be admitted, often so misleading and mischievous. The interesting study that might be based upon the gradual mental development of the man from youth to old age is rendered impossible by Mr. Sparks's methods of treating the written record, and consequently the real character of Washington as a man is as little known today as it was to the generation that followed him." (**Preface to Writings of George Washington,** vol. 1, pp. 18 and 19.)

In 1925 John C. Fitzpatrick compiled Washington's **Diaries,** which were published in four volumes by Houghton, Mifflin & Co. These had been widely scattered. Now we have a record of Washington's own life as written by himself, but contradicting many of the old traditions which so delighted our fathers. Mr. Ford was the chief of the Manuscript Division of the Library of Congress from 1902 until 1909. Mr. Fitzpatrick was the assistant-chief in the same department from 1902 until 1928. In 1926 Mr. Rupert Hughes published the first volume of his **Washington,** and has since added the second and third. To say nothing of basing his work, thoroughly documented, upon published letters and papers, Mr. Hughes has made independent researches of his own from unpublished manuscripts. Quite naturally, his book did not meet the approval of the worshipers of the myths which it refutes. Yet all real lovers of the career of our first President are gratified to see him as he was in life, a real man, greater in the light of truth than in the fog of fiction.

Washington in character and manner was reserved. He kept his own counsel, and few had his confidence. He expressed himself only when he thought it necessary to do so. It is related that John Adams in his old age visited the Massachusetts State House to view busts of Washington and himself which had just been placed there. Pointing to the compressed lips on the face of Washington, he said, "There was a man who had sense enough to keep his mouth shut." Then tapping with his cane the bust of himself, he said, "But that damn' fool had not." Having today Washington's diaries, letters and private papers as he wrote them, we are in a position to to know more of the real man than was known by his contemporaries. To them he was an enigma.

Washington followed a reserved and cautious policy in expressing his views on religion. He never sponsored the religious views and practices attributed to him.

It has been vigorously asserted, for the greater part by those who have had an interest in doing so, that George Washington was a very religious man, and a devout member of the Protestant Episcopal Church, of which he was also vestryman. They say:

That he was one of the most regular of church attendants; that no contingency could arise which would keep him from the house of God on the Sabbath; that if he had company he would go regardless, and invite his visitors to accompany him.

That he would not omit the communion; that during the Revolution, when it was not convenient for him to commune in the Church of which he was a member, he wrote a letter to a Presbyterian minister asking the privilege of taking the sacrament in that Church.*

That he was a man of prayer, and was often found at his private devotions.

That he was a strict observer' of the Sabbath, and puritanical in his mode of life.

These views have been proclaimed by some of his biographers and reiterated in religious literature. In the minds of many they have been established as incontrovertible facts. Yet Washington had not been dead a third of a century before all these statements were as strongly contested by some as they were affirmed by others. Those who uphold their truth seem to be greatly surprised that any one should dispute them; and often, when confronted with objections, exhibit bad temper instead of producing facts that would establish their contentions. All that concerns us is to inquire if evidence can be found that will either prove of refute them. Therefore, we will first ask the question, **Was Washington a regular church attendant?** The Rev. Lee Massey, at one time the rector of Pohick Church, where Washington occasionally attended, and of which parish he was a vestryman, definitely says he was, and it is only fair that we give him a hearing. Says Mr. Massey:

"I never knew so constant an attendant in church as Washington. And his behavior in the house of God was ever so deeply reverential that it produced the happiest effect on my congregation, and greatly assisted me in my pulpit labors. No company ever withheld him from church. I have often been at Mt. Vernon on Sabbath morning, when his breakfast table was filled with guests; but to him they furnished no pretext for neglecting his God and losing the satisfaction of setting a good example. For instead of staying at home, out of false complaisance to them, he used constantly to invite them to accompany him." (Quoted in **The True George Washington**, by Paul Leicester Ford, pp. 77-78.)

This would be quite convincing were it confirmed by Washington himself; but unfortunately in the four large volumes of his **Diaries,** where he tells, "Where and How My Time Is Spent," he directly and positively contradicts it.

We will divide the Diary into four periods, using only such years as are complete. First, before the Revolution; second, after the Revolution; third, while he was President, and fourth, after his second term was ended. During the Revolution he discontinued the Diary. We find in 1768 that he went to church 15 times, in 1769, 10 times, in 1770, nine times, in 1771, six times, and the same number in 1772. In 1773, he went five times, while in 1774 he went 18 times, his banner year outside of the Presidency. During this year he was two months at the First Continental Congress in Philadelphia, where he was in church six

---

*According to one story, he wrote a letter. According to another, he made a verbal request.

times, three times to the Episcopal, once to Romish high mass, once to a Quaker meeting and once to a Presbyterian. In 1784, after the Revolution, he was in the West a long time looking after his land interests, so we will omit this year. In 1785 he attended church just **once**, but spent many of his Sundays in wholly "secular" pursuits. In 1786 he went once. These last two years he was so busy with the work on his farm and other business affairs that he seems to have forgotten the Church almost entirely. In 1787 he went three times. This was the year he was present at and presided over the Constitutional Convention in Philadelphia. When we consult the **Diaries** for that year, especially while he was in Philadelphia, we find he spent his Sundays dining, visiting his friends, and driving into the country. Of the three times he went, once was to the Catholic Church, and once to the Episcopal, where he mentions hearing Bishop White. In 1788, he attended church once. The **Diaries** deal many hard blows to the mythical Washington, above all to the myth that he went regularly to church.

In 1789, he became President, during which time the Diary is incomplete, and it is impossible to account for all the Sundays. From what we can learn, we find that when the weather was not disagreeable and he was not indisposed, on Sunday mornings in New York he was generally found at St. Paul's Chapel or Trinity. In Philadelphia he attended either Christ Church, presided over by Bishop White, or St. Peter's, where the Rev. Dr. Abercrombie officiated. This was to be expected. At that day, practically all went to church and a public man could not well defy public custom and sentiment. Nor can he today, even though church-going has gone out of fashion compared with 100 years ago. Washington spent his Sunday afternoons while President writing private letters and attending to his own business affairs. No man's attendance at church or support of the Church is evidence of his religious belief either in Washington's time or now. Any honest minister will admit this. After Washington retired from the Presidency his own master, and free from criticism, he went to church as few times as possible, for in 1797 he attended four times, in 1798, once, and in 1799, the year of his death, twice. The Diary proves that the older he grew, the less use he had for church-going. And only twice in the Diary does he ever comment upon the sermon; once, when he called it "a lame discourse," and again when he said it was in German and he could not understand it. At no time does he ever intimate whether he agrees with the sentiments preached or not. This is significant.

We are compelled to agree with the comment of Mr. Paul Leicester Ford, who, in speaking of the Rev. Mr. Massey's* statement, said: "This seems to have been written more with an eye to the effect upon others than to its strict accuracy." Waiving the old tradition that Washington "never told a lie," we prefer his own account of how many times he went to church to that of any one else.

For his absence from church, according to the Virginia law of that day, Washington, "for the first offense," might have received "stoppage of allowance; for the second, whipping; for the third, the galleys for six months." Law enforcement at this time was evidently very lax.

That Washington was a vestryman has no special significance religiously. In Virginia, this office was also political. The vestry managed the civil affairs of the parish, among others, the assessment of taxes. Being the largest property holder in the parish, Washington could hardly afford not to be a vestryman, which office he would have to hold before he could become a member of the House of Burgesses. Thomas Jefferson, a pronounced unbeliever, was also a vestryman, and for the

---

*Bishop Meade says the Rev. Mr. Massey was originally a lawyer.

same reasons. General A. W. Greeley once said, in **The Ladies' Home Journal**, that in that day "it required no more religion to be a vestry-man than it did to sail a ship." It is remarkable, after the civil functions of the vestry were abolished in Virginia, in 1780, how few times Washington attended church. He no longer had a business reason for going. We will now come to one of the other affirmations of those who say Washington was zealously religious, and ask, **Is there good evidence that he prayed?**

In the fall of 1925 I was on a visit to New York City after an absence of some years. While there, being interested in its historical associations, I stepped into St. Paul's Chapel, located on the corner of Broadway and Vesey Street. I took a look at the pew in this old church, erected in 1776, in which it is said George Washington sat when he attended services while President of the United States, when the seat of government was located in New York City. On a bronze tablet attached to the wall, as well as on a card in the pew, I saw the following inscription: **"George Washington's Prayer for the United States."**

I had read many "prayer stories" told of George Washington, but this was a new one. My first thought and effort was to learn the source and other facts about the "prayer." I wrote the vicar of St. Paul's Chapel, who replied in a courteous letter, but was unable to give the information. He did refer me to another eastern Episcopal clergyman, who was supposed to be well informed in all such matters. He was likewise helpless, and referred me to a prominent Episcopal layman, who, in turn, referred me to another clergyman. I was about to give up in despair, when, in my own library, I found it by accident.

In 1783, shortly before Washington resigned his commission as commander-in-chief, a financial stringency, accompanied by anarchy and riots, swept the country. The soldiers demanded their pay, which Congress was unable to provide. Something had to be done to alleviate the distress and discontent. Washington appealed to the governors of the States. writing each of them a letter, urging that they all take some action to relieve the prevailing distress and to restore confidence. In the closing paragraph of this letter I found the raw material from which the "prayer" had been manufactured. I quote them here, italicizing in the "prayer" those words the prayer-makers have interpolated, and in the original, the words they have omitted.

The Alleged Prayer

Almighty God, we make our earnest prayer that Thou wilt keep these United States in Thy holy protection, that **Thou** wilt incline the hearts of the citizens to cultivate a spirit of subordination and obedience to government; to entertain a brotherly affection and love for one another and for their fellow citizens of the United States at large. And finally that **Thou** wilt most graciously be pleased to dispose us all to do justice, to love mercy and to demean ourselves with that charity, humility and pacific temper of mind which were the characteristics of the Divine Author of our blessed religion, and without an humble imitation of Whose example in these things we can never hope to be a happy nation. **Grant our supplication, we beseech Thee, through Jesus Christ our Lord. Amen.** (Engraved on a bronze tablet in St. Paul's Chapel, Broadway and Vesey Streets, New York City.)

Its Source

"I now make it my earnest prayer, that God would have you, and the state over which you preside, in **his** holy protection; that **he** would incline the hearts of the citizens to cultivate a spirit of subordination and obedience to government; to entertain a brotherly affection and love for one another, for their fellow-citizens of the United States at large, **and particularly for their brethren who have served in the field;** and finally, that he would most graciously be pleased to dispose us all to love justice, to love mercy, and to demean ourselves with that charity, humility and pacific temper of mind which were the characteristics of the Divine Author of our blessed religion, and without an humble imitation of whose examples in these things, we can never hope to be a happy nation.

"**I have the honor to be, with much esteem and respect, sir, your Excellency's most obedient and most humble servant.—G. Washington.**" (Found in Ford's **Writings of Washington,** vol. x, p. 265.)

In making a prayer from this last paragraph of a letter to civil magistrates the prayer promoters have committed sins both of omission and commission:

Instead of "Sir," with which Washington begins his letter to the governors, they have written, "Almighty God, we make our earnest prayer, etc." Washington in the original speaks in the first person, singular. He does not speak directly to God, but he makes an earnest prayer, or **wish** that God will do a certain thing. The prayer makers use the first person plural and speak to God directly. They have omitted "and the state over which you preside," and "for their brethren who have served in the field." Instead of Washington's closing, "I have the honor to be, sir, etc.," they have substituted, "Grant our supplication, we beseech Thee, through Jesus Christ our Lord. Amen."

That they should add this last phrase, with which all the prayers in the Episcopal prayer book terminate, was unfortunate when we consider that nowhere in Washington's writings does he mention directly or by name Jesus Christ. When he was a boy of 13, he wrote in a copy book:

Assist me, Muse divine, to sing the morn,
On which the Savior of mankind was born.

(See Sparks's **Washington,** p. 519.)

The only other case is in this letter to the governors, where he speaks "of the Divine Author of our blessed religion." In Rupert Hughes' **Washington,** vol. 3, p. 290, is a facsimilie of the last page of the letter, proving that it is not in the handwriting of Washington, but in that of one of his secretaries. While there is no doubt that Washington wrote or dictated the original, the words in his own handwriting do not exist. He gave his ideas to his secretaries, who used their own embellishments. A legal definition of forgery reads, "Forgery consists not only in signing a false name to an instrument, but also in the alteration of an instrument that was otherwise genuine, the rule requiring that the alteration should be in a material part."

It must be conceded that this "prayer" closely approaches the definition of forgery. As evidence of how fictions will circulate, and become more powerful as they go, **The New York World Almanac,** for 1930, p. 906, says: "This prayer, **it is said,** was made by Washington at St. Paul's Church, following his inauguration in the old Federal Building on the North side of Wall Street, facing Broad Street." It was probably hoped that those not familiar with the history of the prayer, which means the majority, would assume this to be an accepted fact.

Washington must have been "powerful in prayer" if we are to believe two other stories told of his attempts to reach the "throne of grace." Some 30 years ago it was proclaimed that in his youth he composed a prayer book for his own use, containing a prayer for five days, beginning with Sunday and ending with Thursday. The manuscript of this prayer book was said to have been found among the contents of an old trunk. It was printed and facsimilies published. Clergymen read it from the altar, one of them saying it contained so much "spirituality" that he had to stop, as he could not control his emotions while reading it.

Yet, while this prayer book was vociferously proclaimed to have been written by Washington, there was not an iota of evidence that he ever had anything to do with it, or that it even ever belonged to him. A little investigation soon pricked the bubble. Worthington C. Ford, who had handled more of Washington's manuscripts than any other man except Washington himself, declared that the penmanship was not that of Washington. Rupert Hughes (**Washington**, vol. 1, p. 558) gives facsimilie specimens of the handwriting in the prayer book side by side with known specimens of Washington's penmanship at the time the prayer book was supposed to have been written. A glance proves that they are not by the same hand.

Then in the prayer book manuscript all of the words are spelled correctly, while Washington was a notoriously poor speller. But the greatest blow it received was when the Smithsonian Institute refused to accept it as a genuine Washington relic. That Washington did not compose it was proved by Dr. W. A. Croffutt, a newspaper correspondent of the Capital, who traced the source of some of the prayers to an old prayer book in the Congressional Library printed in the reign of James the First.

Even the Rev. W. Herbert Burk, rector of the Episcopal Church of Valley Forge, although a firm believer in Washington's religiosity, thus speaks of these prayers: "At present, the question is an open one, and its settlement will depend on the discovery of the originals, or upon the demonstration that they are the work of Washington."

While the "Washington Prayer Book" was thoroughly discredited, there is another prayer yarn told of him that will not die so easily. United States histories, Sunday School papers and religious tracts have sustained its life. The United States government has emblazoned it in bronze on the front of the Subtreasury building in New York City. In 1928, the Postmaster-General issued $2,000,000 in postage stamps to commemorate it. When he was informed that it was a fiction and the real facts presented to him, he replied that he was too busy to correct the mistakes of history. As a romance it is always worth telling. The scene was laid in Valley Forge, in the winter of 1777-78, while Washington's army was in winter quarters, suffering from hunger, nakedness and cold, when many had abandoned all hope of success. There, Isaac Potts, a Quaker, at whose house Washington is said to have had his headquarters, when walking in the woods on a cold winter day, saw Washington on his knees in the snow engaged in prayer, his hat off and his horse tied to a sapling.

This story was first told by our old acquaintance, Weems, the great protagonist of Washington mythology. He does not give his authority for telling it, but others have added to the account. We can clear Isaac Potts of all complicity in foisting it upon the world, as he never told it or certified to its truth. The nearest we can approach him is that some old person **said** he had told it. The Rev. E. C. M'Guire, in a book entitled **The Religious Opinions and Character of Washington**, published in 1836, quotes a man 80 years old, one Devault Beaver, who claims he received the story from Potts and his famliy.

In 1862, James Ross Snowden wrote a letter to the Rev. T. W. J. Wylie, minister of the First Reformed Presbyterian Church of Philadelphia, in which he said his father, N. R. Snowden, had heard the incident from Potts. He said he could not find his father's papers, in which it is claimed he wrote an account of it. He admits that Weems told the story in a different manner from his father's version, but insists that his father told it correctly. As in all of these fables, when

evidence is sought, some link in the chain is lost. The character of the
proof is shady. The word of very old men is always to be taken with
a grain of allowance, especially when uncorroborated. I once talked
with an old man or 87 who claimed that he had seen Lafayette, Charles
Carroll, of Carrollton, and Martha Washington. Upon an investigation,
I found it possible that he had seen the first two, but as his birth
record showed him to have been born in 1802, the year Martha Washington died, it is certain that he never saw her.

We sometimes speak of incredible stories as "old wives' tales," not
thinking that similar stories told by old men are in the same category.
This prayer story is told with variations. According to Weems, Potts
accidentally finds Washington at prayer. Being attracted by a sound in
"a venerable grove," he looks into it and finds him pouring forth his
soul to God, his countenance being of "angelic serenity," these two
expressions being added to give a dramatic and romantic effect. Weems
makes Potts a patriot, who, after watching Washington's struggle with
the Almighty, rushes into his house with great glee, and shouts to his
wife, "Sarah! My dear Sarah! all's well! all's well! George Washington
will yet prevail!" telling her what he had seen. According to the story
as told by the Rev. Mr. M'Guire, Potts was a Tory, as most Quakers
were, and he makes him say to his wife, not calling her by any Christian
name, "Our cause is lost." He seemed to think the revolutionary conflict would be settled by Washington's prayer. Instead of Potts's coming
upon Washington suddenly, hearing a sound in the grove, and upon
investigating finding the Commander-in-Chief at his orisons, as told by
Weems, M'Guire makes him follow the General for some time to see
where he was going and what he was going to do, when, lo, he saw
him get down on his knees in the snow and pray. According to the
Snowden account, Potts's wife's name was not Sarah, but Betty. He
represents him as now willing to support the cause of America, but
does not tell what his views were previously. The prayer causing the
Quaker to change from a Tory to a patriot was no doubt the work of
some later artist who wished the fable to be more effective.

The Rev. M. J. Savage says:

"The pictures that represent him on his knees in the
winter forest at Valley Forge are even silly caricatures. Washington was at least not sentimental, and he had nothing
about him of the Pharisee that displays his religion at street
corners or out in the woods in the sight of observers, or where
his portrait could be taken by 'our special artist!'"

Benson J. Lossing, in his **Field Book of the Revolution** (vol. 2, p.
336), also gives an account of this historical prayer, but does not mention the source from which he obtained it. Like Weems, he tells that
Potts was attracted by a noise in the grove, but while none of the
other chroniclers say anything about Washington's having a horse,
Lossing speaks of "his horse tied to a sapling," and instead of the General's face being a "countenance of angelic serenity," he says it was
"suffused with tears." A reasonable question to ask is, "Can there be
found any evidence that Washington was a 'praying man?'"

Bishop White, whose church he attended on and off for 25 years in
Philadelphia, says he never saw him on his knees in church. This
ought to settle the question. If he did not kneel in church, who will
believe that he did so on the ground, covered with snow, with his hat
off, when the thermometer was probably below zero?

As further proof that the story is fictitious, there is reason to believe that Isaac Potts did not live in Valley Forge at the time Washington's army was there, in the winter of 1777-1778. Mr. Myers, of the
Valley Forge Park Commission, recently admitted this.

That Potts did not own the house at the time is established by
Washington's account book, where it is proved that the rent for headquarters was paid to Mrs. Deborah Hawes, and the receipts were made
out in her name. Potts bought the house when the war was over.

There is yet another story of Washington's praying in the bushes
at Princeton, which we will not dilate upon now. But Valley Forge was
the most prolific in legends. During the same winter that Potts caught
Washington praying in the snow, the Rev. John Gano, Baptist preacher,
is said to have cut the ice in the river, and baptized the commander-
in-chief by immersion in the presence of 42 people, all sworn to secrecy!
And this has been confirmed by a grandson of the Rev. Gano in an
affidavit made at the age of 83 years! But the entire story is discredited
by the fact that the Rev. Gano was not at Valley Forge, and that he
served with Clinton's, and not with Washington's, army. For proof, see
Biographical Memoirs of the Rev. John Gano, also Headingly's **Chaplains of the Revolution.**

Thwarted in their attempts to find evidence that Washington was
publicly a pious man, those interested have tried to prove that he was
privately devout, and prayed clandestinely. If any were in a position
to know of this it would be his own family. His adopted daughter, and
step-granddaughter, Nellie Custis, wrote Mr. Sparks in 1833, when Washington's alleged piety was called into question and it was necessary to
find evidence to prove it, "I never witnessed his private devotions. I never
inquired about them." (See Sparks's **Washington**, p. 522.) She professes
to think he was a believer, and mentions persons having told her they
had seen him pray years ago, but all of the evidence is of this character—always second hand. It will be necessary to show what interest
Washington had in making the public think he was not religious, when
in fact he was in private. In this he would be as much of a deceiver
as those who are religious in public and not in private. And a really
religious man believes in "letting his light shine." If, like Washington,
he is not a religious man, and at the same time honest, not wishing to
offend his friends who are religious, he will take a non-committal attitude. The more we know of the real character of George Washington, the more we find him to have been a man who refrained from
subterfuge.

George Washington Parke Custis. a step-grandson and adopted son
of Washington, wrote, from time to time, a series of articles for newspapers. giving his recollections of his adopted father. He was but 18
when Washington died, in 1799. and his own death occurred in 1857.
His articles were, after his death, collected and edited by B. J. Lossing
and published in book form. His statements vary greatly when compared
with those of others who knew Washington. In fact, he, as a mythol-
ogist. is assigned next place to Weems. He says that Washington,
standing, was in the habit of asking the blessing at the table. Of the
hundreds who had dined with Washington, no one confirms this. But
it is interesting to read the statement of one who did dine with him and
thought he was asking the blessing. but found for it no confirmation.

Commissary-General Claude Blanchard dined with Washington,
and gives in his Journal the following account:

> "There was a clergyman at this dinner who blessed the
> food and said grace after they had done eating and had
> brought in the wine. I was told that General Washington said
> grace when there was no clergyman at the table. as fathers of
> a family do in America. The first time that I dined with him
> there was no clergyman and I did not perceive that he made
> this prayer. yet I remember that on taking his place at the
> table, he made a gesture and said a word, which I took for a

piece of politeness, and which was perhaps a religious action. In this case his prayer must have been short; the clergyman made use of more forms. We remained a very long time at the table. They drank 12 or 15 healths with Madeira wine. In the course of the meal beer was served and grum, rum mixed with water."

This, rather than proving that Washington prayed at the dinner, rather proves that they all liberally celebrated the sacrament. Those who think they find in Washington's praying in the snow at Valley Forge an evidence of the efficacy of prayer will find that a long time elapsed between the time he besought God, and the realization. During the remainder of his life he was not without trials and tribulations. After the battle of Monmouth, in 1778, he did not fight another battle for three years, chiefly because of want of guns, clothing and ammunition for his men. In the meantime the British raided the coast of Connecticut, burning and destroying. Arnold's treason almost succeeded, in which case, all would have been lost. The British invaded and conquered Georgia and the Carolinas. They subdued the inhabitants with great cruelty, and were about to subject Virginia to the same fate. Whether prayer was responsible for it or not, the real Providence of Washington and the country manifested itself in the form of French assistance. At Yorktown, in 1781, Washington, with 9,000 of his own troops, General Rochambeau with 7,000 French soldiers, Admiral De Grasse with 42 French ships of the line and 19,000 French seamen, surrounded Lord Cornwallis, who had an inferior force, and compelled him to surrender. This would not have been possible had Thomas Paine and John Laurens not journeyed to France in February, 1781, and on August 25 returned to Boston with a shipload of clothing, arms and ammunition, and 2,500,000 livres of silver, to clothe Washington's ragged and unpaid soldiers and place in their hands arms fit to use in battle.

But it is not likely that the Valley Forge prayer story will die soon. It is too good a "property" to abandon, for the Rev. W. Herbert Burk, the Valley Forge rector, is working hard to erect a million dollar church to commemorate it. He also stands sponsor for the prayer in St. Paul's Chapel in New York City. Bishop Warburton once said: "A lie has no legs and cannot stand, but it has wings and can fly far and wide."

Was Washington a Communicant? Here we must also enter the realm of myth before looking at homely facts. While the Episcopal Church has nursed the myths of Washington's praying, in the Presbyterian Church are embalmed those asserting that he took communion. Strange to say, the Episcopal Church, while claiming him as a member and believer, seldom claims him as a communicant. The evidence of clergymen who knew Washington and whose churches he attended is very destructive to this myth.

In the Philadelphia Presbyterian Hospital is a large painting of Washington taking the communion at an out-door service, supposed to have been held under the apple trees in Morristown, N.J. Those who hold that this picture represents an historical incident are agreed as to the place, but they differ as to the date. One says it happened in 1777, while another says 1780. As the story is generally told, Washington addressed a letter to a Presbyterian minister, the Rev. Dr. Johnes, asking him if he would admit to the communion a member of another Church. The clergyman replied, "Certainly, this is not a Presbyterian table, but the Lord's table," as Jared Sparks relates it in the chapter in his **Life of Washington** which is devoted to the first President's religious opinions and habits. Accordingly, we are told, Washington attended the meeting and partook of the sacrament. Sparks gives as his

authority Dr. Hosacks' **Life of De Witt Clinton**. Dr. Hosack's authority
was the Rev. Samuel H. Cox, who tells us he had it "from unquestion-
able authority . . . a venerable clergyman, who had it from Dr. Johnes
himself." But he thinks that "to all Christians, and to all Americans, it
cannot fail to be acceptable." (Sparks's **Washington**, pp. 523, 524.) As in
other cases, a link in the chain of evidence is missing, and we are asked
to accept the story on our faith as Christians and our patriotism as
Americans. But in 1836, Asa C. Colton could find no evidence that it
was a fact. He found a son of the Rev. Dr. Johnes, who had no recollection of the alleged event, and could give no testimony. His wife was
more accommodating, but all she could say was that it was "an unquestioned family tradition," which it might have been, though "tradition" is always suspicious. A report was then circulated that the Rev.
Dr. Richards, of the Auburn Theological Seminary, had in his possession the letter of Washington to Dr. Johnes. When appealed to, he denied that he had it or had ever seen it, though he said the story was
"universally current," and "never contradicted," which is about as weak
as evidence can be made.

Fortunately for the truth of history, we are not obliged to rely upon
the word of unnamed "venerable clergymen," or "universally current
traditions" to prove that George Washington was not a communicant.
We can produce well-known men of character and truthfulness, ministers of the gospel whose churches he attended for years and who had
his personal acquaintance and confidence, who not only say he did not
take the sacrament, but that they had no evidence that he was a believing Christian. If he did not accept the communion in the churches
he regularly attended, is it probable that he would beg that privilege of
another minister in another church? This is not in accordance with
common sense, and therefore not good argument. Moreover, these
clergymen who are in a position to know whereof they speak, have left
us written statements, recorded in reliable histories.

One of the most honored clergymen of the Episcopal Church in the
latter part of the 18th Century and the early part of the 19th, was the
Rev. Dr. James Abercrombie, rector of St. Peter's Church, in Philadelphia. Here Washington sometimes attended while he was President.
Dr. Abercrombie was a scholar and at one time a correspondent of
Samuel Johnson. Sprague's **Annals of the American Pulpit**, vol. 5, p.
394, says: "One incident in Dr. Abercrombie's experience as a clergyman,
in connection with the father of his country, is especially worthy of
record: and the following account of it was given by the doctor himself in a letter to a friend, in 1833, shortly after there had been some
public allusion to it." Then follows Dr. Abercrombie's letter:

> "With respect to the inquiry you make, I can only state
> the following facts: that as pastor of the Episcopal Church, ob-
> serving that, on sacramental Sundays George Washington,
> immediately after the desk and pulpit services, went out with
> the greater part of the congregation—always leaving Mrs.
> Washington with the other communicants—she invariably be-
> ing one—I considered it my duty, in a sermon on public wor-
> ship, to state the unhappy tendency of example, particularly of
> those in elevated stations, who uniformly turned their backs on
> the Lord's Supper. I acknowledge the remark was intended
> for the President; and as such he received it. A few days after,
> in conversation, I believe, with a Senator of the United States,
> he told me he had dined the day before with the President,
> who, in the course of conversation at the table, said that, on
> the previous Sunday, he had received a very just rebuke from
> the pulpit for always leaving the church before the administra-

tion of the sacrament; that he honored the preacher for his integrity and candor; that he had never sufficiently considered the influence of his example, and that he would not again give cause for the repetition of the reproof; and that, **as he had never been a communicant,** were he to become one then, it would be imputed to an ostentatious display of religious zeal, arising altogether from his elevated station. Accordingly, he never afterwards came on the morning of sacrament Sunday, though at other times he was a constant attendant in the morning."

Here is honest, straightforward talk, both on the part of Washington and the clergyman. What is more, it is confirmed by others. The Rev. Dr. Wilson, the biographer of Bishop White, in his sermon on the "Religion of the Presidents," says:

"When Congress sat in Philadelphia, President Washington attended the Episcopal Church. The rector, Dr. Abercrombie, told me that on the days when the sacrament of the Lord's Supper was to be administered, Washington's custom was to arise just before the ceremony commenced, and walk out of the church. This became a subject of remark in the congregation, as setting a bad example. At length the Doctor undertook to speak of it, with a direct allusion to the President. Washington was heard afterwards to remark that this was the first time a clergyman had thus preached to him, and he should henceforth neither trouble the Doctor or his congregation on such occasions; and ever after that, upon communion days, 'he absented himself altogether from church.'"

Dr. Wilson's sermon was published in the Albany **Daily Advertiser,** in 1831. Mr. Robert Dale Owen, then a young man, was attracted by it, and went to Albany to interview Dr. Wilson, and gives the substance of the interview in a letter written on November 13, 1831, which was published in New York two weeks later:

"I called last evening on Dr. Wilson, as I told you I should, and I have seldom derived more pleasure from a short interview with anyone. Unless my discernment of character has been grievously at fault, I met an honest man and a sincere Christian. But you shall have the particulars. A gentleman of this city accompanied me to the Doctor's residence. We were very courteously received. I found him a tall, commanding figure, with a countenance of much benevolence, and a brow indicative of deep thought, apparently 50 years of age. I opened the interview by stating that though personally a stranger to him, I had taken the liberty of calling in consequence of having perused an interesting sermon of his, which had been reported in the **Daily Advertiser** of this city, and regarding which, as he probably knew, a variety of opinions prevailed. In a discussion, in which I had taken part, some of the facts as there reported had been questioned; and I wished to know from him whether the reporter had fairly given his words or not. I then read to him from a copy of the **Daily Advertiser** the paragraph which regards Washington, beginning, 'Washington was a man,' etc., and ending 'absented himself altogether from church.' 'I endorse,' said Dr. Wilson with emphasis, 'every word of that. Nay, I do not wish to conceal from you any part of the truth, even what I have not given to the public. Dr. Abercrombie said more than I have repeated. At the close of our conversation on the subject his emphatic expression was—for I well remember the very words—"Sir, Washington was a Deist."'"

Dr. Wilson further said in this same interview:

"I have diligently perused every line that Washington ever gave to the public, and I do not find one expression in which he pledges himself as a believer in Christianity. I think anyone who will candidly do as I have done, will come to the conclusion that he was a Deist and nothing more."

As Dr. Wilson was the biographer of Bishop White, we will hear from him again.

Our next witness will be "a venerable clergyman," but not unknown and unnamed—the Rt. Rev. William White, the first bishop of Pennsylvania, one of the most distinguished men in the history of the American episcopacy, a man of intellect, high character and honor. He was one of the few Anglican ministers who did not take the side of England during the Revolution. Washington attended his church, Christ's, in Philadelphia, for about 25 years when he happened to be in that city. The two men, the prelate and the soldier and statesman, were personal friends. I recently visited this church, and the verger told me that Bishop White is yet the biggest part of the church. His episcopal chair still stands by the side of the altar, while his body rests beneath it. On August 13, 1835, Colonel Mercer, of Fredericksburg, Va., wrote Bishop White this letter:

"I have a desire, my dear sir, to know whether General Washington was a member of the Protestant Episcopal Church, or whether he occasionally went to the communion only, or if he ever did so at all. No authority can be so authentic and complete as yours on this point."

Bishop White replied:

"Philadelphia, Aug. 15, 1835.

"In regard to the subject of your inquiry, truth requires me to say that General Washington never received the communion in the churches of which I am the parochial minister. Mrs. Washington was an habitual communicant. I have been written to by many on that point, and have been obliged to answer them as I now do you. I am respectfully,

"Your humble servant,

"William White"

(**Memoir of Bishop White**, pp. 196, 197.)

The Rev. Bird Wilson, in the **Memoir of Bishop White**, p. 188, says: "Though the General attended the churches in which Dr. White officiated, whenever he was in Philadelphia during the Revolutionary War, and afterwards while President of the United States, he was never a communicant in them."

In a letter to the Rev. B. C. C. Parker, dated November 28, 1832, in reply to some inquiries about Washington's religion, Bishop White said:

"His behavior in church was always serious and attentive, but as your letter seems to intend an inquiry on the point of kneeling during the service, I owe it to the truth to declare that I never saw him in the said attitude. . . . Although I was often in the company of this great man, and had the honor of often dining at his table, I never heard anything from him which could manifest his opinions on the subject of religion. . . . Within a few days of his leaving the Presidential chair, our vestry waited on him with an address prepared and delivered by me. In his answer he was pleased to express himself gratified by what he had heard from our pulpit; but there was nothing that committed him relatively to religious theory."

(**Memoir of Bishop White**, pp. 189-191.)

In another letter to the Rev. Mr. Parker, dated December 31, 1832, the Bishop says even more distinctly:

"I do not believe that any degree of recollection will bring to my mind any fact which would prove General Washington to have been a believer in the Christian revelation further than as may be hoped from his constant attendance upon Christian worship, in connection with the general reserve of his character." (**Memoir of Bishop White**, p. 193.)

Ward's **Life of Bishop White**, p. 72, says, "Washington was not himself a communicant of the church."

It was early in the 1830's that the supposed piety of Washington was called into question and evidence of its being a fact demanded. This accounts for the letters we have quoted being written during that decade. The Rev. Dr. Abercrombie wrote the letter I have quoted, in 1831; the Rev. Bird Wilson preached his sermon on the religious beliefs of the founders of the republic in the same year; Bishop White wrote his letter to the Rev. B. C. C. Parker in 1832, and his letter to Colonel Mercer in 1835. Jared Sparks wrote to Nellie Custis for evidence of Washington's taking the communion in 1833. The Rev. Mr. M'Guire, in 1836, made fruitless inquiries about Washington's Presbyterian communion. We have observed that no evidence could be found, except unsupported tradition, that Washington prayed, communed, or in any way gave outward indication of being a religious man, except that he attended church sometimes; while Bishop White and the Rev. Drs. Abercrombie and Wilson positively say that he was not religious.

In 1831, Mr. Robert Dale Owen, afterwards a member of Congress, where he introduced the bill establishing the Smithsonian Institute, and who later was Minister to Naples, held a newspaper debate with the Rev. Origen Bacheler, which was afterwards published in book form and had a large circulation. Mr. Bacheler insisted that Washington was a communicant and appealed to the Rev. William Jackson, rector of Alexandria, Va., for evidence. Mr. Jackson eagerly sought it, but failed to find it and wrote Mr. Bacheler, "I find no one who ever communed with him." (Bacheler-Owen Debate, vol. 2, p. 262.)

Still Mr. Bacheler was not satisfied, and begged Mr. Jackson to seek further. After trying again, he wrote, "I am sorry, after so long a delay in replying to your last, that it is not in my power to communicate something definite in reference to General Washington's church membership," and in the same letter he says, "Nor can I find any old person who ever communed with him." (Bacheler-Owen Debate, quoted in John E. Remsburg's **Six Historic Americans**, pp. 110-111.)

In the fall of 1928 I visited Pohick Church, which Washington occasionally attended and in which he was a vestryman. I asked the caretaker if there was any evidence in the parish records that Washington took communion. At first he evaded my inquiry by saying that in the Episcopal Church no one took communion unless he was confirmed, and there being no bishops in this country at the time, confirmation was impossible. I then asked if Episcopalians dispensed with the communion in this country until they had bishops. He again evaded a direct answer, but, pointing to the pews of Washington, George Mason and George William Fairfax, who, like Washington, were vestrymen, said, "There is no evidence that any of these men communed." Nearly all well-informed Episcopal clergymen know Washington was not a communicant, but they find it very inconvenient to admit it. To a Christian believer the communion is the most sacred rite. All of them take it when they feel themselves worthy. Some do not take it when they feel they are unworthy. To say Washington was a Christian in the ortho-

dox sense and **never** partook of it—and so far as we know this is true—
cannot be a compliment to him.

I have cited four churches which Washington attended. The ministers of two of them say emphatically that he did not commune. One of
them says just as emphatically that he was not a believer, only a
Deist. The other says he had no evidence of his Christian belief other
than that he attended church, which is no evidence at all. In the other
two, in both of which he was a vestryman, no evidence could be found
that he ever stood at the Lord's table.

On February 20, 1833, Mr. Sparks wrote to Nellie Custis, then Mrs.
Lewis, for evidence that her step-grandfather communed. She answered,
on February 26, as follows: "On communion Sundays, he left the church
with me after the blessing, and returned home, and we sent the carriage
back after my grandmother." (Sparks's **Washington**, p. 521.) Sparks
himself, on p. 523, expresses his regrets at this in these words:

"The circumstance of his withdrawing himself from the
communion service, at a certain period of his life, has been
remarked as singular. This may be admitted and regretted,
both on account of his example, and the value of his opinion
as to the importance and practical tendency of the rite."

The probability was that he thought the rite had no "practical
tendency," and unlike many others then and now he was not hypocrite
enough to go through a form which he considered meaningless. But to
undertake to say, as Sparks afterwards does, that this is no reflection
upon Washington as a Christian is begging the question. It is true that
Ralph Waldo Emerson resigned from the ministry because he refused
to celebrate the Lord's Supper, but no one knew better than Mr. Sparks
that Emerson's religion was of a far different type than that he tries
to prove Washington had.

Myths about Washington compared with kindred myths. When
we read these various stories about Washington and compare them with
other myths of American history, now conceded to be nothing but
myths, we will perceive that they are all cut from the same cloth. In
Watson's **Annals of Philadelphia**, p. 422, we read of the following incident at a session of the first Continental Congress:

"It was on this occasion that General Washington, then
a member from Virginia, was observed to be the only member to **kneel**, when Bishop White first offered his prayer to the
throne of grace—as if he were early impressed with a sense of
his and their dependence on the God of battles."

Here the author out-did himself. When Bishop White wrote to the
Rev. B. C. C. Parker that he had never seen Washington on his knees,
apologists might be able to say that he no doubt forgot this time in
Congress, were it not for the fact that the prayer at this Congress
was not offered by Bishop White, but by the Rev. Jacob Duche, who
afterwards turned traitor and tried to induce Washington to do the
same. Yet this fable, like the prayer at Valley Forge, has been celebrated
in picture and by the Peter Parleys who have written history.

We have been told that John Brown, while on his way to the scaffold, stopped and kissed a Negro child. This has been written in United
States history, with a touching engraving attached. Andrew Hunter,
who prosecuted Brown, has firmly denied it, saying that a cordon of
soldiers surrounded him; that no one, particularly no Negro, was permitted to get near him. Oswald Garrison Villard, in his **Life of John
Brown Fifty Years After** (p. 554), says: "No little slave child was held
up for the benison of his lips, for none but soldiery was near and the
street was full of marching men."

The story of General Lee surrendering his sword to General Grant has likewise been popular in histories, and Grant has been eulogized for his great "magnanimity" in returning it. General Grant, in his **Memoirs**, thus disposes of the story: "The much talked of surrendering of Lee's sword and my handing it back, this, and much more that has been said about it, is the purest fiction." (Vol. 2, p. 494.)

The **Western Christian Advocate** published a story about Lincoln, which, though it was copied in a score of Lincoln biographies, was without the slightest basis in fact. It was to the effect that upon the reception of the news of Lee's surrender, Lincoln and all his cabinet got down upon their knees in prayer. In 1891, Hugh McCullough, Lincoln's last Secretary of the Treasury, was yet living. Through an old acquaintance, Mr. N. P. Stockbridge, of Fort Wayne, Ind., he was approached, and this is what he had to say:

"The description of what occurred at the Executive Mansion, when the intelligence was received of the surrender of the Confederate forces, which you quote from the **Western Christian Advocate**, is not only absolutely groundless but absurd. After I became Secretary of the Treasury I was present at every cabinet meeting, and I never saw Mr. Lincoln or any of his ministers upon his knees or in tears." (See Remsburg's **Six Historic Americans**, Lincoln section, p. 83.)

One of the best known myths of American history was enshrined by one of our greatest poets, John Greenleaf Whittier in "Barbara Frietchie." We have all read it, and some of us have recited it when we went to school. It is a noble poem, and stirs our patriotism. Yet, except for the fact that there really was such an aged woman living in Frederick, Md., in 1862, when Stonewall Jackson's army marched through that town, the poem represents only fiction. Whittier, in a letter written on October 19, 1880, does not vouch for its historicity, but states that he told it as it was told to him without asking whether it was a fact. The **Americana Encyclopedia** says, "Recent investigations have thrown some doubt upon the authenticity of the account." Two Confederate generals, Henry Kyd Douglas and Jubal A. Early, have denied that any such occurrence took place. They both say there were no flag demonstrations when their army marched through Frederick, except by little children, and to these no attention was paid. The army did not even march along the street on which Barbara Frietchie lived, and had they done so they would have seen no flag, for she did not fly one. The only foundation for the story is that once Barbara took a Union flag and hid it in a Bible, saying there no rebel would ever look to find it, and we are not quite sure that this is true. But when the poet says,

"Up the street came the rebel tread,
Stonewall Jackson riding ahead;

Under his slouched hat, left and right,
He glanced, the old flag met his sight.
'Halt!'—the dust-brown ranks stood fast!
'Fire!'—out blazed the rifle blast."

we must hold our breath. One fact has been proved above all others, which is that Stonewall Jackson a few days before had been injured by a fall from a horse, and was carried through Frederick in an ambulance.*

For the persistence with which myths are accepted as facts, even when they are admitted to be myths, we can find no better illustration

---

*For the facts about Barbara Frietchie, see **Munsey's Magazine**, vol. 26, p. 542, January, 1902. Article by Marian West.

than Edward Everett Hale's **Man Without a Country**. It was written in 1862, to stimulate patriotism during the rebellion. The story was of Philip Nolan, a young lieutenant in the United States Army, who, at the time of Aaron Burr's alleged treason, was heard to remark, "Damn the United States! I wish I may never hear of the United States again!" For this he was tried by a court-martial and sentenced to imprisonment for life on a United States man-of-war that would never make an American port, and whose officers were told to see that he would never hear the name of his country again. Such a man as Philip Nolan never lived, the story is wholly fictitious, and Dr. Hale published it as such. Yet there were people who were willing to vouch for the truth of the narrative. Dr. Hale said, in a late edition of the book:

"The story having once been published, it passed out of my hands. From that moment it has gradually acquired different accessories for which I am not responsible. Thus I have heard it said that at one bureau of the Navy Department they say that Nolan was pardoned in fact, and returned home to die. At another bureau, I am told, the answer to questions is that though it is true that an officer was kept abroad all of his life, his name was not Nolan. The Hon. James Savage, who discredited all tradition, still recollected this 'Nolan court-martial.' One of the most accurate of my younger friends had noticed Nolan's death in the newspaper, but recollected that it was in September and not in August. A lady in Baltimore wrote me in good faith that Nolan had two widowed sisters living in that neighborhood. A writer in the New Orleans **Picayune**, in a careful historical paper, explained at length that I had been mistaken all through; that Philip Nolan never went to sea but to Texas; that there he was shot in battle, March 21, 1801; and by orders from Spain every fifth man of his party was to be shot, had they not died in prison. Fortunately, however, he left his papers and maps, which fell into the hands of a friend of the **Picayune's** correspondent.

"With all these suggestions the reader need not occupy himself. I can only repeat that my Philip Nolan is pure fiction. I cannot send his scrap-book to my friend who asks for it, because I have it not to send." (Edition of 1917, pp. 103-104.)

When we read of the persistence of these myths, and that some love them as a cat loves to lap milk, and a donkey to chew thistles, we are sometimes inclined to agree with Napoleon when he said that history consists "of lies agreed upon." For a knowledge of how myths concerning religion are born, grow and flourish, consult the great **Ecclesiastical History** of Mosheim.

The well-known historian, Henry C. Lea, in an address upon "The Ethical Values of History," published in the **American Historical Review**, for January, 1904, said:

"History is not to be written as a Sunday-school tale for children of a larger growth. It is, or should be, a serious attempt to ascertain the severest truth as to the past and to set it forth without fear or favor. It may, and it generally will, convey a moral, but that moral should educe itself from facts."

I think this applies to the fables told of Washington, and those who tell them sometimes say they should not be controverted because of the "moral" they teach. But what type of a moral is taught when you tell about a man that which is absurdly untrue, and what kind of morality is that built upon such a foundation We are not required to go beyond the truth in the life of George Washington to find him to have been one of the greatest of men. To what purport is it to say that he went regularly to church when we know he did not, prayed in the woods though he never prayed in church; wrote a prayer book at that period of his life when his chief thoughts were of war and the girls; asked a Presbyterian minister's permission to take communion in his church, when he declined to take it in the church he regularly attended? **Was Washington a Sabbath Keeper and a Puritan?** Some who have endeavored to prove that George Washington was sound in his theological views and in the practices pertaining to them have also declared that he was sound in his personal conduct, from the Puritan standpoint. I say Puritan standpoint advisedly, lest I inadvertently cast a reflection upon Washington; knowing that all good men do not endorse this standpoint.

We are told that he was a strict observer of the Sabbath, and we are sometimes referred to an incident in Connecticut, when he would not travel on Sunday. The entry in his **Diary** telling of this is dated Sunday, November 8, 1789, and reads as follows: "It being contrary to law and disagreeable to the people of this State (Connecticut) to travel on the Sabbath day—and my horses, after passing through such intolerable roads, wanting rest, I stayed at Perkins' tavern (which, by the bye, is not a good one)—all day—and a meeting house being a few rods from the door, I attended morning and evening services, and heard a lame discourse from a Mr. Pond." (**Diaries**, vol. 4, p. 50.)

Yet when we read Washington's own account of his later trip through the southern States, we find he continually traveled on Sunday, and seldom attended church. On Sunday, September 19, he was on a trip inspecting his lands. He did not call upon his tenants for their rent, because he says they were "**apparently** very religious," and "**it** was thought best to postpone going among them until tomorrow." The italics are Washington's own. In both of these cases he was aiming not to offend other persons' conscientious scruples, not carrying out his own.

It has been said Washington did not receive visitors on Sunday. So far as his home in Mt. Vernon was concerned, a glance at the **Diaries** will prove this to be untrue. When he had no guests there on the first day of the week, he made it a subject of special comment. While he was President he did not receive visitors on Sunday for the very good and practical reason that he wanted the day to himself to attend to his own private business. Let us look at a few instances, typical of many:

Sunday, July 11, 1790. "At home all day—despatching some business relative to my own private concerns." (**Diaries**, vol. 4, p. 142.)

Sunday, February 14, 1790. "At home all day writing letters to Virginia." (Ibid, p. 87.)

Sunday, October 11, 1789. "At home all day writing private letters." (Ibid, p. 19.)

Sunday, June 27, 1790. "Went to Trinity church in the morning—employed myself in writing business in the afternoon." (Ibid, p. 130.)

Sunday, May 2, 1790. "Went to Trinity church in the forenoon—writing letters on private business in the afternoon." (Ibid, p. 126.)

Sunday, April 18, 1790. "At home all day—the weather being stormy and bad, wrote private letters." (Ibid, p. 115.)

Sunday, March 21, 1790. "Went to St. Paul's chapel in the forenoon—wrote private letters in the afternoon. Received Mr. Jefferson, Minister of State, about one o'clock." (Ibid, p. 106.)

It would be useless to quote further, as this is practically the fact about all of his Sundays, so far as the **Diaries** are complete, while he

was President. Paul Leicester Ford says, in speaking of his attending
to his own private business on Sunday: "It was more or less typical of
his whole life." (**The True George Washington**, p. 78.)

We find that he was engaged in many "secular" pursuits on Sunday. Mr. Ford adds: "He entertained company, closed land purchases,
sold wheat, and, while a Virginia planter, went fox-hunting on Sunday." (Ibid, p. 79.) A few specific instances of this will be given. On
Sunday, March 31, 1771, he was engaged "on the arbitration between
Dr. Ross and Company and Mr. Semple." (**Diaries**, vol. 2, p. 12.) Sunday,
October 13, 1771, he spent his time "plotting and measuring the sur-
veys which Capt. Crawford made for the officers and soldiers." On
Sunday, December 25, of the same year, he "agreed to raise Christopher
Shade's wages to 20 pounds per annum." One week prior to this, De-
cember 18, he "went to Doeg Run and carried the dogs with me, who
found and run a deer to the water." (**Diaries**, vol. 2, pp. 45 and 46.)
On Sunday, October 25, 1772, he was "assisting Crawford with his sur-
veys" (ibid, p. 840), while on Sunday, November 4, he "set off for the
Annapolis races." (Ibid, p. 82.)

Washington danced, and the **Diaries** are full of instances of his
going to assemblies and balls. During the Revolution he, with Generals
Greene, Knox, Wilkinson and others, signed a subscription paper to
pay the sums set beside their names "in the promotion and support of
a dancing assembly." Once he danced for three hours with Mrs. Greene
without sitting down. Once the entire party danced all night. At New-
port General Rochambeau gave a ball and Washington danced the first
figure, while the French officers took the instruments from the mu-
sicians and furnished the music. He frequently traveled to Alexandria
to attend balls, and danced until he was 64 years old. (See **The True
George Washington**, pp. 183, 184.)

The theater was the bane of our Puritan ancestors. As late as 1792
a performance of Sheridan's **School for Scandal** was stopped by the
sheriff in Boston. New York was about the only city in the northern
colonies where performance of plays was permitted. Pennsylvania
passed an act prohibiting theaters in 1700. In 1759 this law was evaded
by the erection of a theater outside the limits of Philadelphia. The ministers petitioned the legislature to suppress it and were successful, but
the King and Council in London vetoed the act. There was peace until
1779, when, taking advantage of the fact that Pennsylvania was independent of England, the ministers were successful in having passed a
law imposing a fine of 500 pounds on anyone who erected a theater.
The law was re-enacted in 1786, but the penalty was reduced to 200
pounds. On March 2, 1789, this law was repealed on petition of leading citizens of Philadelphia. Theaters were now permitted.

All his life, Washington's **Diaries** prove, he attended the theater
whenever an opportunity offered. In Philadelphia he did not hesitate
to defy the stern puritanical element that opposed the theater, and
for this he was criticized. On January 9, 1797, he records: "Went to the
theatre for the first time this season. The Child of Nature and the
Lock and Key were performed." (**Diaries**, vol. 4, p. 248.) On the 24th
of the same month he attended the Pantheon. There bareback and
fancy riding were the attraction. On January 26, Washington sold the
proprietor a fine white horse, named Jack, for $150. On February 27,
five days before his term as President expired, he "went to the Theatre
in the evening." The play on the boards this time was **The Way to get
Married**, followed by a comic ballet entitled, **Dermot and Kathleen, or
Animal Magnetism**.

Bishop Meade has denied that Washington went fox-hunting, attended theaters, or that he would stoop to cards or dice. (**Old Churches,**

Ministers and Families of Virginia, vol. 2, pp. 242-55.) We can only say the good Bishop was mistaken. His father, who was a member of Washington's staff during the Revolution, ought to have told him better. Cards and dice were a favorite amusement with Virginia gentlemen. Washington partook of them. He did not play for heavy stakes, but in a carefully kept ledger is to be found an account of his losses and gains. In his "Ledger B,"* 1772-1774, his net loss was six pounds, three shillings and three pence, not bad for two years, and 63 games, of which he lost 36 and won 27.

What would shock our modern Puritans more than all things else is the well-known fact that he not only drank liquor, wine and beer, but manufactured and sold them. When Congress passed the first excise law in 1794, placing a tax on distilled spirits, it caused a rebellion in western Pennsylvania. Washington himself regarded this law as an incentive to make money, so he installed a distillery at Mt. Vernon, and made whisky, "from rye chiefly and Indian corn in a certain proportion."

Mr. Ford says: "In 1798, the profit from the distillery was 344 pounds, 12 shillings, and seven and three quarter pence, with a stock carried over of 755¼ gallons." (**The True George Washington,** p. 123.)

Yet we must remember that the Puritans of Washington's day did not take umbrage at the manufacture of rum, as their descendants do today. In New England it was the leading industry. While Washington was careful not to give offense to his pious countrymen in things pertaining to doctrine, all his life he set his face against their puritanical practices. But those who still believe that Washington was a Puritan can console themselves with the fact that while he was a big grower of tobacco, he did not personally use it.

While he is usually looked upon as a grave, solemn man, Washington was fully capable of both making and enjoying a joke. He was popular with women, but there is no record of any improprieties. Far from being the walking manikin some would have us believe he was, we find him a real man of flesh and blood. The excellence of Washington's character did not consist in loud professsions of superior righteousness, and in giving attention to forms; but we find him a superior man because at all times he was honest, honorable, reliable, recognized the rights of others, was patient under difficulties and disappointments, always exercising that uncommon thing known as common sense. These are the reasons why his contemporaries esteemed him and had confidence in him, and why, with all of the light shown upon his career, he yet holds his place in history.

The Public Attitude of Washington toward the Church and Religion. The public attitude of Washington toward the Church as an institution, and religion in general, is interesting, but it has no bearing on his private opinions, which he never expressed. To Lafayette, on August 15, 1787, he wrote:

> "I am not less ardent in my wish that you may succeed in your plan of toleration in religious matters. Being no bigot myself, I am disposed to indulge the professors of Christianity in the church that road to heaven which to them shall seem the most direct, plainest, easiest and least liable to exception."

To Sir Edward Newenham, he wrote, on October 20, 1792:

> "Of all the animosities which have existed among mankind, those which are caused by difference of sentiment in religion appear to be the most inveterate and distressing, and ought most to be deprecated. I was in hopes that the enlight-

---

*See vol. 2, of Rupert Hughes' **Washington,** pp. 208, 209, in which the ledger pages are reproduced.

ened and liberal policy which has marked the present age would at least have reconciled Christians of every denomination, so far that we should never again see their religious disputes carried to such a pitch as to endanger the peace of society."

After Washington was inaugurated as the first chief magistrate, representatives of the different religious bodies waited upon him and presented him with addresses, to which he replied. From these replies I select the following excerpts:

"While all men within our territories are protected in worshipping the Deity according to the dictates of their consciences, it is rational to be expected from them in return, that they will all be emulous of evincing the sanctity of their professions by the innocence of their lives and the beneficence of their actions; for no man, who is profligate in his morals, or a bad member of the civil community, can possibly be a true Christian, or a credit to his own religious society." (To the General Assembly of the Presbyterian Church, May, 1789.)

"If I could have entertained the slightest apprehension that the Constitution framed in the convention, where I had the honor to preside, might possibly endanger the religious rights of any religious society, certainly I would never have placed my signature to it; and, if I could now conceive that the general government might ever be administered as to render liberty of conscience insecure, I beg you will be persuaded that no one would be more zealous than myself to establish effectual barriers against the horrors of spiritual tyranny, and every species of religious persecution." (To the General Committee Representing the United Baptist Churches of Virginia.)

"The liberty enjoyed by the people of these States, of worshipping Almighty God agreeably to their conscience, is not only among the choisest of their **blessings**, but also of their **rights**. While men perform their social duties faithfully, they do all that society or the state can with propriety demand or expect; and remain responsible to their Maker for the religion or modes of faith which they may prefer or express." (To the Quakers, 1789.)

"As mankind becomes more liberal they will be more apt to allow that all those who conduct themselves as worthy members of the community, are equally entitled to the protection of civil government. I hope ever to see America among the foremost nations in examples of justice and liberality. I rejoice that a spirit of liberality and philanthrophy is much more prevalent among the enlightened nations of the earth, and that your brethren will benefit thereby in proportion as it shall become still more extensive." (To the Hebrew Congregation of Savannah, May, 1790.)

"On this occasion, it would ill become me to conceal the joy I have felt in perceiving the fraternal affection, which appears to increase every day among the friends of genuine religion. It affords edifying prospects, indeed, to see Christians of different denominations dwell together in more charity, and conduct themselves in respect to each other with a more Christian-like spirit than ever they have done in any former age, or in any other nation." (To the Episcopalians, August 19, 1789.)

"Of all the dispositions and habits which lead to political prosperity, religion and morality are indispensable supports. In vain would that man claim the tribute of patriotism who should labor to subvert these great pillars of human happiness, these firmest props of the duties of men and citizens. The mere politician, equally with the pious man, ought to respect and cherish them. A volume could not trace all their connections with private and public felicity. Let it simply be asked, Where is the security for property, for reputation, for life, if the sense of religious obligation desert the oaths, which are the instruments of investigation in courts of justice? And let us with caution indulge the supposition that morality can be maintained without religion. Whatever may be conceded to the influence of refined education on minds of peculiar structure, reason and experience both forbid us to expect that national morality can prevail in exclusion of religious principle. It is substantially true that virtue or morality is a necessary spring of popular government."* (From the Farewell Address.)

Every public man, every office holder and politician realizes that organized religion, socially, politically and economically, is a factor to be recognized and dealt with. Washington, not only as Commander-in-Chief, but more so as President, was obliged to have the united support of all the people, regardless of his individual views. He was careful to warn all these Churches against the great vice of the world, religious bigotry, intolerance and persecution. Because a motive is inspired by religion, it may not always be right, but religion is a powerful motive, right or wrong. Washington, in all these addresses, had in mind that religious controversy and dissension breed discord. At the same time, he realized that to secure independence and erect the new government, the cooperation of the Churches and the ministers was essential. He wanted their support, and to have their enmity would have been unfortunate.

There have been few Clemenceaus, Bradlaughs, Berts and Gambettas in public life who openly opposed the Church. These did so under extraordinary circumstances. Had Washington been as firm an Agnostic as Ingersoll, it would have been to his advantage to remain silent on the subject. He is careful to refer to religion in general, not to any particular belief or Church. He says nice things to them all, but commits himself to none. His use of the word "Christian" at times means nothing definite. Christianity might mean Roman Catholicism or Unitarianism, or "mere morality," just as its user prefers. Of course every man must give special homage to the religion of the country in which he lives. In the "Farewell Address," he often refers to "religion and morality." This might mean any religion, and the other excerpts also confirm us in thinking that he meant all religions and none in particular.

Thousands of men today hold that religious institutions should be upheld because of the prop they give to morality. They support the Church for that reason, while they are indifferent to its theological teaching. They believe, as did Draper: "The tranquility of society depends so much on the stability of its religious convictions, that no one can be justified in wantonly disturbing them." They think religion is necessary for other people, while not needed by themselves. It will also be noticed that Washington, while he sometimes couples morality and religion, stresses the former, and ends by saying that "virtue or morality is a necessary spring of popular government."

Among the addresses sent to Washington when he became Presi-

---

*All these answers to the addresses of the Churches will be found in the Washington section, pp. 151-157. of Harpers' **Encyclopedia of United States History**, and Mr. Ford's **Writings of Washington**.

dent was one from the First Presbytery of the Eastward, which objected to the new Constitution because it did not recognize God and the Christian religion, in these words: "We should not have been alone in rejoicing to have seen some explicit acknowledgement of the only true God, and Jesus Christ, whom he hath sent, inserted somewhere in the Magna Charta of our country." To this, Washington replied:

"The path of true piety is so plain as to require but little political direction. . . . In the progress of morality and science, to which our government will give every furtherance, we may confidently expect the advancement of true religion and the completion of our happiness."

Here, as on similar occasions, he is too canny to say what "true piety" is. His statement that "true piety" will be advanced through the "progress of morality and science," would place him at the present day in the ranks of Rationalism.

Washington knew, at the same time, as did Madison, that religion, legally united with the state, is no aid either to "virtue or morality." For that reason he said, in the treaty with Tripoli, made in 1796, and ratified by the Senate in 1797: "The Government of the United States of America is not, in any sense, founded upon the Christian religion." He was too shrewd to oppose the orthodoxy of his time, and equally shrewd in not committing himself to its teachings. Socially, he conformed to the religious customs of his day, just enough to maintain the good will of the Churches, ministers and religious people.

What Was Washington's Belief? It is said that some one asked of Lord Beaconsfield his religion. He replied, "The religion of wise men." Thereupon, his interlocutor again asked, "What religion is that," and my Lord answered, "Wise men never tell." Washington was a wise man and never told.

In classifying these Presidents, placing them in one Church or another, whenever they actually were believers in the doctrines of that Church, I have had no difficulty in securing indubitable evidence, except in the case of President Pierce, whose religious affiliations it required some effort to learn. The proofs have been culled when possible from the spoken or written words of the Presidents themselves, combined with their public attitudes, in which I could make no mistake.

Washington never made a statement of his belief, while his actions rather prove that if he was not a positive unbeliever, he was at best an indifferentist. We have seen that he was not a regular attendant at church services—rather an irregular one. I have examined 14 years of his complete Diaries, 13 of them when he was at home, with two Episcopal churches within eight or 10 miles. One of these years, 1774, was his banner year for church attendance, when he went 18 times. Yet we find, in these 14 years, his average attendance to have been but six times a year—not a very good record.

That Washington did not commune is established beyond all doubt by reputable witnesses. The evidence of Bishop White, the Rev. Dr. Abercrombie and the Rev. Dr. Wilson certainly outweighs the very shady assertion that he once took communion in a Presbyterian church, which rests upon questionable and anonymous evidence, to say nothing of its utter improbability.

Bishop White says Washington did not kneel in prayer. Nellie Custis says he stood during the devotional service. She also admits that she never saw him pray, but that someone long dead had told her that he had seen him praying many years before. The Valley Forge prayer is a myth of even a weaker type than the Presbyterian communion story. The "Prayer for the United States" is a demonstrated fabrication. These fictions would not be necessary were there true evidence that Washington was religious. During the Revolution, forged letters were published in London attacking his personal moral character. It has been said that letters written by Washington were in existence that cast reflections upon him, but no one has ever been able to produce them. Between the fictions, forgeries and falsehoods told to make Washington either a plaster saint or a rake, it is difficult to say which would have disgusted him the more.

Jared Sparks says:

"After a long and minute examination of the writings of Washington, public and private, in print and in manuscript, I can affirm, that I have never seen a single hint, or expression, from which it could be inferred, that he had any doubt of the Christian revelation, or that he thought with indifference or unconcern of that subject. On the contrary, wherever he approaches it, and indeed wherever he alludes in any manner to religion, it is done with seriousness and reverence." (**Life of Washington**, p. 525.)

If Dr. Sparks found from Washington's writings that he never had a "doubt of the Christian revelation," neither could he find among them anything proving his belief in the same. He may have thought about it, and it is likely that he did, but as to expressing his views, he surely was indifferent and unconcerned. The truth is that the majority of unbelievers, especially men of prominence in political or social life, make no statement of their unbelief. True, when Washington spoke of religion, he spoke with "seriousness and reverence," but he so spoke of all religions and not of any particular one. That an unbeliever is necessarily flippant, it is the prerogative of Mr. Sparks to assert. Scholarly Freethinkers consider religion an important subject, even though they reject its orthodox interpretation. While not necessarily reverent in their attitude, they discuss it seriously from the standpoint of science, logic and history.*

Most important of all, there stands out the fact that while in Washington's writings there is nothing affirming or denying the truth of Christian revelation, there is also nothing inconsistent with Deism. Deists of the time believed in God and his Providence. They accepted all of moral value in the Christian Bible and in all other sacred books, holding it to be a part of natural religion. They held in high esteem the moral teachings and character of Jesus. Even the orthodox never tire of quoting complimentary things said about him by Paine and Rousseau. Many Deists prayed and believed in prayer.

Nor can Dr. Sparks find anything in the writings of Washington tending to prove that he believed in Jesus as the Christ and the son of God. Nor will he find anything which will prove that a future existence had any firm place in his calculations, though Deists, as a rule, hope for "happiness beyond this life." During Washington's sickness and death religion was not mentioned. No minister was called in, though three doctors were present.

Dr. Moncure D. Conway says:

"When the end was near, Washington said to a physician present—an ancestor of the writer of these notes—'I am not afraid to go.' With his right fingers on his left wrist, he counted his own pulses, which beat his funeral march to the grave. 'He bore his distress with astonishing fortitude, and conscious as he declared, several hours before his death, of his approaching dissolution, he resigned his breath with the greatest com-

---

*That I may not be justly accused of unfairness, I reproduce in its entirety, in the Appendix, the chapter in Sparks's **Life of Washington** that deals with his religious views.

posure, having the full possession of his reason to the last moment,' so next day wrote one present.* Mrs. Washington knelt beside his bed, but no word passed on religious matters. With the sublime taciturnity which marked his life he passed out of existence, leaving no word or act which can be turned to the service of superstition, cant or bigotry."

He died like an ancient pagan Greek or Roman. This has puzzled many who have tried to fit Washington with orthodox garments.

In his letters to young people, particularly to his adopted children, he urges upon them truth, character, honesty, but in no case does he advise going to church, reading the Bible, belief in Christ, or any other item of religious faith or practice. Once he wanted mechanics for his estate. He did not demand that they be Christians, but he wrote to his agent, "If they be good workmen, they may be from Asia, Africa, or Europe; they may be Mohammedans, Jews, or Christians of any sect, or they may be Atheists."

Except the legal phrase, "In the name of God, Amen," there are no religious references in Washington's will, something unusual in wills made at that time. While he liberally recognizes his relatives he leaves nothing to churches or for other religious purposes, but he does remember the cause of education.

We have already quoted Bishop White to the effect that when the vestry of Christ Church waited upon Washington with an address, he expressed gratification at some things he had heard from their pulpit, but said not a word that would indicate his own religious views. Just before he left the Presidency, all the ministers of Philadelphia waited upon him, also bearing an address. We will let Thomas Jefferson tell the story, as he wrote it in his **Diary**, for February 1, 1800, just six weeks after Washington's death:

"Feb. 1. Dr. Rush tells me that he had it from Asa Green that when the clergy addressed General Washington on his departure from the Government, it was observed in their consultation that he had never on any occasion said a word to the public which showed a belief in the Christian religion and they thought they should so pen their address as to force him at length to declare publicly whether he was a Christian or not. They did so. However, he observed, the old fox was too cunning for them. He answered every article in their address particularly except that, which he passed over without notice. Rush observes he never did say a word on the subject in any of his public papers except in his valedictory address to the governors of the States when he resigned his commission in the army, wherein he speaks of the benign influence of the Christian religion.

"I know that Gouverneur Morris, who pretended to be in his secrets and believed himself to be so, has often told me that General Washington believed no more in the system (Christianity) than he did." (**The Writings of Thomas Jefferson,** vol. 1, p. 284.)

Dr. Benjamin Rush was one of the ablest physicians of his time and a patriot of the Revolution. The Asa Green spoken of was one of the most noted Presbyterian ministers of the day, and was the chaplain of Congress while the seat of the government was located in Philadelphia. The object of these ministers was to find, if possible, what Washington's religious views were, and to draw from him some sentiment they could use to combat the infidelity of Thomas Paine. The

---

*See Appendix for the account of Washington's sickness and death as written by his secretary, Tobias Lear, from whom Dr. Conway quotes.

result was that orthodoxy received no more comfort than heterodoxy. A glance at an entry in Washington's **Diary** for October 10, 1785, throws great light upon his attitude toward the Church and religion. It will speak for itself: "A Mr. John Lowe on his way to Bishop Seabury for ordination, called and dined here—could not give him more than a general certificate founded on information, respecting his character—having no acquaintance with him, nor any desire to open a correspondence with the **new** ordained bishop."

Washington for social and matrimonial reasons could attend church as little as possible—an average of six times a year at home. He could be a vestryman because that was a political office from whence he went to the House of Burgesses and from whence his taxes were assessed. This was in his interest. He could meet and dine with clergymen and treat them with courtesy. When they addressed him he could say some nice things in reply, just enough to keep them from barking at his heels. But to be involved in a correspondence with a bishop over an ordination or to be mixed up in any of the church imbroglios of the time was more than he could stand and here he drew the line. He has been well called "the sly old fox," and nowhere did he demonstrate this quality better than when he was obliged to deal with the Church, the clergy and religion.

Theodore Parker says:

"He had much of the principle, little of the sentiment of religion. He was more moral than pious. In early life a certain respect for ecclesiastical forms made him vestryman in two churches. This respect for outward forms with ministers and reporters for newspapers very often passes for the substance of religion. It does not appear that Washington took a deep and spontaneous delight in religious emotions more than in poetry, in works of art, or in the beauties of Nature . . . Silence is a figure of speech, and in the latter years of his life I suppose his theological opinions were those of John Adams, Dr. Franklin, and Thomas Jefferson, only he was not a speculative man, and did not care to publish them to the world." (**Six Historic Americans.**)

The Rev. Dr. Abercrombie said, "Washington was a Deist." The Rev. Dr. Wilson said, "I think any one who will candidly do as I have done, will come to the conclusion that he was a Deist and nothing more." Gouverneur Morris said he no more believed in the system of Christianity than Morris did himself. His intimate friend, Bishop White, who perhaps was the best qualified to judge, denies that Washington ever took communion to his knowledge, though he attended Dr. White's church more often than any other while he was President. He also admits that he never heard Washington utter a word which would indicate him to have been a believer; and what is more, he says he never saw him on his knees during prayer, an attitude all Episcopalians assume when performing that function of religion. The positive evidence, I admit, is meagre, but combined with the facts and circumstances to which I have called the reader's attention, it is strong. That he was an evangelical Christian has never been proved and is improbable. That he was a Deist is not inconsistent with any known fact.

Mr. Parker says that silence is a figure of speech. We may add that it is sometimes more eloquent and convincing than words.

The facts of the mythical character of Washington's alleged piety have been before the world for many years. Historians and biographers, not desiring to give offense to the religious public, taught to accept his religiosity as infallibly true, have either not mentioned them at all or spoken of them in whispers. But, as historians develop more courage and more of them speak the truth out loud, more of them admit his Deistic sentiments. William Roscoe Thayer, in his **Life of Washington** (published by Houghton, Mifflin & Co.), says: "I do not discover that he was in any sense an ardent believer. He preferred to say 'Providence,' rather than 'God,' probably because it was less definite." "For a considerable period at one time of his life he did not attend the communion." (p. 239.) "He believed in moral truths and belief with him was putting into practice what he professed." (Ibid.) **"He had imbibed much of the deistic spirit of the 18th Century."** (p. 240.)

Mr. Rupert Hughes has not yet completed his biography of Washington, but three volumes so far having been published. From personal acquaintance with him, however, I know that his view of Washington's religious opinions is substantially in accord with the view of Mr. Thayer and others whom I have cited.

Another recent writer, W. E. Woodward, speaks of them without hesitation in these words:

"He seemed, according to the evidence, to have had no instinct or feeling for religion." "The name of Jesus Christ is not mentioned even once in the vast collection of Washington's published letters. He refers to Providence in numerous letters, but he used the term in such a way as to indicate that he considered Providence as a synonym for destiny or fate." (p. 142.) "Bishop White, who knew him well for many years, wrote after Washington's death that he never heard him express an opinion on any religious subject." "He had no religious feeling himself, but thought religion was a good thing for other people—especially for the common people. Any one who understands American life will recognize the modern captain-of-industry attitude in this point of view." "He considered religion a matter of policy. Of that we might have been sure—knowing as we do his type of mind." "He said nothing about religion—nothing very definite—and was willing to let people think whatever they pleased." (p. 143.)

I think I have given in this chapter plenty of evidence to sustain these writers' opinions. When Messrs. Hughes' and Woodward's books were published, their critics did not deny the truth of their statements of fact, but denounced them for making them. Others, like Woodrow Wilson, in his **Life of Washington,** and Paul Haworth, in his **Washington: The Country Gentlemen,** thinking his religious opinions to be a dangerous subject, have said nothing about them. It is often dangerous to speak the truth.

CHAPTER II

PRESIDENTS WHO WERE PRESBYTERIANS

ANDREW JACKSON

Born, March 15, 1767. Died, June 8, 1845. President, 1829-1837.
The story of the early religious background of the United States is of interest when we consider the beliefs of its people. The wilds of America were early settled by representatives of the then most prominent forms of the Christian faith. While a large number of them emigrated to find on this western continent religious liberty, most of them, if strong enough, sought to to establish, by law, the Church they brought with them.

In New England, with the exception of Rhode Island, Congregationalism was the State Church. In New York, it was at first the Dutch Reformed. Later, the English governors sought to establish the Church of England but the opposition was so strong that they were not successful except in theory. In New Jersey, the same attempt was made, though there was not an Episcopal church in the colony at the time. Pennsylvania granted liberty to all "who confess and acknowledge the one Almighty and eternal God"; but the holders of office "shall be such as profess faith in Jesus Christ." The constitution of Delaware, formed in 1776, declared that all persons professing the Christian religion "ought forever to enjoy equal rights and privileges," but to hold office the acknowledgement of the trinity and the inspiration of the scriptures was mandatory. Maryland was first settled by Catholics. Then the Puritans arrived, obtained power and persecuted them. Later the Church of England was established. The so-called freedom of conscience law of Maryland is a myth. It granted liberty to trinitarian Christians only, the Jew, the Unitarian and the unbeliever being excluded. It punished blasphemy by boring the tongue with a red-hot iron. The first act favoring absolute religious liberty passed in America, and, for all we know to the contrary, in the modern world, was enacted in Rhode Island. There, 20 years before Maryland was settled, Roger Williams proclaimed freedom to all, Christian, Jew, Pagan and Infidel. In 1647, two years before the Maryland law, which did not provide freedom at all, these sentiments of Williams were enacted into a statute.

In Virginia, the Church of England was established, and the penalties for heresy and non-conformity were very severe, even up to the Revolution. The same establishment was set up in the Carolinas. Georgia, under the benevolent Oglethorpe, had no established Church, but Romanists were excluded. When, in 1752, the colony lost its charter, the Church of England was made the State Church.

Among the early settlers was a large proportion of those holding the doctrines of John Calvin. The Puritans of New England, the Dutch settlers of New York, the Scotch and the Ulsterites all held Presbyterian doctrines, though all did not hold to the Presbyterian form of church government. Hence, it is natural that this Church should leave its impress upon the people of the United States and upon some of its

---

*For a full and accurate history of religious laws in the thirteen colonies, see **The Rise of Religious Liberty in America**, by Sanford H. Cobb. Published by Henry Holt & Co., New York City.

statesmen, as it did upon Andrew Jackson, the seventh President. His
parents emigrated from the North of Ireland and settled in South Carolina. Although he was not a communicant until after he retired from
the Presidency, he was a believer in the Christian religion, as taught by
John Calvin, and a fairly regular church attendant.

Andrew Jackson is one of the most picturesque characters in American history. As a boy, he fought in the Revolution, was taken prisoner,
and had his arm cut to the bone by the sword of a British officer because he refused to clean the officer's muddy boots. A planter, frontier
lawyer and judge; a congressman and senator from Tennessee immediately after that State's admission to the Union; a militia general, Indian fighter, hero of the Battle of New Orleans, he became, after a
bitter struggle, President of the United States, the first "man of the
people" to hold this high office. He was so accustomed to the wild life
of the frontier that he did not feel at home anywhere else. He has been
described, when young, as "reckless, impetuous, quarrelsome, and pas-
sionate in temper; thoroughly disinclined to learning of any sort, his
favorite pursuits being racing, gaming and cock-fighting; but he was
possessed of invincible determination, dauntless courage and excelled
in marksmanship and riding, qualities which later served him well." He
fought during his lifetime two duels, in one of which he "killed his
man," and in the other received a slight wound himself. His political
enemies many times published lists of his fights and escapades.

John Parton, one of the best of Jackson's biographers, describes
the circumstances under which he joined the Church, as they were related to him by the Rev. Dr. Edgar, who received the ex-President into
the fold:

> "Ere long a 'protracted meeting' was held in the little church
> on the Hermitage farm. Dr. Edgar conducted the exercises, and
> the family at the Hermitage were constant in their attendance.
> The last day of the meeting arrived, which was also the last
> day of the week. General Jackson sat in his accustomed seat,
> and Dr. Edgar preached. The subject of the sermon was the
> interposition of Providence in the affairs of men, a subject
> congenial with the habitual tone of General Jackson's mind.
> The preacher spoke in detail of the perils which beset the life
> of man, and how often he is preserved from sickness and sud-
> den death. Seeing General Jackson listening with rapt atten-
> tion to his discourse, the eloquent preacher sketched the career
> of a man who, in addition to the ordinary dangers of human
> life, had encountered those of the wilderness, of war, and of
> keen political conflict; who had escaped the tomahawk of the
> savage, the attacks of his country's enemies, the privations
> and fatigues of border warfare, and the aim of the assassin.
> How is it, exclaimed the preacher, that a man endowed with
> reason and gifted with intelligence can pass through such
> scenes as these unharmed, and not see the hand of God in his
> deliverance? While enlarging upon his theme, Dr. Edgar saw
> that his words were sinking into the General's heart, and he
> spoke with unusual animation and impressiveness."

We judge from this that Dr. Edgar had learned his business
well, as those who are familiar with the psychology of conversions
can testify. The biographer continues:

> "The services ended, General Jackson got into his carriage
> and was riding homeward. He was overtaken by Dr. Edgar on
> horseback. He hailed the Doctor and said he wished to speak
> with him. Both having alighted, the general led the clergyman
> a little way into the grove. 'Doctor,' said the general, 'I want
> you to come home with me tonight.' 'I cannot come tonight,'

was his reply: 'I am engaged elsewhere.' Dr. Edgar said he had promised to visit that evening a sick lady, and he felt bound to keep his promise. General Jackson, as though he had not heard the reply, said a third time and more pleadingly than before, 'Doctor, I **want** you to come home with me tonight.' 'General Jackson,' said the clergyman, 'my word is pledged; I cannot break it; but I will be at the Hermitage tomorrow morning very early.'

The anxious man was obliged to be contented with this arrangement, and went home alone. He retired to his apartment. He passed the evening and the greater part of the night in meditation, in reading, in conversing with his beloved daughter and in prayer. He was sorely distressed. Late at night when his daughter left him, he was still agitated and sorrowful. What thoughts passed through his mind as he paced his room in the silence of the night, of **what** sins he repented and **what** actions of his life he wished he had not done, no one knows or ever will know."

Those who have studied the human mind in relation to the emotions will think all of this has a natural interpretation. Many a man and woman view their past careers, think of their errors and realize they must be corrected or their lives will be failures. Many have abandoned their vices and bad habits owing to the fear of losing their health and the respect of their neighbors and friends. Some give up their vices through sheer disgust with them. Self condemnation is not the exclusive property of supernaturalism. Thoughtful people are coming to recognize that the **facts** of religion can be traced to natural causes. The chief aim of the religion of General Jackson's day, as represented by Dr. Edgar, was to save the soul through faith in the supernatural attributes of Christ. It was the teaching of the Presbyterian Church of that day, and is yet the teaching of its creed, that good conduct cannot save in lieu of faith. Such has been the teaching of all other orthodox Churches. They have merely followed the teaching of Paul that faith can be counted for righteousness. Martin Luther said, "If any one says that the Gospel requires works for salvation, I say flat and plain, he is a liar."

Jackson's biographer concludes the story of the General's conversion: "In the morning the Rev. Dr. Edgar appeared soon after sunrise. General Jackson told the joyful history of the night and expressed a desire to be admitted into the Church with his daughter that very morning. The usual questions respecting doctrine and experience were satisfactorily answered by the candidate. Then there was a pause in the conversation. The clergyman said at length: 'General, there is one more question it is my duty to ask you. Can you forgive all your enemies?' The question was evidently unexpected, and the candidate was silent for a while. 'My political enemies,' said he, 'I can freely forgive; but as for those who abused me when I was serving my country in the field, and those who attacked me **for** serving my country—Doctor, that is a different case.'

"The Doctor assured him it was not. Christianity, he said, forbade the indulgence of enmity absolutely and in all cases. No man could be received into a Christian Church who did not cast out of his heart every feeling of that nature. It was a condition that was fundamental and indispensable.

"The Hermitage church was crowded to the utmost of its small capacity; the very windows were darkened with the eager faces of the servants. After the usual services the General rose to make the required public declaration of his concur-

rence with the doctrines, and his resolve to obey the precepts
of the Church. He leaned heavily upon his stick with both hands;
tears rolled down his cheeks. His daughter, the fair young ma-
tron, stood beside him. Amid a silence the most profound the
General answered the questions proposed to him. When he was
formally pronounced a member of the Church, and the clergyman was about to continue the service, the long restrained
feelings of the congregation burst forth in sobs and exclama-
tions which compelled him to pause for several minutes. The
clergyman himself was speechless with emotion, and abandoned himself to the exaultation of the hour. A familiar hymn
was raised in which the entire assembly joined with a fervor
which at once expressed and relieved their feelings."

The conversion of General Jackson gives us an idea of the emotional religion so prevalent a century ago, and which still lingers
among us today. Once the question was put to Bishop White, one of
the pastors of George Washington, "What is your opinion of revivals?"
The Bishop answered, "They have one great evil, in that they cause
some to mistake their animal for their spiritual nature." Those who
want evidence of this should read the chapter in Henry A. Wise's
Seven Decades of the Union, in which he tells of Tangier Island, located in Chesapeake Bay, and a part of Virginia, where revivals were
a regular feature of the island's life. After a visit from a prominent
evangelist the ministers of Pittsburgh met and resolved that they would
give no more countenance to traveling evangelists.

It must be remembered that General Jackson was of a very emotional nature, and all his life was imbued with strong passions. In
all his career these prevailed. Sometimes he was desperately right,
while at other times he was equally desperately wrong. He was not
a thinker, a student or even a reader, except of the newspapers. Although he had been admitted to the bar, it is said he never read a law
book through. He was emphatically a man of action and in that
sphere he shines in American history. Later he forgot that he had
agreed to forgive his enemies, and shortly before he died he said the
greatest mistake he had ever made was when he did not hang John
C. Calhoun, the leader of the South Carolina nullifiers. To the end
of his life he delighted to show his friends the pistol with which he
had killed Charles Dickinson in a duel.

It must be remembered that those who have led rough, irregular
lives in their youth often become fanatically religious in old age.
"Old Hickory," as he was called owing to his unbending nature, except for his military exploits, does not stand as well in history as
he stood in the estimation of his contemporaries. Yet in his com-
mendable qualities many think it would not be an evil to have more
men of his stamp in public life today.

JAMES KNOX POLK

Born, November 2, 1795. Died, June 15, 1849.

President, March 4, 1845—March 4, 1849.

When James Knox Polk, of Tennessee, was nominated by the Dem-
ocratic party for President, in 1844, after he had been in Congress 14
years, Speaker of the House of Representatives for two terms and
Governor of his own State, he was but little known outside of it. His
selection was a surprise even to his own party. Governor Letcher, of
Virginia, exclaimed, "Polk, great God, what a nomination!" Stephen
A. Douglas remarked, "From henceforth no private citizen is safe!"
The Whigs sang in a campaign song:

> "Ha! Ha! Ha! Such a nominee,
> As James K. Polk of Tennessee."

He was nominated because the current issues were the annexation of Texas and the extension of slavery, two things he could be depended upon to accomplish. From 1840 to 1860 is known in our history as the era of weak men in the White House. All were mere politicians and "trimmers," when a real principle was broached. As was the case with a President in our time, the arduous duties of his office caused President Polk to break down in health. He left Washington an incurably sick man and died within a few months after he had returned to his home in Tennessee.

The Polk family, like most families of Scotch ancestry, was Presbyterian. Mrs. Polk was of the same faith and prohibited dancing and card playing in the White House. During the Tyler administration the Presidential mansion was the scene of gaiety and grand entertainments; but on the inauguration of President Polk it was said the reign of the Cavalier ended and that of the Puritan began. Yet the President was not a member of any Church and had never been baptized. While he was an habitual attendant of the Presbyterian Church, with his wife, his own private opinions leaned toward Methodism. McCormac's **Life of Polk**, the only one in existence so far as we know, on page 721, contains the following statement:

"The Polk family, as well as Mrs. Polk, were Presbyterians, but the ex-President was not a member of any Church. He went regularly with his wife to the Church of her choice, though his preference was for the Methodist denomination. A few days before his death his aged mother came from Columbia bringing her own pastor in the hope that her son might accept baptism and unite with the Presbyterian Church. But the son recalled a promise once given to the Rev. Mr. McFerren, of the Methodist Church, that, when he was ready to join the Church, the Rev. McFerren should baptise him. Having thus formally embraced Christianity, he felt prepared to meet the 'great event.' "

Theodore Parker says that on his deathbed he acknowledged that his good works had been as "filthy rags." But he was safely on board the old ship of Zion before she weighed anchor and spread her sails for the Elysian fields.

JAMES BUCHANAN
Born, April 22, 1791. Died, June 1, 1868.
President, March 4, 1857—March 4, 1861.

James Buchanan was the last of the pre-Civil War Presidents. He had been in the House and Senate for 20 years, had been Secretary of State and Minister to England. Born in Pennsylvania and descended from Scotch emigrants, he was a Presbyterian by inheritance; but like Presidents Jackson and Polk he never joined the Church until he retired to private life. All his life, however, he had been a regular attendant, and a contributor to all Churches, including the Catholic.

In August, 1860, his last year in the White House, President Buchanan was stopping at Bedford Springs, a summer resort in Pennsylvania, where the Rev. Dr. William M. Paxton, pastor of the First Presbyterian Church of New York City, was also a guest. Having had some previous acquaintance with the reverend doctor he one day invited him into his room, where he opened his heart. He said:

"I think I may say that for 12 years I have been in the habit of reading the Bible and praying daily. I have never had any one with whom I have felt disposed to converse, and now that I find you here, I have thought you would understand my feelings, and that I would venture to open my mind to you upon this important subject, and ask for an explanation of some things I do not clearly understand."

He then asked Dr. Paxton what a religious experience is, and wanted to know how a man might know he was a Christian, to which the doctor gave replies that satisfied him. Thereupon the President said: "Well, sir, I thank you. My mind is now made up. I hope I am a Christian. I think I have had some of the experience which you describe, and as soon as I retire from my office as President, I will unite with the Presbyterian Church."

Dr. Paxton here became excited. It is not often a minister has an opportunity to gather a President of the United States into the fold. Then he was an old man, and might die, as did President Harrison, who so sorely disappointed the Rev. Dr. Hawley. Therefore he exclaimed, "Why not **now**, Mr. President? God's invitation is **now** and you should not say **tomorrow**." President Buchanan replied with deep feeling and a strong gesture: "I must delay, **for the honor of religion**. If I were to unite with the Church now, they would say hypocrite, from Maine to Georgia." Here he was different from some statesmen of today who seem to take no interest in religion until they get into politics, when "the honor of religion" does not disturb them.

Shortly after the 4th of March, 1861, President Buchanan kept his word and was received into the Presbyterian Church of Lancaster, Pa., his home city. He was fortunate in living 80 years ago instead of today. Now he would not be permitted to serve his term in office. He would be compelled to run successfully the clerical gauntlet before he could be elected.

GROVER CLEVELAND
Born, March 18, 1837. Died, July 24, 1908. President, March 4, 1885—March 4, 1889. March 4, 1893—March 4, 1897.

The first Democratic President to be elected after the Civil War was the son of the Rev. Richard Cleveland, a Presbyterian minister. Like many other mininsters, the Rev. Mr. Cleveland supported a large family on a small salary. His children were therefore obliged to work as soon as they were able. Grover worked in a store in Fayetteville, N.Y., where his father held his last charge before his death. In this place, we are informed by a living sister of Mr. Cleveland, he joined the church of which his father was the pastor.

Later he went to New York City, where he taught for a while in a school for the blind. Here he became acquainted with Fanny Crosby, the noted hymn writer. He moved from New York City to Buffalo, where he studied law, was admitted to the bar, entered politics and laid the foundation of his later eminence. While in Buffalo, he kept his name on the roll of his father's old church in Fayetteville. That he was a member of the Church in Buffalo is doubtful. While living there, he had the reputation of being a blunt, honest man of the world, whose attendance at the house of Bacchus was more regular than his attendance in the house of God.

He loved to play pinochle in favorite saloons, and had he not been a drinking man would perhaps not have been elected Mayor of Buffalo, from which office he stepped into the Governor's chair and afterwards into the Presidency. He happened to be in a saloon drinking a glass of beer and eating a lunch, when in came a number of Democratic politicians looking for a candidate for mayor. One of them in a joking manner said, "Let us nominate Grover." The joke became serious. He was nominated and elected; then nominated and elected governor by the greatest majority a governor ever received; and in less than four years after he stood in front of the saloon bar, was inaugurated President of the United States.

Those who, like the present writer, recall the presidential campaign of 1884 between James G. Blaine and Grover Cleveland, remember the

bitter, abusive, acrid personalities of that year. Mr. Blaine had a
vulnerable public record, and his opponents flaunted the "Mulligan
letters" with all their strength. His private life, however, had been
beyond reproach. When he was nominated, Mr. Cleveland was an almost
unknown man outside of his own State, but his public record as sheriff,
mayor and governor commended him to the people of the United
States. His adversaries then launched an attack upon his private life.
One charge was that he had not done his duty to his country during
the Civil War by enlisting in the army, but had hired a substitute. The
fact was that owing to two brothers having enlisted, he had to remain
home as the sole support of his mother and two sisters. When the draft
came, he borrowed $300 to hire a man to go in his stead.

The second charge was not so easily met. A certain Rev. George
H. Ball, of Buffalo, charged him with seduction and bastardy. This
preacher of that "charity that thinketh no evil" prayed God not to
strike him dead because he had voted for Cleveland for governor. The
friends of Mr. Cleveland prepared to issue a denial, but he would not
permit them. He said, "It is true. Tell the truth!" He held that while
he was willing to defend all his public acts, his private acts did not
concern the public. He was quite justified in this view. Another minister, the Rev. Mr. Burchard, in his "Rum, Romanism and Rebellion"
speech, quite neutralized the attack of the Rev. Mr. Ball on the youth-
ful morals of Mr. Cleveland, who was elected, the first Democratic
President in a quarter of a century. The illegitimate child of which so
much was said afterwards became a prominent professional man and
an honored citizen of Buffalo. His father was twice elected President
of the United States, the Rev. Mr. Ball received much free advertising,
and when the smoke cleared away no one was injured beyond recovery.

After Grover Cleveland entered the White House, he gave more
attention to the Church, as he also did to matrimony, marrying his
ward, Miss Frances Folsom, a young lady of great personal charm. It
was not until his second term, on which he entered March 4, 1893, that
he became prominently religious. A wave of piety swept over the
country during this year of the great panic, as had happened in the
two former periods of financial distress, in 1857 and 1873. The Churches
registered their protests against the inaugural ball, which, almost
from the foundation of the government, had been an occasion of great
gaiety. The new President was prompt to unite with the Churches in
voicing his disapproval.

This was also the year of the World's Columbian Exposition in
Chicago. The Churches had been organizing for three years to prevent the doors from opening on Sunday. Religious societies had met
in conventions and pledged themselves not to attend unless the Sabbath was strictly observed. The question was carried into the courts.
The ministers demanded that Cleveland call out the military, if necessary, to shut the gates, but while he sympathized with the Sabbatar-
ians he did not go that far.

In the fall, he recognized Jesus Christ in his Thanksgiving Proclamation, something no other President had ever done. The pace for
religious legislation having been set during the administration of President Harrison, President Cleveland was now looked upon as the patron
saint of the "National Reformers" and other theocratic organizations.
During Cleveland's second administration, a Sunday law was introduced for the District of Columbia, as was also the "Christian amendment," placing God in the Constitution and making Christianity the
official religion of the State. The late William Jennings Bryan was
preparing to advocate such an amendment when he died.

Nor can the sincerity of Mr. Cleveland be doubted. While he had
not been a "practical Christian" at all times, he seemed to revert to
the piety of his youth as he grew older. This happens to many who

have never given the foundation of religion their attention. On January 7, 1904, after the death of his oldest daughter Ruth, he wrote to a friend:

"I had a season of great trouble in keeping out of my mind the idea that Ruth was in the cold, cheerless grave instead of in the arms of her Saviour. It seems to me I mourn our darling Ruth's death more and more. So much of the time I can only think of her as dead, not joyfully living in heaven. God has come to my help and I have felt able to adjust my thought to dear Ruth's death with as much comfort as selfish humanity will permit. One thing I can say: not for a moment since she left us has a rebellious thought entered my mind."

His sister writes that she knew "his boyhood's faith brightened his dying hours." The grief of a father for the death of a loved child is not a proper subject for discussion, and we can be pleased to think that under the circumstances he found consolation. We could say the same had he been a Buddhist, a Mohammedan, a Mormon or a Confucian.

Yet President Cleveland was not a Puritan, and if he were alive today, he would not stand well on the Anti-Saloon League's card-index. He liked beer, fished on Sunday and kept a store of good liquor for himself and his friends.

John S. Wise, in his **Recollections of Thirteen Presidents**, says there were two men in American history who above all others were attacked by venomous personal abuse, Grover Cleveland and Robert G. Ingersoll. This was because of their holding unpopular ideas. Fifty years ago, to be a Democrat in some sections was synonymous with being a traitor, an enemy of your country, its prosperity and happiness; while to say openly that you did not accept the orthodox Christian religion was to place yourself outside the pale of social recognition and to be looked upon as having hoofs and horns.

Years ago, I knew an old man in a rural community who was an outspoken "Infidel." A woman who knew him remarked: "I do not see why some people are so bitter at Mr. —————. He does not appear to be any different from other men." Since the partisan prejudices that swayed the minds of his contemporaries have become extinct, history has been just toward President Cleveland. Now, regardless of party, he is considered to have been one of our most efficient Presidents.

BENJAMIN HARRISON
Born, August 20, 1833. Died, March 13, 1901. President, March 4, 1889—March 4, 1893.

Benjamin Harrison, the 23rd President of the United States, was a great-grandson of Benjamin Harrison, who signed the Declaration of Independence, and a grandson of William Henry Harrison, the ninth President, at whose house he was born, in 1833. He was a Presbyterian, an elder in the Church, and the first President who was unquestionably a communicant in an orthodox Church at the time he was elected. Grover Cleveland was a communicant in his youth and late in life, but there is no evidence that he was such when he was first elected.

President Harrison was deeply religious, a believer in divine providence, and thought himself an object of its particular care. Knowing this, during his administration the Churches were successful in introducing bills in Congress to promote religion by law. On May 21, 1888, Senator Henry W. Blair, of New Hamphire, introduced a "National Sunday Rest Bill," the preamble of which read, "A bill to secure to the people the enjoyment of the first day of the week, commonly known as Sunday, as a day of rest, and to promote its observance as a day of religious worship." A great outcry was raised against this bill, as worded, and on December 9, 1889, Senator Blair re-introduced it, making the title read, "A bill to secure to the people the privilege of rest and religious worship, free from the disturbance of others, on the first day of the week." Except that it granted exemption from the penalties those "who conscientiously believe in and observe any other day than Sunday as the Sabbath or day of religious worship," its provisions were not different from the first. Not since 1829 had a bill for the enforcement of a Sunday law been introduced in the national legislature. As the bill entered into the realm of conscience and the field of religious controversy, it was not reported from the committee room and died a natural death. Similar bills have been since introduced and have met the same fate. Four days after introducing his Sunday bill, Senator Blair introduced an "Educational Amendment" to the Constitution of the United States, section 2 of which read: "Each State in this Union shall establish a system of public schools, adequate for the education of all the children living therein, between the ages of six and 16 years inclusive, in the common branches of knowledge, and in virtue, morality, and the principles of the Christian religion." This, like his Sunday bill, was very deceptive, and, like it, was laid on the table. Senator Blair having failed, Mr. W. C. P. Breckinridge, of Kentucky, who was later to acquire an unsavory reputation, introduced, on January 6, 1890, a Sunday bill for the District of Columbia, which also failed. President Harrison's well-known orthodox predilection had encouraged the sponsors of these bills. Religious legislation has always been unpopular, except with the extremists in the Church, yet it is an ever present danger.

General Harrison had an undistinguished though honorable record as an officer in the Civil War, and was Senator from Indiana for one term. He was a splendid platform speaker, and publicly had a great influence over the masses. In private he had the reputation of being cold and distant.

WOODROW WILSON
Born, December 28, 1856. Died, February 3, 1924. President, March 4, 1913—March 4, 1921.

Our World War President was Presbyterian through a long line of Scotch and Irish ancestors on both his father's and mother's side. His father, the Rev. James Ruggles Wilson, was a Presbyterian minister who was born in Ohio, of Irish ancestry. His mother's father, the Rev. Thomas Woodrow, after whom he was named, came from Scotland, and was a graduate of the University of Glasgow. Each held a high position in the Church, and both are known in its history.

The father of the future President moved from Ohio to Virginia early in the 50's. Woodrow Wilson was born at Staunton, Va.; later, the Wilson family moved to Augusta, Georgia. While in Ohio the Rev. Wilson seemed to take no particular interest in the then all-absorbing question of slavery. But in 1861, he was a delegate to the National Assembly of the Presbyterian Church, held in Philadelphia, where a resolution was passed reading out of the Church all slave-holders. The Rev. Mr. Wilson at once took up the cudgel for his adopted section, and invited southern Presbyterians to meet with him in Augusta, where he organized the Southern Presbyterian Church. He cast his fortunes with the South during the war and became a chaplain in the Confederate Army, while his brothers were fighting in the Union Army. After the war, when, upon a visit to Ohio, he was asked if he was a reconstructed rebel, his reply was, "No, only a whipped one." When his son was first proposed as a teacher in Princeton University, objection was raised against him because of his southern antecedents.

The Rev. Joseph Ruggles Wilson was an interesting character. He had all the geniality of the Celt, and was far from being puritanical.

He loved a good dinner, enjoyed smoking his pipe, and sometimes took a nip of "Old Scotch." This, of course, was before the crusade for Prohibition had captured the Protestant Churches. His Irish wit, combined with his knowledge and interesting conversation, made him a social favorite, as those who remember him when he passed his latter years at the home of his son will recall.

The maternal uncle of the World War President also had an interesting history, which is recorded in the chronicles of his adopted country. The Rev. James Woodrow was originally a printer and publisher, and sometimes, to hasten work, it was necessary for his printers to work nights. He would permit no Sunday work. At midnight Saturday he compelled his employes to cease their labors, but promptly at two minutes after 12 on Monday morning they resumed. In this way the work was accomplished, but the old Scotch custom of Sabbath keeping was not invalidated. Yet while he was a very religious man, and conformed to the standards of the Presbyterian Church, he finally got into trouble, and had to leave the Church. He believed in and preached Evolution. A minority in the Church defended him, but he was ousted from the Presbyterian seminary in Columbia, S. C., where he was a teacher of the natural sciences. Andrew D. White, in **The Warfare Between Science and Theology in Christendom**, vol. 1, pp. 317-318, thus speaks of his case:

"This hostile movement became so strong that, in spite of the favorable action of the directors of the seminary, and against the efforts of a broad-minded minority in the representative bodies having ultimate charge of the institution, the delegates from the various synods raised a storm of orthodoxy and drove Dr. Woodrow from his post. Happily, he was at the same time professor in the University of South Carolina in the same city of Columbia, and from his chair in that institution he continued to teach natural science with the approval of the great majority of thinking men in that region; hence, the only effect of the attempt to crush him was, that his position was made higher, respect for him deeper, and his reputation wider."

Dr. Woodrow was a real man, and would not compromise as many ministers have done. He finally left the Church and became the president of a bank. He was a member of a number of learned scientific societies both in Europe and America. His trial for heresy, in the 1880's, aroused national attention. Nearly 40 years later, when his nephew was President of the United States and the Fundamentalists had renewed the old battle against Evolution, some one wrote to President Wilson asking whether he believed in Evolution. He replied: "Of course, like every other man of education and intelligence I do believe in organic Evolution. It surprises me that at this late date such questions should be raised." It is good that while these Scotch Presbyterians are often very stubborn in maintaining their opinions, when they change them, they are equally stubborn in defending their new ones.

It will, at this point, be pertinent to consider President Wilson's views upon the relation of science to certain problems. He once said that college instructors could "easily forget that they were training citizens as well as drilling pupils"; that a college should be "a school of duty." When he was once attacked for being hostile to science, he replied:

"I have no indictment against what science has done: I have only a warning to utter against the atmosphere which has stolen from laboratories into lecture rooms and into the general air of the world at large. Science has not changed the nature of society, has not made history a whit easier to understand, human nature a whit easier to reform. It has won for us a great liberty in the physical world, a liberty from superstitious fear and disease, a freedom to use nature as a familiar servant, but it has not freed us from ourselves. We have not given science too big a place in our education; but we have made a perilous mistake in giving it too great a preponderance in method over every other branch of study."

On the subject of the relation of science to religion, there are three sets of opinions: those of the Fundamentalists, who reject science; of the Rationalists, who reject the claims of religion; of the Modernists, of whom President Wilson was one, who accept science in the physical world, but will not be bound by its laws in the spiritual.

Mr. Wilson was the first president of Princeton University who was not a minister. When he moved there, he found two Presbyterian Churches, the First and the Second. He thought but one was needed, and tried to unite them. He joined the Second and was elected an elder, but afterwards left it and gave his support to the First. His entire family attended church services, but the children did not go to Sunday School. Mrs. Wilson taught them the Sunday School lesson and the Westminster catechism at home. President Wilson often led the chapel exercises in the college, but his talks took a practical trend. For instance, he once took as his text a verse from Paul's address to Agrippa: "Whereupon, O King Agrippa, I was not disobedient unto the heavenly vision." (Acts, 26:19.) He then enlarged upon the necessity of all having a vision, or a purpose in life.

President Wilson was not a Puritan. His daughter says that, like his father, he was a mixture of dignity and gaiety. He liked to play whist, euchre and backgammon, was a remarkable mimic and could tell endless dialect stories. Shortly after his entrance into the White House, in 1913, his Secretary of State, William Jennings Bryan, suggested over the telephone that he make his administration a temperance, or white ribbon, affair, and, conforming to the custom in President Hayes' day, not serve wine. Mr. Wilson replied he would not do this for three reasons: first, it had been the custom to serve wine at public dinners, except in one administration, since the foundation of the government; second, he was not a Prohibitionist, and, third, he liked a drink sometimes himself. The Volstead Act was passed and went into effect without his signature.

Yet anomalies are associated with both Bryan and Wilson. The first, an apostle of peace, rests in a military cemetery. The second, of the sturdiest Presbyterian stock, found his last resting place in a gorgeous Episcopal cathedral.

CHAPTER III.

PRESIDENTS WHO WERE UNITARIANS

In point of numbers the Unitarian Church has always been among the minor religious bodies. Yet its influence upon the intellectual, moral and literary forces of the United States has been far greater proportionately than its numerical strength. No other Church has contributed to this country so many distinguished men and women in all departments of human activity. A few words touching the history of this Church, particularly in America, will enable us better to comprehend the subject.

From the earliest history of the Christian Church there was controversy over disputed theological questions. Among these none occupied greater attention than the nature of God. Some held to his unity, others to the trinity. Those holding the first view were almost successful in making it the dogma of the whole Church. They were specially strong in the West. They were called Arians, after their leader, Arius; sometimes Socinians and later Unitarians. The Council of Nice, the first ecumenical council of the Church, held in the city of that name in southeastern France, was assembled to consider two questions: the canon of the Bible, and the "Arian controversy," as the question of the Godhead was then called. This council sent Arius into exile and condemned his doctrines. Afterwards, he died suddenly, and, as his friends maintained, through the treachery of his enemies.

Wherever Unitarianism penetrated, it was persecuted and stamped out. The last two heretics burned at the stake in England (in 1612), Bartholomew Legate and Edward Wightman, were put to death for denying the trinity. A special law for the punishment of this offense by death was passed during the Commonwealth. In the toleration act of 1689 all dissenters except Unitarians were granted freedom of worship. In spite of persecution they grew, and one of the most distinguished writers on Christian evidence, Dr. Nathaniel Lardner, was a Unitarian, and Unitarian views were held by John Milton, the poet, Sir Isaac Newton, the scientist, and John Locke, the philosopher.

In the last quarter of the 18th Century they had two distinguished advocates in Richard Price and Joseph Priestley, the latter, the discoverer of oxygen. In Birmingham, a mob attacked the house of Dr. Priestley, burned it to the ground, destroying all his valuable scientific apparatus. He was driven out of the city and took refuge in the United States where he died in Pennsylvania, in 1804. Some of his descendants are still among us. In 1813 toleration was granted the Unitarian Church.

The invasion of Unitarian thought among the puritanical churches of New England began in the last quarter of the 18th Century. There was an intellectual and moral revulsion against the doctrines of original sin, predestination, election, hell, and the blood atonement. King's Chapel, built in 1749, the oldest Episcopal church in New England, became Unitarian. James Truslow Adams, in his **New England in the Republic**, p. 220, quotes from G. W. Cooke's **Unitarianism in America**, p. 75:

> "In Boston a visitor wrote in 1791 that the ministers there were so diverse in their views that they could not agree in any one point in theology. Ten years later there was but **one minister in that city who accepted the doctrine of the Trinity.**"

In 1810 the great controversy upon the subject was still on, and by 1825 Unitarianism had captured a large number of the New England churches, and some of the ablest ministers gave their adherence to its views. In Massachusetts, Church and State were united. The town elected the minister and the people were taxed for his support. Should the majority vote for a Unitarian, he was declared the town minister. The orthodox were then obliged to give up the meeting house, and hold services in the school house or in a hall, or build another church. In the rebellion against the rigid Calvinistic dogmas so many churches were lost to the orthodox that in 1833 they were glad to separate Church and State, and support their ministers without the aid of public taxation.

Two of the greatest Unitarian preachers of the first half of the 19th Century were William Ellery Channing and Theodore Parker. The latter came to deny the truth of the miracles of the New Testament, and after a while the Church was divided between the supernaturalists and the naturalists. Today, while they have their differences, none are supernaturalists. Unitarians have always held that character, not speculative theology, is the chief consideration in religion. As to their doctrines, we can do no better than to quote from one of their best-known present day ministers.[*]

"Unitarianism simply asserts that any man, white or black, rich or poor, ignorant or educated, Jew or Gentile, bond or free, Christian or pagan, orthodox or heterodox, theist or atheist, is entitled to think as he sees fit and yet not be denied the right of religious fellowship. It asserts that every man has a right to enter into religious fellowship without being obliged to recognize the authority of certain officers or documents, and without promising to confine his search after truth to the limitations imposed by certain Roman bulls and Protestant creeds. It established a hundred years ago and maintains today amid the almost infinite variety of Churches, one where a man may follow truth to the uttermost bounds and speak the truth as he finds it to the uttermost consequences and be responsible not to any outside authority, either ecclesiastical or biblical, but only to his own conscience.

"Without going into detail as to its growth and influence, I might say that there are nearly 500 churches affiliated with this organization, some called by other names than Unitarian, of which at least half are in New England, chiefly in Massachusetts. These churches are absolutely free in doctrine and polity, so that they vary considerably, each church in its belief and in its practise being determined largely by the training which it has received from the pulpit. Some of them are not very far removed from the liberal type of Congregationalism, while others have discarded almost every vestige of traditional Christianity and are seeking to build a rational religion upon the foundation of the results of modern science; some cling to the theological interpretation of human experience while others have adopted a purely scientific attitude toward life; some are ardently theistic while others are enthusiastically humanistic.

"The very foundation stone of the Unitarian faith is the belief that truth should be taken as authority and not authority as truth. The only thing to which intellectually a free Unitarian can afford to bow is truth."

---

[*]The Rev. John H. Dietrich, minister of the First Unitarian Church, Minneapolis, Minn.

It is well to add that the influence of Unitarian thought is not
and has not been limited to its own organizations and pulpits. It has
affected all other Churches and ministers of all other denominations.

No other Church in the United States has had so many distinguished adherents. Four Presidents have been outspoken Unitarians:
John Adams, John Quincy Adams, Millard Fillmore, and William
Howard Taft. Were we to add to these, four others, who held expressed Unitarian views, but were not members of the Church, Thomas
Jefferson, Abraham Lincoln, Rutherford B. Hayes, and George Washington (whose only expressed religion was simple Deism), we would
have more Unitarian Presidents than can be found in any other denomination. We do not include them in this chapter because we do not
want to attach to any man a label which he never adopted himself.

Of our great statesmen, John C. Calhoun, Hannibal Hamlin, Dan-
iel Webster, Thomas Pickering, Edward Everett, Charles Sumner, Fisher
Ames, John A. Andrew, Robert M. La Follette, and many others, were
Unitarians.

Four Justices of the U.S. Supreme Court (two of them Chief
Justices), John Marshall, Joseph Story, Stanley Matthews and William
Howard Taft, have been Unitarians.

Many of our great writers, Bryant, Longfellow, Lowell, Whittier,
Holmes, Emerson, Bayard Taylor, George W. Curtis, Helen Hunt, Thomas
Wentworth Higginson, Edward Everett Hale, Brete Harte, Richard Stod-
dard, E. C. Steadman, Thomas Bailey Aldrich, Henry D. Thoreau, Louisa
M. Alcott, and many others, have professed the Unitarian faith. Among
educators included in this denomination are Horace Mann, Peter Cooper,
Ezra Cornell, David Starr Jordan, and every president of Harvard
University for 120 years.

The same can be said of many of our great historians, including
Bancroft, Motley, Prescott, Sparks, Palfrey, Parkman and Fiske.

Among American scientific men who preferred Unitarianism were
Agassiz, Peirce, Bowditch and Draper.

Noted women of the Unitarian faith include, Margaret Fuller,
Lydia M. Child, Lucretia Mott, Helen Hunt Jackson, Mary A. Livermore,
Dorothea Dix, Julia Ward Howe, author of the "Battle Hymn of the
Republic," Charlotte Cushman, the great actress, Maria Mitchell, the
astronomer, Elizabeth Cady Stanton, Lucy Stone and Susan B. Anthony.*

In the Hall of Fame, in New York City, are the busts of 63 eminent
Americans. Twenty-two of these, more than a third, were Unitarians,
and one-third more of them were of Unitarian belief, though never
connected with any organization. No intelligent American can afford
to ignore the influence of Unitarians and Unitarian thought in our
history.

Then we must not fail to notice the one great vicarious atonement
heresy has offered to the Moloch of orthodoxy in the United States,
in Thomas Paine. Surely he was despised and rejected of men, and
received many stripes. Yet four of his contemporaries, Washington,
John Adams, Jefferson and Benjamin Franklin, held substantially his
religious views, though they did not shout them from the house top,
as did Paine when he wrote the **Age of Reason**. And it would be difficult
to decide which was the more bitter in his repudiation of the orthodox
religion, Paine, Jefferson or John Adams. Yet this was the creed of
Paine as written by himself:

"I believe in one God and no more! and I hope for happiness
beyond this life. I believe in the equality of man, and I believe

---

*An English Unitarian, Sara Flower Adams, wrote the well-known hymn,
"Nearer, My God, to Thee."

that religious duties consist in doing justice, loving mercy, and endeavoring to make our fellow creatures happy.

"Nothing that is here said can apply, even with the most distant disrespect, to the **real** character of Jesus Christ. He was a virtuous and amiable man. The morality he preached and practised was of the most benevolent kind; and though similar systems of morality have been preached by Confucius, and by some of the Greek philosophers, many years before, and by Quakers since, and by many good men in all ages, it has not been excelled by any."

This would make Thomas Paine, were he alive today, a Unitarian of the most conservative kind.

JOHN ADAMS
Born, October 30, 1735. Died, July 4, 1826. President, March 4, 1797—March 4, 1801.

The Adams family, in the number of its representatives in public service and in other positions of prominence, is one of the most noted in American history. Few families have produced distinguished representatives in more than one generation. In the Adamses we have two generations of Presidents, three of diplomats, and many of them have demonstrated marked ability in various fields of endeavor.

Its first representative, John Adams, was one of the first to take a stand against the aggressions of England. He was a member of the first Continental Congress, a signer of the Declaration of Independence, Minister to France, Holland and England, the first Vice President and the second President, as such the first to occupy the White House as a residence when the seat of government was transferred to Washington. John Adams came of sturdy New England farmer stock, and a sturdy man he ever was. Entering Harvard College, his first intention was to study for the orthodox ministry, but he abandoned it for the law. The reason can be surmised, when later we read in his **Works** his opinion of the orthodoxy of his time, and the relative merits of the ministry and the law:

"People are not disposed to inquire for piety, integrity, good sense or learning in a young preacher, but for stupidity (for so I must call the pretended sanctity of some absolute dunces), irresistible grace, and original sin." (**Works**, vol. 1, p. 37.) "The pulpit is no place for you, young man! and the sooner you give up all thoughts of it the better for you, though the worse for it."

When he had fixed his eyes upon the law, he said: "If I can gain the honor of treading in the rear, and silently admiring the noble air and gallant achievements of the foremost rank, I shall think myself worthy of a louder triumph than if I headed the whole army of orthodox preachers." (**Works**, vol. 2, p. 31.)

In 1764, he married Miss Abigail Smith, daughter of the minister of Weymouth. The Rev. Mr. Smith did not take a fancy to his prospective son-in-law any more than the son-in-law was favorably impressed by orthodox ministers. Mr. Smith had promised his daughters that on the Sunday following their marriage they would be at liberty to select the text for his sermon. His older daughter Mary married first and chose, "Mary hath chosen the better part." When Abby was married to John Adams, she selected, "John came neither eating nor drinking, and ye say, He hath a devil."

John Adams' grandson, Charles Francis Adams, his biographer and editor of his **Works**, thus states Mr. Adams' position upon the subject of religion:

"He devoted himself to a very elaborate examination of the religion of all ages and nations, the results of which he committed to paper in a desultory manner. The issue of it was the formation of his theological opinions very much in the mold accepted by the Unitarians of New England. Rejecting, with the independent spirit which in early life had driven him from the ministry, the prominent doctrines of Calvinism, the trinity, the atonement and election, he was content to settle down upon the Sermon on the Mount as a perfect code presented to men by a more than mortal teacher."

While the cautious Washington was reticent upon the subject of religion, blunt-spoken John Adams did not hesitate to say what he thought. In a letter written to Thomas Jefferson in 1817 he said:

"Twenty times in the course of my late readings, have I been on the point of breaking out, 'This would be the best of all worlds if there were no religion in it!' But in this exclamation I should have been as fanatical as Bryant or Cleverly. Without religion, this world would be something not fit to be mentioned in polite company—I mean hell. So far from believing in the total and universal depravity of human nature, I believe there is no individual totally depraved. The most abandoned scoundrel that ever existed never wholly extinguished his conscience, and while conscience remains there is some religion. Popes, Jesuits, Sarbonnists, and Inquisitors have some religion. Fears and terrors appear to have produced a universal credulity—but fears of pain and death here do not seem so unconquerable as fears of what is to come hereafter." (**Works**, vol. 10, p. 254.)

These were bold words for his day. Jefferson in reply said if by religion was meant the orthodox type, Mr. Adams was wholly correct in saying "This would be the best of all worlds if there were no religion in it."

Speaking of revelation, Mr. Adams said, "The human understanding is a revelation from its maker, and can never be disputed or doubted." "No miracles, no prophecies are necessary to prove celestial communication." (**Works**, vol. 10, p. 66.)

Of eternal damnation, a doctrine insisted upon by the orthodox of his day, he said: "I believe in no such thing. My adoration of the author of the Universe is too profound and too sincere. The love of God and his creation—delight, joy, triumph, exultation in my own existence—though but an atom, a **molecule organique**, in the Universe—these are my religion."

He does not believe in demoniacal possession. Even if the Evangelists do, he does not: "Howl, snarl, bite, ye Calvinistic, ye Athanasian divines, if ye will. Ye will say I am no Christian. I say ye are no Christians, and there the account is balanced. Yet I believe all the honest men among you are Christians in my sense of the word." (Vol. 10, p. 67.)

In other words, he believed that all good men are Christians regardless of their theological belief.

John Adams' **Diary** and his letters to Mrs. Adams are among the most interesting of our Revolutionary literature, and nothing throws more light upon the times. Mrs. Adams was a most delightful and intellectual woman, religious without being a bigot. For some years Mr. Adams and Thomas Jefferson was estranged, owing to the bitterness of political differences. Through the influence of Mrs. Adams their friendship was renewed, and in their old age they corresponded with each other; among other things upon the subject of religion, on which they were in hearty agreement. When Mrs. Adams died, in 1818, Jef-

ferson wrote Adams a beautiful letter of sympathy,* to which John
Adams made the following acknowledgement:

> "I do not know how to prove physically, that we shall
> meet and know each other in a future state; nor does Revelation,
> as I can find, give us any positive assurance of such a felicity.
> My reasons for believing it, as I do most undoubtedly, are that
> I cannot conceive such a being could make such a species as
> the human, merely to live and die on this earth. If I did not
> believe in a future state, I should believe in no God. This Uni-
> verse, this all would appear, with all of its swelling pomp, a
> boyish firework. And if there be a future state, why should the
> Almighty dissolve forever all the tender ties which unite us
> so delightfully in this world, and forbid us to see each other in
> the next?" (vol. 10, pp. 362-363.)

John Adams wrote a **History of the Jesuits**, whom he did not admire. He was a member of the Massachusetts constitutional conventions of 1779 and 1820. There he made a strenuous fight to separate
Church and State, but failed, the opposition being too strong for him
to overcome. His aim was, however, achieved, seven years after his
death. He presented his home town, Quincy, with a church building,
which today houses a prosperous Unitarian congregation. Here he
was buried, as was his son, John Quincy Adams.

JOHN QUINCY ADAMS
**Born, July 11, 1767. Died, February 23, 1848. President, March
4, 1825—March 4, 1829.**

John Quincy Adams, the oldest son of John Adams, enjoyed many
advantages. He came from sound stock, both on his father's and
mother's side, and he was trained by his father, whom he accompanied,
when he was but 12 years old, on his mission to France, in 1779. He
was placed in a school at Paris, and later attended the University of
Leyden, in Holland. When he was but 15 years old he was secretary to
the American minister to Russia.

He returned home, was graduated from Harvard in 1788, became a
lawyer, and his political, diplomatic and literary career began. Under
the **nom de plume** of "Publicola," he wrote a reply to Paine's **Rights
of Man**, probably at the instigation of his father.

This book had just begun to circulate in the United States, and
was dedicated to President Washington, who was at that time trying
to make a treaty with England. That country had not yet given up
Detroit and other military posts in the West which were supposed to
be surrendered at the close of the Revolution. Washington was anxious
to secure these as well as to make a new commercial treaty. As **The
Rights of Man** was an attack upon the English government, it was
thought that its endorsement by Washington would interfere with the
consummation of the treaty. But while the Federal party looked askance
at the **Rights of Man**, it was warmly welcomed by the Republicans, at
whose head stood Thomas Jefferson. When the treaty with England
was concluded, it was greatly disliked, and made Washington, for a
time, extremely unpopular.

John Quincy Adams was a member of the Massachusetts State
Senate in 1802, and in 1803 he was elected to the United States Senate.
After serving three years as Professor of Rhetoric at Harvard College,
he was sent by President Madison as Minister to Russia, where he
remained four and a half years. In 1814, he, together with Gallatin and

---

*For this letter of Thomas Jefferson, see the chapter dealing with his
religious views.

Bayard, negotiated the treaty of peace with England. Then he became Minister to England, where he stayed until President Monroe made him Secretary of State. Occupying this office, he was the real author of the "Monroe Doctrine."

In the Presidential election of 1824 no candidate received a majority of electoral votes. Andrew Jackson received 99, John Quincy Adams, 84, W. H. Crawford, 41 and Henry Clay, 34. For the second time, the election was thrown into the House of Representatives. There, Mr. Clay switched his votes to Adams, who was thus elected. His administration was not eventful, though the country was prosperous. Thereafter, there was a new division of the nation politically, into the Whig and Democratic parties.

Distinguished as Mr. Adams' career had been, history would not have accorded him the place which it does, had it not been for his services in Congress after he had left the White House. In 1830 the Plymouth district of Massachusetts elected him to Congress on the Anti-Masonic ticket. Here he remained until his death, in 1848. Here he became famous as the defender of "The right of petition." When he introduced petitions from Abolitionist societies praying for the abolition of slavery, the southern members were in an uproar. Some charged him with treason, while others favored his expulsion. So ably and courageously did he defend himself that he acquired his well-known title of "The Old Man Eloquent." His enemies said he introduced the petitions because he was angry with the southern members for voting against him in the election of 1825.

Mr. Adams, like his father, kept a diary. Here he gives us many sidelights upon the events of his time. Strange to say, this work was for years neglected by his own countrymen, but recently it has been issued by an English publisher. He also wrote a small volume of **Poems**, though none of them has taken a permanent place in American literature.

Like his father, John Quincy Adams was a Unitarian. At the age of 21, when most young men are devoted to frivolous matters, he was studying religion from the liberal standpoint, as well as other serious subjects. He was then a law student in Newburyport, Mass., and in his diary refers to a young man there who was very orthodox:

> "This young fellow, who was possessed of most violent passions, which he with great difficulty can command, and of unbounded ambition, which he conceals perhaps, even to himself, has been seduced into that bigoted, illiberal system of religion, which, by professing vainly to follow purely the dictates of the Bible, in vainly contradicts the whole doctrine of the New Testament, and destroys all the boundaries between good and evil, between right and wrong. But, like all the followers of that sect, his practise is at open variance with his theory. When I observe into what inconsistent absurdities those persons run who make speculatve, metaphysical religion a matter of importance, I am fully determined never to puzzle myself in the mazes of religious discussion, to content myself with practising the dictates of God and reason so far as I can judge for myself, and resign myself into the arms of a being whose tender mercies are all over his works." (**Life in a New England Town**, 1787-1788, p. 161.)

He also speaks of a liberal minister in Newburyport in these words: "However, the people in this town are so bigoted that a man of Mr. Andrews' liberal religious sentiments will not be half so popular a preacher as one who would rave and rant and talk nonsense for an hour together in his sermon." (Ibid, p. 131.)

Speaking of the Rev. William Hawley, the rector of St. John's Church, Adams said, in his diary for December 23, 1821:

"Mr. Sparks, the Unitarian, preached for the first time at the Capitol to a crowded auditory. His election as chaplain to the House of Representatives occasioned much surprise, and has been followed by unusual symptoms of intolerance. Mr. Hawley, the Episcopal preacher at St. John's Church, last Sunday preached a sermon of coarse invective upon the House, who, he said, by this act had voted Christ out-of-doors; and he enjoined upon all the people of his flock not to set their feet within the Capitol to hear Mr. Sparks."   ,

This gives an idea of the religious prejudice in this country a century ago. In our time another Unitarian, Edward Everett Hale, was a chaplain of Congress, yet today we have seen orthodox ministers protest when a Unitarian was called upon to fill the position of chaplain. Adams had no sympathy with the sabbatarianism of his time. In the diary of January 21, 1844, he speaks of it in the following words:

"The question about keeping the Sabbath holy as a day of rest is one of the numerous religious and political excitements which keep the free people of this Union in perpetual agitation. They seem to be generated by the condition of the country—in a state of profound peace. There are in this country, as in all others, a certain proportion of restless and turbulent spirits—poor, unoccupied, ambitious—who must always have something to quarrel about with their neighbors. These people are the authors of religious revivals."

Ben. Perley Poore, in his **Reminiscences**, tells the following anecdote of John Quincy Adams: "Senator Tazewell, Mr. Randolph's colleague, was a first-class Virginia abstractionist and an avowed hater of New England. Dining one day at the White House, he provoked the President by offensively asserting that he had never known a Unitarian who did not believe in the sea-serpent." This was a strange remark, but it proves that Adams' Unitarianism was common knowledge.

During one session of Congress John Quincy Adams, owing to ill health, was not able to take his seat until February 17. As he walked in, all the members instinctively arose, out of respect to the venerable man who had come down to them from a former generation. Finally, in 1848, while sitting at his desk in the House, he was stricken with paralysis, and lived but a few days. His body was taken to Quincy, his and his father's old home, where his funeral was held in the Unitarian church.

MILLARD FILLMORE
Born, February 7, 1800. Died, March 8. 1874. President, July 9, 1850—March 4, 1853.

Millard Fillmore became the 13th President of the United States on July 9, 1850, following the death of General Zachary Taylor, who was elected in 1848. He was not one of our greatest Presidents, although some momentous events took place during his administration. Born in western New York, Fillmore was of New England stock. He attained considerable distinction as a lawyer, and served a number of terms in the lower House of Congress, after which, in 1844, he was the Whig candidate for governor of New York, but was defeated by Silas Wright, the Democratic candidate. In 1847, he was elected comptroller of New York.

In his career in state politics he was frequently at odds with William H. Seward, who also assumed leadership of the Whig party of the State. One point of contention between Fillmore and Seward was the division of the public school funds. The Catholics of New York demanded a share of these funds for their parochial schools. Seward favored complying with their demand, but Fillmore resolutely refused to consent to the division of state school funds with sectarian educational institutions, thereby upholding the American idea.

After he became President on the death of Taylor, he was again in conflict with Seward, who, with Thurlow Weed, refused to make any concession to the South on the slavery question. President Fillmore took the side of Henry Clay and the southern Whigs. He signed the Fugitive Slave law, for which he has been greatly condemned, an act which paved the way for the repeal of the Missouri Compromise. It was a time of great excitement, and these concessions delayed, but did not prevent, the secession of the southern States.

The foreign policy of President Fillmore was very vigorous. During his term of office the principle of protecting U.S. citizens at home and abroad was strictly enforced. The fleet of Commodore M. C. Perry visited Japan and opened up trade with that country. The American, or "Know Nothing." party nominated Fillmore for President in 1856, but he obtained only one electoral vote, in Maryland.

He was an avowed Unitarian and took an interest in the progress of that Church. When Abraham Lincoln stopped off in Buffalo on his way to be inaugurated, in 1861, he was entertained by ex-President Fillmore, and one Sunday morning both went together to services in the Unitarian Church.

WILLIAM HOWARD TAFT
Born, September 15, 1857. Died, March 8, 1930. President, March 4, 1909—March 4, 1913.

Ohio has outranked Virginia as the "Mother of Presidents." The latter State has given the country five Presidents—Washington, Jefferson, Madison, Monroe and Tyler—while from Ohio have come W. H. Harrison, Grant, Hayes, Garfield, McKinley, Taft and Harding, seven in all.

William Howard Taft's long career in the public service is fresh in the minds of the people. He was born in Cincinnati, in 1857. His father, Alphonso Taft, was a delegate to the Republican national convention of 1856, which nominated Fremont, and was a judge of the Superior Court of Cincinnati from 1865 until 1872. In 1876, Alphonso Taft was appointed Secretary of War, by President Grant, but served only two months, after which he was appointed Attorney-General. Later, he was minister to Russia.

His son, William Howard, after holding a number of smaller positions in Cincinnati, was for three years a judge of the Superior Court, like his father. President Harrison appointed him Solicitor-General, and in 1892 made him a judge of the United States Circuit Court. From this position he was appointed, in 1899, first Governor-General of the Philippine Islands, in which office he distinguished himself. President Theodore Roosevelt tendered him a nomination as a Justice of the U.S. Supreme Court, which he at this time refused, as he believed that his work in the Philippines was not yet completed. Later, he accepted an appointment as Secretary of War.

As the term of President Roosevelt drew to a close, he did what no other President except Jackson had ever done—he dictated who should be his successor. His choice, William Howard Taft, was elected, after which Roosevelt went to Africa to hunt lions.

While Roosevelt had said that Taft possessed "a standard of absolutely unflinching rectitude on every point of public duty, and a literally dauntless courage and willingness to bear responsibility," the latter did not capture the public interest as did his predecessor. He did not have Roosevelt's dramatic force which for years had thrilled the country. In his race for a second term, Taft was overwhelmingly defeated, carrying only two States, Vermont and Utah. He accepted this disappointment gracefully, and became a teacher of law in Yale University, after which President Harding placed him on the bench as Chief Justice of the Supreme Court.

William Howard Taft had a Unitarian heritage. His father was one of the pillars of the Unitarian Church in Cincinnati, in the late 1850's, when Dr. Moncure D. Conway, author of **The Life of Thomas Paine**, was its minister. In the same congregation was George Hoadley, afterwards Governor of Ohio, and Stanley Matthews, afterwards United States Senator, and a Judge of the Supreme Court.

Article VI, section III of the Constitution of the United States says, "No religious test shall ever be required as a qualification to any office or public trust under the United States." We have already seen that some of our early public officials were anything but orthodox in their religious opinions. Today, this provision, while holding good in law, in practice is "more honored in the breach than in the observance." The entire church membership of the United States is but a small minority of the population. Yet a portion of this church membership (we are pleased to say not all of it) has decreed that public officials must be sound (according to their idea of soundness, of course) in their theological views as well as on other issues. In a certain western city the ministerial association passed a resolution warning their flocks not to vote for a certain candidate for mayor because he was a Unitarian. In another city, the ministers opposed another candidate because they said he was "an Atheist."

At the time Taft was nominated for President, an "anti-Catholic" movement was beginning in this country. Such movements occur periodically, spread for a while and slowly die.

Before Taft was nominated, the guns of bigotry began to belch. The first broadside, strange to say, was aimed at Mrs. Taft, who was accused of being a Roman Catholic. This proved to be a boomerang, as the lady was not a Catholic and never had been. As a result, President Roosevelt wrote a strong letter condemning the mixing of religion and politics, and calling the attention of the people to the fact that there were no religious tests for office, and to assume that there are is an impertinence. It is safe to say that Mr. Roosevelt's virile pen never wrote a stronger document than this proved to be.

Taft's opponent in the Presidential race of 1908 was the late William Jennings Bryan, who felt he had received a divine call to maintain strict orthodoxy of religious opinion everywhere. Wherever he went Bryan raised the **odium theologicum** against Taft, saying, among other things, that "the American people would never elect a man President who disbelieved in the virgin birth and the divinity of Christ." What Bryan might have accomplished had his Fundamentalist hosts been organized in 1908 we do not know, but the fact remains that Taft beat him by 1,269,804 votes.

The most highly irritated was the evangelist, "Billy" Sunday, who, wherever he held meetings, denounced unsparingly the Unitarian Church as having been "born in hell." When he was once told that he ought to modify his language, as the President of the United States was a Unitarian, his reply was "To hell with President Taft."

When the evangelist went to Boston to hold meetings he changed his tactics, not because he became more tolerant or more of a gentleman, but because of pecuniary considerations. There he was told that some of the wealthiest men in the city, from whom large contributions were expected, were Unitarians, and that he had better cease his fulminations. He did so, as he also had done in Omaha, Nebraska. Here, the president of the street railway company was a Unitarian, and as a big donation was hoped for from them, it was thought he had better place a stop on his zeal. If Unitarians did come from hell and return

thither, their money in this world was not taken at a discount.
President Taft never pushed his religious views to the front. His
only public appearance in their behalf was when he was the chairman
of a Unitarian conference held in Detroit. He was friendly with all denominations, was tolerance personified, yet he did not escape the attacks of bigots. These resulted from the action he took as Governor of
the Philippines, in the matter of the "Friar lands." These clerics had
been in the Islands from their earliest settlement. The Spanish government from time to time had granted them great landed possessions
and had turned over to them certain civil functions. They were very
unpopular with the natives, who accused them of immoralities, tyranny
and great exactions.

After Taft arrived, he made a thorough examination of the "Friar
question." He found their title to the lands valid, yet so long as they
remained in possession peace among the natives could not be restored;
and as long as they were the owners of the property, it was impossible
to evict them. The only thing to do was to buy them out. Taft went,
with a number of advisers, to Rome, to consult Pope Leo XIII. Arrangements mere made by which Congress was to appropriate $7,200,000
to pay the religious orders for their lands, after which they were to
move. As a result, Governor Taft received blows from both sides. Some
Catholic journals accused him of unfairness to their Church, while
certain sectarian Protestant papers accused him of unduly favoring
the Catholic Church, and of giving it more than the land was worth.
The Church, owning the lands in the end, seemed to be satisfied with
the settlement.

The truth is that religious corporations are not essentially different
from those that are not religious. In dealing with the government,
they all try to get all they can, and often complain that they are not
getting enough; though in many cases they are obtaining more than
they should have. If the Catholic Church here received more than it
was entitled to, other Churches have been equally fortunate.

During his campaign for reelection, in 1912, President Taft was
obliged to issue a bulletin defending himself against anti-Catholic
organizations, who had charged him with granting the Catholic Church
special favors. The ground of his offense lay in some western government Indian schools where nuns had been employed to teach, and who
performed their duties wearing their religious garb. An Indian school
official, one Valentine, discharged the nuns, holding it to be illegal
for teachers in a government school to perform their functions in the
uniform of a religious order. An appeal was made to the President, who
restored the nuns to their positions, while at the same time he removed
Valentine. This action caused great indignation, for the President himself admitted that the wearing of a religious garb in a public school
was illegal, and that none who wore it should, in the future, be hired
as teachers; but that it would be unjust to discharge those who were
already employed. In this attitude, he displayed undue solicitude, as
the Church would look after these nuns, and none of them would suffer by losing their positions. This point, and the discharge of Mr. Valentine, placed a weapon in the hands of his enemies, which they
wielded effectively.

In the bulletin he issued in his own defense, Taft denied that he
had granted any special favors to the Catholic Church, but that in all
the public positions he ever held, it had been his object to "encourage
all the Churches wherever he could do so without making any invidious
distinctions." Here he only made the mistake politicians often are unfortunate in makng. In this country where Church and State are separate, each Church must support itself, and it is not the business
of the government to "encourage all" or any of them. The only duty
of the American government, so far as the Church and religion are

concerned, is to protect all Churches and all religions in their equal rights, and as the Supreme Court of Ohio, where President Taft had often practiced, once declared, "to see that religious sects keep their hands off each other." (**Ohio Reports**, vol. 23, p. 250.) Yet, politicians, to curry favor with the religious, will grant favors to Churches, which it is often necessary for the courts to set aside. The trouble arises when one Church receives more favors than others. It was in such troubled waters that President Taft found himself.

Washington turned his back upon the communion; Jefferson proved by his writings as well as some of his acts that he was an opponent of orthodoxy; Lincoln was known by his intimate friends to be a Free-thinker; the two Adamses and Fillmore did not suffer because they were Unitarians. Therefore, the experiences of President Taft would seem to indicate that the spirit of religious liberty and toleration has gained but little in the past 140 years. And through all the attacks upon him, political and religious, President Taft maintained his smile and genial good nature.

CHAPTER IV

PRESIDENTS WHO WERE EPISCOPALIANS

FRANKLIN PIERCE

Born, November 23, 1804. Died, October 8, 1869. President, March 4, 1853—March 4, 1857.

Had Franklin Pierce, of New Hampshire, left the Presidency as popular a man as he went into it, he would undoubtedly been the most popular of our chief executives. In the election of 1852 he carried every State but four. No President, except Franklin D. Roosevelt, has been elected by such an overwhelming popular and electoral vote. But when President Pierce left the White House, he was completely out of public favor, and remained in obscurity for the remainder of his life. Not until 1914 did the State of New Hampshire erect a statue in commemoration of the only chief magistrate it had given to the nation. He was called "a northern man with southern principles," and was elected on a wave of sentiment which proclaimed that the only way to save the Union and prevent secession was to accede to all the demands of the slave-holders. Jefferson Davis was Pierce's Secretary of War and the future President of the Confederacy dictated his policies.

Information concerning Franklin Pierce is meager. Until recently the only biography of him available was that written, in 1852, by his college-mate, the well-known American author, Nathaniel Hawthorne, as a "campaign document." Of Pierce's religion, Hawthorne said:

"General Pierce has naturally a strong endowment of religious feeling. At no period of his life, as is well known to his friends, have the sacred relations of the human soul been a matter of indifference with him; and of more recent years, whatever circumstances of good or evil fortune may have befallen him, they have served to deepen this powerful sentiment. Whether in sorrow or success he has learned, in his own behalf, the good lesson, that religious faith is the most valuable and most sacred of human possessions; but with this sense, there has come no narrowness or illiberality, but a wide sympathy for the modes of Christian worship and a reverence for religious belief, as a matter between the Deity and man's soul, and with which no other has a right to interfere." (Hawthorne's **Life of Franklin Pierce**, p. 123.)

This is rather meager information, coming as it does from so intimate a friend of Nathaniel Hawthorne, the last night of whose life was spent in the company of Pierce. The same could be said of a Catholic or a Protestant, a Mohammedan, a Buddhist or a Zoroastrian. The document issued by the State of New Hampshire, giving an account of the ceremonies at the unveiling of Pierce's statue in Concord, on November 24, 1914, says nothing of his religious belief or church affiliation. He was a member of the constitutional convention of New Hampshire in 1850. There he made a strenuous fight as did John Adams in Massachusetts, to abolish that portion of the State Constitution which made the Protestant religion the official religion of the Granite State. Although Pierce, like Adams, was unsuccessful, his actions indicate that his religious views were in advance of his time.

However, in my researches I discovered that President Pierce was always orthodox in his belief, even while in college, but that he did not

join a Church until a few years before his death, when he united with
and became a communicant of St. Paul's Episcopal Church, of Concord. While I was looking for definite information, I was informed
that Professor Roy F. Nichols, of the Department of History, in the
University of Pennsylvania, was engaged in writing a life of Pierce.*
I applied to him for information, and he responded in a private letter,
as follows:

"Pierce expressed himself in writing at least twice on the
subject of religion, once in a manuscript fragment written in
later life describing his beliefs in college which show them to
be decidedly orthodox. The other was a letter he wrote to his
law partner in the early 1840's still expressing belief in orthodoxy but showing no vivid religious experience. He was a constant attendant at church. In Concord he attended the South
Congregational Church and while President in Washington
he attended Presbyterian churches, most frequently that on
4½ Street (now John Marshall Place). I think you may discount the statement that he attended St. John's Church. In
all probability he went there once in a while but I doubt very
much that he made it a regular practice. In later life, during
the Civil War, he was baptized, confirmed and became a regular
communicant in St. Paul's Episcopal Church, in Concord."

Like most public men of his time President Pierce was a man of
convivial habits, and, like some others, he sometimes drank too much.
When it was proposed to nominate him for the Presidency, this greatly
alarmed his friends, who called on him to talk the matter over. He
promised them that if elected he would at once cease drinking, and remain a total abstainer while his term lasted. He honorably kept his word.

FRANKLIN DELANO ROOSEVELT
Born, January 30, 1882—   President, March 4, 1933—

The 32nd President of the United States is the third Democrat
elected since the Civil War. Like the Harrison and Adams families,
the Roosevelts have furnished two Presidents of the United States.
Franklin D. Roosevelt is the fifth President to come from the State
of New York.

The Roosevelt family in America is of Dutch origin, all being
descendants of Klaes Martensen Roosevelt, who emigrated from Holland
to the then colony of New Netherlands, in 1644. The subject of this
sketch is a fifth cousin of Theodore Roosevelt, who occupied the Presidential chair from September 14, 1901, until March 4, 1909. Both of
the Roosevelts were graduated from Harvard, both were members of
the New York legislature, and Assistant-Secretary of the Navy. Each
had been Governor of New York. Each has been a candidate for Vice
President. Both have been prolific writers. While one was a liberal Republican, the other has been an equally Progressive Democrat.

Franklin Delano Roosevelt was born in Hyde Park, N.Y., on January 30, 1882. His father was James Roosevelt, and his mother, still
living, Sarah Delano, whose family was of Flemish origin. Philip, the
founder of the American branch of the Delano family, came to this
country in 1624. They were a sea-faring family and are said to have
owned and operated ships in all parts of the world.

As Franklin Delano Roosevelt descended from two old American
patrician families, he began life with many advantages. In 1904 he was
graduated from Harvard University, later studying at Columbia University Law School, and he practiced for several years in New York

---

*This book by Professor Nichols was published in 1932.

City. He was elected and reelected to the New York State Senate, and under President Wilson was Assistant-Secretary of the Navy. In 1920 he was nominated for Vice President on the Democratic ticket, his running-mate being James M. Cox, of Ohio. Roosevelt supported Alfred E. Smith for the Presidential nomination in 1924, and worked for him when he was nominated in 1928. At Smith's suggestion, Roosevelt consented to become the Democratic candidate for Governor of New York, in 1928. He was successful, and was again elected in 1930, by a majority of 725,000 votes, the largest that any candidate ever received in the history of the State.

Roosevelt had a strong Republican legislature to oppose him, as well as Tammany Hall, the local New York City Democratic organization, yet he effected many reforms. He soon became the most prominent contender for the Democratic Presidential nomination, and in Chicago, on June 27, 1932, he was nominated on the fourth ballot, receiving 945 out of 1,154 votes. During the campaign he visited all sections of the country and was frequently heard over the radio.

The campaign was an exciting one. For three years the United States had been in the throes of the worst economic crisis of its history, and the Hoover administration had become thoroughly discredited. The people were also in rebellion against Prohibition, which most right-minded persons held to be ineffective, a farce and a disgrace to the land. It soon became apparent that the Republican candidate, Herbert Hoover, was not to be considered in the running. He carried but six States, while Roosevelt carried 42, with a popular majority of 7,000,000. It was the greatest Presidential victory since 1852, when the Democratic party elected Franklin Pierce.

On February 15, 1933, the President-elect narrowly escaped assassination when he was shot at by a demented Italian, one Zangara, in Miama, Fla. Mayor Anton Cermak of Chicago was hit instead by the bullet and after lingering for a few days died.

There can be no doubt that President Roosevelt has faced greater and more serious problems than has any other peace-time President, and that he has handled these problems with great courage and vigor.

In 1905, Franklin D. Roosevelt married Miss Anne Eleanor Roosevelt, a distant cousin. They have five children. Mrs. Roosevelt, like the President, takes an active interest in social welfare, which she manifests by her various activities and by her public utterances.

Both are members and communicants in the Protestant Episcopal Church, the President being a vestryman in the church of Hyde Park, N.Y. It is said that no pressure of public duties has ever interfered with his duties to his Church. Yet, unlike many, he does not make merchandise of his religion, and his speeches, messages and other public utterances are singuarly free from religious cant and platitude so commonly resorted to by politicians to catch the church vote. His Thanksgiving proclamation in 1933 was one of the briefest ever known.

The clergy seem to be cold toward him because he advocated the repeal of the 18th Amendment. This led a Methodist bishop to call him an "alley President," while another Methodist minister, the Rev. Clarence True Wilson, in comparing him with his Presidential namesake, said that Theodore Roosevelt was "100% American," while Franklin Delano Roosevelt was "2%," both of which statements illustrate the malignity of the clerical mind under opposition. The collapse and repeal of their favorite law, which was a failure for the purposes for which it was enacted, to say nothing of bringing in its wake other evils, has put a considerable crimp in the political activities of the Churches.

It is said that while President Roosevelt is a church member and a church official, he is a more irregular attendant upon church services than some Presidents who were not professing Christians.

CHAPTER V

PRESIDENTS WHO WERE NOT MEMBERS OF ANY CHURCH

WILLIAM HENRY HARRISON
Born, February 9, 1773. Died, April 4, 1841. President, March 4—April 4, 1841.

William Henry Harrison, a son of a signer of the Declaration of Independence, was the last President who had witnessed scenes in the Revolution, and the first to die in office, which he held but 30 days. He early went into the army, distinguished himself in Indian wars, commanded at the battle of Tippecanoe, where he defeated Tecumseh, the Indian chief who was so troublesome to the settlers. It was to General Harrison that Commodore Perry sent the famous message, "We have met the enemy and they are ours." Later he fought a battle on the River Thames, in Canada, where the British were defeated, and their ally, Tecumseh, was slain.

After the War of 1812, General Harrison was continually in public life, a member of Congress, the State Senate of Ohio and the U.S. Senate, a presidential elector and minister to the United States of Columbia. The Whigs thought a military hero was needed as a candidate for President; hence in 1836 he was nominated to oppose Martin Van Buren, by whom he was defeated. In 1840, the two opposing candidates were before the people again, and General Harrison won, in the famous hard cider and log cabin campaign.

When he took the chair, in 1841, General Harrison was 68 years old, and in feeble health. He had taken cold on the day of the inauguration. He over-exerted himself, and died when but a month in office. President Harrison had never been a church member, as is proved by the following account of his funeral, to be found both in Montgomery's **Life of Harrison**, and in **The Diary of John Quincy Adams.**

"At half past 11 o'clock, the Rev. Mr. Hawley, Rector of St. John's Church arose, and observed that he would mention an incident connected with the Bible, which lay on the table before him (covered with black silk velvet). 'This Bible,' said he, 'was purchased by the President on the fifth of March. He has since been in the habit of daily reading it. He was accustomed not only to attend church, but to join audibly in the services, and to kneel humbly before his maker.'

"Dr. Hawley stated that had the President lived, and been in health, he intended on the next Sabbath to become a communicant at the Lord's table."

This proves that, at the age of 68, President Harrison did not own a Bible, and had not thought religion worthy of his attention, for if he had was he not derelict in his duty all his life? Or, did he suddenly take an interest because he was in public office? This would appear suspicious in a politician. And was it any credit to the Rev. Hawley to convert a broken-down old man, whom, when he was in the bloom of youth and health, all the Churches and ministers had failed to draw into the fold? For all this, we have no evidence except the word of the clergyman. Yet if all he has said is true, the transaction sheds no luster on either President Harrison or himself.

ANDREW JOHNSON
Born, December 29, 1808. Died, July 31, 1875. President, April 15, 1865—March 4, 1869.

The successor of Abraham Lincoln as President of the United States, and the third to become President through death, Andrew Johnson, is one of the interesting characters of American history. Springing from that class of people called in the South, "poor white trash," he was without educational advantages in his youth. A tailor by trade, he learned to read while working in a shop. After his marriage, his wife taught him to write. He began at the bottom of the ladder politically, serving as alderman, mayor, member of the legislature of Tennessee, a member of Congress, Senator, and finally President.

Until recently Andrew Johnson was one of the most misrepresented men in American history, and one of the most common errors concerning him is the statement that he was a member of the Methodist Church. Anyone who will only take the trouble to investigate will learn that this was not a fact, as will be proved in this chapter. Johnson had the courage to stand firm against the political spoilsmen of his time. This was "the head and front of his offending."*

The truth is, that after the death of Lincoln, Johnson determined to follow the policy of the deceased President in the reconstruction of the States lately in rebellion. This did not please demagogues like Thaddeus Stevens, Benjamin F. Wade and Charles Sumner, who stood at the head of the party seeking revenge upon the South and an opportunity to persecute and plunder its people. Had Lincoln lived, he would have had the same conflict on his hands—in fact, it had begun before his assassination.

When the cotton States seceded in 1861, and their Senators and Congressmen went South to aid in the rebellion, Andrew Johnson was the only one who stood by the Union and remained in his seat in the Senate. President Lincoln sent him to Tennessee, in 1862, as military governor of that State. At the risk of his life he did his duty, brought his State back into the Union, restored the authority of the national government, and as a reward was elected Vice President, with Lincoln, in 1864.

In spite of this service, malignant partisans have called him a traitor. He was even accused of complicity in the murder of Lincoln. Articles of Impeachment, born of malice, were framed-up against him, that he might be expelled from the White House, and one of the South-hating radicals put in his place. It was a close contest; Johnson escaped impeachment by only one vote. There were, however, enough honest men in the then corrupt Senate of the United States to prevent this disgrace of the law-making body of the American people. Most of those involved in this great wrong, among them Charles Sumner, who was its chief instigator, afterwards expressed their regret that they were connected with it.

Andrew Johnson was not a Methodist, nor was he a member of any other Church, though he always claimed to be a religious man. At one time William G. ("Parson") Brownlow accused him of being an "Infidel." This is usually a term of reproach. Mr. Johnson replied, "As for my religion, it is the doctrine of the Bible, as taught and practised by Jesus Christ." (See **The Age of Hate**, by G. F. Minton, p. 80.)

Mrs. Eliza Johnson was a Methodist, and, like a loyal husband, Johnson would sometimes accompany her to services. We will now give

*For proof of this statement, see a recent work (1929), **Andrew Johnson, A Study in Courage**, by Lloyd Paul Stryker. The Macmillan Co.

the facts as told by Winston. (**Life of Andrew Johnson**, p. 101):

"I have stated that the influence of Mrs. Johnson over her husband was unbounded, and yet into one place he would not follow her, the organized Church. She might find satisfaction in such a Church, but he could not. Like Lincoln, if he could have found an organization based on the personality of Christ, without creed or dogmas, without class distinctions or the exaltation and deification of money, he was willing to join it 'with all his soul.' But so far as he could make out, there was no such Church. Believing in a rule of right and in a revealed religion, he took Christ as a model, yet he feared that the Christians of his day were further away from the simplicity, the charity and the love- of their fellows, which Christ enjoined, than many a heathen was."

As the Methodist Church was somewhat interested in the impeachment proceedings against President Johnson, the truth of history demands that we say something about that Church at this period. Its clergy have always insisted that Methodism is synonymous with patriotism and all other virtues. This depends largely upon the epoch and the geographical location. During the Revolution it took the side of England, following the example of its founder, John Wesley. As a result, Methodist preachers were obliged to leave the country, or go into hiding, as did Francis Asbury, who afterwards became the first Methodist Bishop in the United States.

Upon the question of slavery, John Wesey said it was "the sum of all villainies." This was said in England, before buying and selling Negroes became profitable in the United States. When it became profitable, from 1820 on, the position of the Church was either in favor of Negro servitude or it was equivocal. At its General Conference, held in Cincinnati, Ohio, in 1836, it censured by an overwhelming vote some members who had attended an Abolition meeting. In 1841, at the meeting of the General Conference, the Church split, and the Methodist Church South was organized.

Most assuredly, the Southern church was pro-slavery. The mistake many make is in assuming that the Northern Church was anti-slavery. The fact is that members of the Northern Church continued to hold slaves without coming into conflict with the Discipline, and it was not until the Conference of 1864, a year after the Emancipation Proclamation, that the Northern Conference came to the conclusion that slavery was wrong. They had plenty of time to think it over, and were now certain they were on the safe side, as all church organizations in politics aim to be. Hence, while the Southern Church was always pro-slavery, that of the North trimmed its sails to float with the tide.

It might be asked why the Methodist Church of the North took such a great interest in the impeachment of President Johnson, and why their Conference of 1868 was so anxious to throw him out of the White House. The reason was that it followed the hue and cry of politicians, expecting thereby to attain some advantage to itself. We have seen such a case in our own day. While our ministers were preaching peace before the United States entered the European war, none were more belligerent than these same reverend gentlemen after we did enter it. They expected their reward, and they received it. They obtained chaplaincies. They were permitted, with the aid of the Government, to stage "drives" for money, which were so remunerative that they tried to continue them after the war was over. The canteen service in the Army was turned over to religious organizations, some of whom obtained as much as they could free of charge, and charged the soldiers all they could, and made millions.

The presiding Bishop at the Conference of 1868 was Matthew

Simpson, who for years had been an astute Republican politician. The Methodists had been influential enough to have President Lincoln appoint James Harlan, who was once one of their preachers, Secretary of the Interior instead of appointing, as he wished to do, his old Illinois friend, Jesse K. DuBois. Harlan served in the Cabinet for about a year under President Johnson, and then resigned. He went back to Iowa, was again elected to the Senate, was on hand in 1868—one of the bitterest enemies of his former chief in the impeachment proceedings. It appeared that there would not be enough Senators opposed to President Johnson to make out a case. As Senator Willey, of West Virginia, was a Methodist, the influence of the Conference was brought to bear upon him, and he voted for the impeachment. Then they offered a resolution for an hour of prayer that they might ask God to cast out the President of the United States. Under these conditions, why ask the Senate of the United States to waste its time further? Why not turn President Johnson over to the Methodist Conference acting under the direct influence of the Almighty? One of their members saw they were in a very ticklish position. He called their attention to the fact that the Senate was under oath to decide the case under the law and the evidence, and that this resolution could only be interpreted as demanding that they violate that oath, and decide regardless of the law and the evidence, for it placed the Methodist Church above both. Bishop Simpson saw the point, and unctuously introduced another resolution praying "to save our Senators from error." This would take them out of a very embarrassing situation, and they had faith that God would understand them just the same. At the same time the white Methodists were in conference in Chicago, the Negro members of that Church were in session in Washington. They also took up the question of President Johnson's impeachment. They did not bother God at all about it. They appealed first hand to the Senate to impeach him.

It is needless to say these proceedings of the Methodists, white and black, did not please the President. Out of courtesy to his wife he had been attending their Church. Now he ceased going, and went to the Catholic St. Patrick's Cathedral to hear Father McGuire, who, he said, "cut out politics." He admired the Catholic Church "because of its treatment of the rich and poor alike. In the cathedral there were no high-priced pews and no reserved seats, the old woman with calico dress and poke bonnet sitting up high and being as welcome as the richest." (**Plebeian and Patriot**, p. 476.)

Andrew Johnson died at his home in Tennessee, in 1875, just after taking his seat as United States Senator from that State. He had been a Mason, and the lodge to which he belonged conducted his funeral.

ULYSSES SIMPSON GRANT

Born, April 27, 1822. Died, July 23, 1885. President, March 4, 1869—March 4, 1877.

The life of U. S. Grant, commanding general of the Union forces in the Civil War, was, in large part, tragic. He was graduated from the U.S. Military Academy, but his scholastic record at West Point was not brilliant. His career in the Mexican War was honorable, but he did not like the army. In the earlier 50's he was sent to California, where, possibly because of the monotony of army life on the frontier, he took to excessive drinking, as a result of which he was obliged to resign. This habit grew on him, to the great detriment of himself and his family.

The opening of the Civil War found him in Galena, Ill., a clerk in the leather store of his younger brothers. With great difficulty he obtained a commission as colonel of an Illinois regiment. Here he found his opportunity in middle life. From small-town clerk to commanding general and, eventually, to the Presidency, was quite a stride for the unknown and almost penniless man of eight years before.

President Grant was wholly unacquainted with and without training in statecraft; he innocently became the victim of dishonest politicians, and his two administrations have passed into history as the most corrupt on record. He was obliged to bear some of the infamy of this, although it is generally agreed that Grant himself retained his integrity.

He was as unfamiliar with business affairs as with politics, and innocently permitted his name to be associated with that of a sharper in a fraudulent banking enterprise. It collapsed, after victims in all sections of the country had been fleeced. General and Mrs. Grant, their children and other relatives were ruined financially in this debacle. An ex-President of the United States, the most successful general of modern times, he was thrown back into the poverty of earlier years, and at the same time he had to endure the implied reflection upon his character. As though this were not enough, General Grant developed a cancer, and, after months of patient suffering, died. We do not believe the history of the world records a case more pathetic. While his health and life capitulated to disease and death, General Grant at no time surrendered his principles or his honor. He was more of a hero as he lay in the cottage at Mt. McGregor, than before Donelson, Vicksburg or in the Valley of Virginia.

It has been erroneously maintained that General Grant was a Methodist. The fact is, he was not a member of any Church, and had not even been baptized. Once, while a cadet at West Point, he failed to attend chapel. For this he received eight demerits, and was placed under arrest. He tells of this incident in a letter written to his cousin, McKinsey Griffith, September 22, 1839. He objected to being compelled to go to church, saying, "This is not republican." (Brown's **Life of Grant**, p. 329.)

Mrs. Julia Dent Grant was a Methodist, a member and attendant of the Metropolitan Methodist Church of New York City, after the Grant family made the metropolis their home. Her husband accompanied her, as many other husbands have done when their wives have been church members. Some men who do not dance accompany their wives to balls. Does this make them dancers?

The minister of this church was the Rev. J. P. Newman, D. D., afterwards a Methodist bishop. He was a lover of notoriety, and ever sought to have his name on the front page of the newspapers, as was demonstrated by the following incident.

In 1869 there was a great controversy in Utah over the subject of polygamy. The government was trying to suppress it, but the Mormons were defending it and chief among their defenses was the plea that it was sustained by the Bible. The Rev. Newman traveled to Utah and challenged the Mormons to debate the question with him. His offer was accepted, and Elder Orson Pratt, one of the leading Mormon preachers, was selected to meet him. The Mormons were so jubilant over the success of their champion that they issued the discussion in pamphlet form as a campaign document, and for years circulated it as a justification of polygamy from a biblical standpoint. When I first visited Salt Lake City, in 1897, I bought a copy of this work at the church bookstore.

From the time General Grant became seriously ill, in the spring of 1885, until his death, on July 23, the Rev. Newman devoted to him almost all his attention. He became a member of the family, leading in family prayer, and endeavoring to point out to the General the way of salvation. He made as inglorious a failure in this endeavor as he did in trying to convince the Mormons that the Bible did not sanction polygamy. He did succeed, as W. E. Woodward says, in "making a fool of himself."

We may well wonder why he was thus permitted to plague the dying man. General Chaffee, one of whose daughters General Grant's son married, enlightens us, in the following words: "There has been a good deal of nonsense in the papers about Dr. Newman's visits. General Grant does not believe that Dr. Newman's prayers will save him. He allows the doctor to pray simply because he does not want to hurt his feelings. He is indifferent on his own account to everything." General Chaffee had formerly been a senator from Colorado, was with Grant frequently during his illness and knew whereof he spoke.

A contemporary journalist said: "His acceptance of the effusive and offensive ministrations of the peripatetic preacher was probably due as much to his regard for the feelings of his family and his tolerance of his ministerial friend as to any faith in religion. All the press can gather now about his religious belief is filtered through Dr. Newman, and must, therefore, be largely discounted." To what extent this writer is telling the truth will appear hereafter.

Yet, the Rev. Newman had a reason of his own for being there, and he was candid enough to tell it. It was not to save from hell the soul of the man who had witnessed so much death, destruction and carnage on the field of battle. He said, "Great men may gain nothing from religion, but religion can gain much from great men." In other words, he was there to obtain publicity for his Church and for himself.

When Stephen A. Douglas, Lincoln's great opponent, who, like General Grant, was not a church member, lay dying in Chicago, Mrs. Douglas, who was a devout Roman Catholic, called in Bishop Duggan, of that Church, to see her husband. Wives who are religious naturally think their husbands ought to be the same, so we can account for the attitude of Mrs. Douglas and Mrs. Grant. The Bishop asked Senator Douglas whether he had ever been baptized according to the rites of any Church. "Never," replied the Senator. "Do you wish to have mass said after the ordinances of the holy Catholic Church?" inquired the Bishop. "No, sir," was the prompt reply. "When I do, I will communicate with you freely." The next day Mrs. Douglas again sent for the Bishop. Coming to the Senator's bedside, he said: "Mr. Douglas, you know your condition fully, and in view of your dissolution, do you desire the ceremony of extreme unction to be performed?" "No," replied the dying man, "I have no time to discuss these things now." The Bishop left the room, as any other clergyman who was also a gentleman would have done.

The Rev. Dr. Newman, however, was a sticker. When he found that General Grant had never been baptized, he did not ask permission to perform the rite. While Grant was asleep, he took a pan of water and sprinkled him. He was determined that General Grant should go to heaven, in spite of himself.

The reverend doctor frequently questioned General Grant, hoping that in his replies he would say something that would commit him to the Methodist faith. When he refused to do this, Dr. Newman put words into Grant's mouth which he never uttered. Once he quoted him as saying: "Three times have I been in the valley of the shadow of death, and three times have I returned thither." Mark Twain called the attention of the public to this misrepresentation, saying the General always spoke in plain, blunt language and never used figures of speech. Mark Twain was a personal friend of the General, frequently called on him while he was sick, and was the publisher of his **Memoirs** after his death. Fortunately, we know just what Grant did say. It was true that his life was despaired of three times and he later recovered. The last time, he was revived by the physicians with the aid of brandy. General Adam Badeau, an old personal friend, who was on his staff during the war, was present at the time and gives the exact facts, and the exact words uttered:

"At this crisis he did not wish to live. 'THE DOCTORS ARE RESPONSIBLE THREE TIMES,' HE SAID, 'FOR MY BEING ALIVE, AND—UNLESS THEY CAN CURE ME—I DON'T THANK THEM.' He had no desire to go through the agony again. For he had suffered death; he had parted with his family; he had undergone every physical pang that could have come had he died before the brandy was administered." (Badeau's **Grant in Peace**, p. 450.)

Quite a difference between these words and those attributed to him by the Rev. Newman, who interpolated "three times have I been in the shadow of death," and "three times have I returned thither," to give the incident a dramatic effect and a pious air.

At another time Dr. Newman asked General Grant what was the supreme thought on his mind when death was so near? The answer was, "The comfort of the consciousness that I have tried to live a good and honorable life." Would that all men could say this when they are about to leave this world, but it did not please the reverend doctor, nor did it please his friends, the religious press. The **New York Independent** commented thus:

"The honest effort 'to live a good and honorable life' may well be a source of comfort at any time, and especially so in the hour and article of death: and we see no impropriety in referring to it as such. But it would be a great mistake to make such an effort, or such a life, even though the best that any man ever lived, the basis on which sinners are to rest for their peace with God and their hope of salvation. Sinners are saved, if at all, through grace, and by the suffering and death of Christ, and upon the condition of their repentance toward God, and faith in the Lord Jesus Christ. This is the gospel plan of salvation as Christ himself taught it and the Apostles preached it. There is no other plan known to the Bible.

"Great men and small men viewed simply as men, as subjects of the moral government of God, and as sinners, stand at a common level in respect to their wants and the method of their relief; and they must alike build their hopes on Christ and his work, accepting him by faith, or they will build in vain. 'A good and honorable life' is no substitute for Christ."

We will let the New York **Commercial Advertiser** tell the story of General Grant's death, and the relation of the Rev. Dr. Newman to that event:

"About 7:15 o'clock on the morning that Grant died Dr. Newman said he thought he would go over to the hotel and get a little breakfast. The physician warned him that a change might occur at any moment, and that he had better not go. He turned to Henry, the nurse, and asked his advice. Henry thought the General would live for an hour. So off went the Doctor and ate his breakfast. In the meantime, Dr. Sands, who had left the cottage at 10 o'clock the previous evening in order to have a good night's rest, came back about 7:50, just in time. Dr. Newman was not so fortunate. After breakfast, he came up the path at so quick a rate, his arms waving, that he was short of breath. Dr. Shrady saw him coming, walked out, and said, 'Hush! he's dead.' The Doctor almost fell. His terrible disappointment was depicted on his face."

The secular press did not hesitate to ridicule the Rev. Newman and call him a mountebank. Other religious journals criticised him, even more severely than did the **New York Independent**. The **New York World** said: "Dr. Newman beautifully remarks that 'some of the last scenes of General Grant's death were pitiful and at the same time eloquent,' which is alike creditable to Dr. Newman's elocution and eyesight, since he witnessed these scenes from the breakfast table at the hotel some distance away from the cottage occupied by the general."

On the morning following the General's death, the **World** said: "General Grant, as it would appear, had no settled convictions on the subject of religion. Having been interrogated during his last illness on the question of religion, he replied that he had not given it deep study, and was unprepared to express an opinion. He intimated that he saw no use of devoting any special thought to theology at so late a day, and that he was prepared to take his chances with the millions of people who went before him."

The **Christian Statesman** said: "It is not on record that he [Grant] spoke at any time of the Saviour, or expressed his sense of dependence on his atonement and mediation." The Nashville **Christian Advocate**, a Methodist organ, rebuked Dr. Newman in these words:

"Some ministers seem to have an incurable itch for claiming that all the men who have figured prominently in public life are Christians. Mr. Lincoln has almost been canonized, and General Grant has been put forward as possessing all the graces, though neither one of them ever joined the Church or made the slightest public profession of faith in Jesus. Has it (Christianity) anything to gain by decking itself with the ambiguous compliments of men who never submitted themselves to its demands? The less of all this the better. We are sick of the pulpit toadyism that pronounces its best eulogies over those who are not the real disciples of Jesus Christ."

After General Grant's death, Dr. Newman issued a statement filled with rhetoric and generalities, but he does not assert that the subject of his great solicitude acknowledged faith in Christ. That was further than he could go in safety.

General Grant was a firm believer in separation of Church and state, and had no patience with clerical interference with the government. In his **Memoirs** (vol. 1, p. 213), he said: "No political party can, or ought to, exist when one of its corner-stones is opposition to freedom of thought. If a sect sets up its laws as binding above the state laws, whenever the two come in conflict, this claim must be resisted and suppressed at any cost.

He was opposed to all types of religious interference with the public schools. In his speech before the Army of the Tennessee, delivered in Des Moines, Iowa, in 1875, General Grant used these words, which are often quoted:

"The free school is the promoter of that intelligence which is to preserve us as a nation. If we were to have another contest in the near future of our national existence, I predict that the dividing line will not be Mason's and Dixon's, but between patriotism and intelligence on one side, and superstition, ambition and ignorance on the other. Let us all labor to add all needful guarantees for the more perfect security of FREE THOUGHT, FREE SPEECH AND FREE PRESS, pure morals, unfettered religious sentiments, and of equal rights and privileges to all men, irrespective of nationality, color or religion. Encourage free schools, and resolve that not one dollar of money be appropriated to the support, of any sectarian school. Resolve that neither the State nor nation, or both combined, shall support institutions of learning other than those sufficient to afford every child growing up in the land the opportunity of a good common education, unmixed with sectarian, pagan or atheistical tenets. Leave the matter of religion to the family altar, the Church, and the private schools, supported entirely by private contributions. KEEP CHURCH AND STATE FOREVER SEPARATE."

Some persons said that General Grant was here attacking the Catholic schools. On this point, his friend, General Sherman, says, "The Des Moines speech was prompted by a desire to defend the freedom of our public schools from sectarian influences, and, as I remember the conversation which led him to write that speech, it was because of the clamor for set religious exercises in the public schools, not from Catholic but from Protestant denominations." (Packard's **Grant's Tour Around the World**, p. 566.)

General Grant believed that church property should be taxed the same as other property. In an annual message to Congress (1875), he used this language:

"In connection with this important question, I would also call your attention to the importance of correcting an evil that if permitted to continue, will probably lead to great trouble in our land before the close of the 19th Century. It is the acquisition of vast amounts of untaxed Church property. In 1850, I believe, the Church property of the United States, which paid no tax, municipal or State, amounted to $87,000,000. In 1860 the amount had doubled. In 1870 it was $354,483,587. By 1900, without a check, it is safe to say this property will reach a sum exceeding $3,000,000,000. So vast a sum, receiving all the protection and benefits of the government, without bearing its proportion of the burdens and expenses of the same, will not be looked upon acquiescently by those who have to pay the taxes. In a growing country, where real estate enhances so rapidly with time as in the United States, there is scarcely a limit to the wealth that may be acquired by corporations, religious or otherwise, if allowed to retain real estate without taxation. The contemplation of so vast a property as here alluded to, without taxation, may lead to sequestration without constitutional authority, and through blood. I would suggest the taxation of all property equally."

Two weeks before he died, General Grant wrote the following note, addressed to his wife, which was found on his person after his death:

"Look after our dear children and direct them in the paths of rectitude. It would distress me far more to think that one of them could depart from an honorable, upright, and virtuous life than it would to know that they were prostrated on a bed of sickness from which they were never to arise alive. They have never given us any cause for alarm on this account, and I trust they never will. With these few injunctions and the knowledge I have of your love and affection, and the dutiful affection of all our children, I bid you a final farewell, until we meet in another and, I trust, a better world. You will find this on my person after my demise."

Here is shown no partiality for any creed, Church or religion. General Grant hoped for a future life, as do all religionists, and even some Agnostics.*

*For the facts about the religious opinions of General Grant, I am largely indebted to **Six Historic Americans**, by John E. Remsburg; to **Grant in Peace**, by Adam Badeau, and to **Meet General Grant**, by W. E. Woodward.

RUTHERFORD BIRCHARD HAYES

Born, October 4, 1822. Died, January 17, 1893. President, March 4, 1877—March 4, 1881.

While Rutherford Birchard Hayes was President of the United States, it was said by his enemies that he was ruled by his wife, who was, in fact, the Chief Executive. While this statement contained an element of truth, it grossly exaggerated the situation, particularly in regard to President Hayes' religious belief.

As is well known, Mrs. Lucy Webb Hayes was a Methodist of the strictest type. When she took charge of the White House, cards, dancing, and low necked dresses were banished. Wine and liquors disappeared from the table—even the glasses in which they had been served were put out of sight. The Discipline of the Methodist Church prevailed. Yet the good lady was unable to convince her husband of the superiority of the doctrines of John Wesley, for President Hayes was not a Methodist, held views contrary to the Discipline, and was not a member of any Church. Many persons were astonished when President Hayes' **Biography** was published, and the real facts of his religious views given to the world.

The mother of President Hayes was a Presbyterian. He attended Kenyon College, where he had Episcopalian instructors, but his biographer, Charles Richard Williams, says: "While he felt himself to be a Christian in all essential respects, he never united with any Church. There were declarations of belief in the orthodox creeds, that he could not conscientiously make." (Vol. 2, p. 435.)

In his **Diary** (May 17, 1890), he states his position: "I am not a subscriber to any creed. I belong to no Church. But in a sense satisfactory to myself, and believed by me to be important, I try to be a Christian and to help do Christian work." (P. 435.)

Before his last sickness he said: "I am a Christian according to my conscience, in belief, not, of course, in character and conduct, but in purpose and wish: not, of course, by the orthodox standard. But I am content and have a feeling of trust and safety." (P. 437.)

He read and admired Emerson, who was not orthodox but a Pantheist. From him he said he obtained "mental improvement, information and kept the mental faculties alert and alive." He thought the Sage of Concord prepared us "for the inevitable, to be content at least for the time, and also for the future," and that he "developed and strengthened character." "How Emerson prepares one to meet the disappointments and griefs of this mortal life! His writings seem to me to be religion. They bring peace, consolation; that rest for the mind and heart which we all long for—content." (Pp. 433-434.)

President Hayes was an admirer of the closing declaration of the will of Charles Dickens, which read: "I commend my soul to the mercy of God through our Lord and Saviour, Jesus Christ, and I exhort my dear children humbly to try to guide themselves by the teachings of the New Testament in its broad spirit, and to put no faith in any man's narrow construction of the letter here, or there." (Dickens attended the old South Place Unitarian Chapel in Finsbury, London.)

Hayes copied this in his **Diary** (p. 437), under date of March 13, 1892. Were President Hayes to be classified religiously, he might find a proper place among the Unitarians of the middle of the 19th Century.

In writing of President Hayes, we cannot forbear mentioning the case of D. M. Bennett; first, because it involved the President himself; second, it involved religion; third, it aroused great controversy in 1879; fourth, it is one of the noted cases in the Federal Reports.

Bennett was a Freethinker and edited a Freethought, or, as some preferred to call it, an "Infidel," weekly in New York City. He smote the popular orthodoxy of his time "hip and thigh." He also published many books and cheap tracts, all attacking the supernatural claims of Christianity. He had no pretensions to learning or literary ability. He was, however, thoroughly honest and earnest, and a "hard hitter." Quite naturally, such a journal would arouse the antipathy of orthodox religionists. The old tactics of suppressing by law those whose ideas one does not like were not out of vogue in the 1870's, nor are they today. The ultra Evangelicals sought a method to put this troublesome man Bennett out of business. As he was a small publisher with little capital, it was hoped that a prosecution followed by a term in prison would accomplish the object. Blasphemy laws were in existence, although they were unpopular; and there was also a law providing severe penalties for sending obscene matter through the mails.

This law was passed in 1873, just at the close of the congressional session. Attention was then called to the nature of the bill. Among other things, it was pointed out that it could be utilized to throttle free press and penalize the discussion of legitimate questions upon which the people ought to be informed. This law was very flexible, and might, and did, result in the imprisonment of those who sent through the mails articles or literature that offended the prejudices of judge or jury. As further evidence of its flexibility, we can point to 84 court decisions in its interpretation, diametrically opposed to 84 other decisions. The law in its operation gave great lattitude to private opinion as to what was or was not "obscene." Nevertheless, it was passed.

An organization called "The Society for the Suppression of Vice," with Anthony Comstock at its head, was formed to enforce this law. Comstock was a puritanical fanatic, an abnormal creature, whose attitude would have been very appropriate to the 17th Century, but who was in the 19th Century an anachronism. Behind this society and Comstock stood the Churches. The Society was a forerunner of the Anti-Saloon League in its methods and functions. The latter is in fact a political organization of the Churches, the difference between the two being that the "Vice Society," as it is often called, undertook to tell the American people what books, newspapers and magazines they could read, what they could discuss and know, what pictures they could look upon, and what plays they could see performed. Both organizations have resorted to the spying and sneaking system of obtaining evidence against their victims. If Anthony Comstock could inveigle Bennett into sending something "obscene" through the mails, and bring him before his favorite federal judge, Charles L. Benedict, Bennett would be sent to prison. God and religion would be avenged and the ministers made happy.

One day in 1878, Comstock, incognito, visited Bennett's place of business, and spent hours looking over his stock, seeking something on which he might base a prosecution. He selected two pamphlets, one, strictly scientific, entitled, "How Marsupials Propagate," the other, an anti-theological tract called, "An Open Letter to Jesus Christ." He then wrote a letter to Bennett ordering them to be sent to him through the mails. Bennett, naturally, mailed the pamphlets. Armed with a warrant and accompanied by a United States marshal, Comstock again descended upon Bennett's book shop, arrested him, took him, with copies of the offending pamphlets, before the United States commissioner, who held him under bail of $1,000. An indictment was found by the grand jury.

Comstock and the Church started well, but they ended badly. Great indignation was aroused over the arrest. Only those who can scent "obscenity" from afar thought these works contained anything improper. Robert G. Ingersoll interested himself in the case. He sent copies of the "evidence" to Charles Devens, Attorney-General of the United States, announcing that if Bennett were prosecuted he would appear in his defense, whereupon Mr. Devens ordered the New York district prosecutor to drop the case. Comstock was angry, and said he "would get even with Bennett yet."

We will now turn our attention to the State of Massachusetts and to the town of Princeton. Here lived Ezra H. Heywood, a graduate of Brown University, who edited a small paper called **The Word**. He was considered something of a "crank," and had written a number of reform pamphlets, dealing with finance, the labor question and social philosophy. Among these was a 15c-pamphlet, entitled **Cupid's Yokes**, which attacked the institution of marriage.

This work was so ineffably dull that it is hard to understand how anyone ever summoned enough interest to read it through. Few persons, then or now, would agree with the views it expressed, but they were stated in proper language, for Mr. Heywood was a scholar. Opinions may be wise or foolish, true or false, but they cannot be good or bad, to say nothing of being "obscene." Only when translated into action can they do harm. Thomas Jefferson said that when absurd opinions arise, give Truth fair play and Reason will laugh them out of doors, and the government need not be troubled with them.

It would have been well had Anthony Comstock and his society taken this advice. Instead, Comstock went to Boston and arrested Heywood for sending **Cupid's Yokes** through the mails. His trial was held on January 18 and 19, 1878, before Judge Clark. The verdict was an anomaly. The jury was out 20 hours, but failed to agree. Then Judge Clark dismissed them for four days while he took a trip. Upon reassembling, they rendered a verdict of guilty, "though they did not find the book obscene within the meaning of the law."

Why, therefore, was Heywood found guilty of a crime? A similar verdict in a similar case brought against Charles Bradlaugh and Annie Besant in England was set aside. Heywood was nevertheless sentenced to a term of two years in the penitentiary at Charlestown, Mass. An appeal was made to President Hayes to rectify this injustice by granting Heywood an executive pardon, and he did so.

The advertisement received by **Cupid's Yokes** through the arrest and trial of its author caused its circulation to rise from a few thousand to tens of thousands. Everybody wanted to read this allegedly bad book, but the prurient were disappointed, as the "obscenity" was not obvious.

In the summer of 1878, a convention was held in Watkin's Glen, N.Y. Heywood's sister-in-law, Miss Josephine Tilden, attended and opened a book-stand where she offered **Cupid's Yokes**. By its side was another stand, at which D. M. Bennett sold his publications. One day while Miss Tilden was at lunch, Bennett tended her stand, and sold several copies of **Cupid's Yokes** to spies sent there for the purpose by the Young Men's Christian Association. Miss Tilden and Bennett were arrested but released on bail. They afterwards returned to Watkins Glen for trial, but the district attorney refused to prosecute, and the case was dropped. Thus far, no one had thought this much-advertised book was sufficiently obscene to justify conviction of those who sold it.

Bennett had neither published nor sold **Cupid's Yokes** before; but, feeling that he had been persecuted and wronged, he determined to defy his persecutors. Therefore, in his paper, **The Truth Seeker**, he announced that he would sell the book, and send it through the mails to any who might want it. Here Comstock saw his opportunity. He wrote Bennett another letter ordering a copy, and it was mailed to him. Comstock then staged another raid on Bennett's office, arrested the proprietor, and seized all copies of **Cupid's Yokes** in sight. The aged publisher was now in the jaws of the lion.

The late Elbert Hubbard was once arrested on a charge of "obscenity." He humbly pleaded guilty and paid a fine of $300. While he was wanting in Bennett's courage, he had what Bennett had not—discretion. Yet free speech and free press have been won by the struggles of men like Bennett, who, in spite of prison, would not cease fighting. Bennett had the spirit which motivated Richard Carlile, who spent nine and and a half years in English prisons, until the government became tired of the game and ceased arresting him.

In 1870, "obscenity" was a terrible and disgraceful crime. Then the individual who innocently published something dealing with marriage or divorce, childbearing or birth control, or anything pertaining to sex—even a physician giving advice to his patients—stood within the shadow of the penitentiary. It made no difference if the choicest and purest language, free from all vulgarity, were used. The "obscenity" law was backed by what has been termed "public consideration," which Gaboriau called "the admiration of fools, the consideration of knaves and the concert of all conceited vanities." All who objected to the law and the methods of its enforcer, Comstock, were at once listed as "advocates of obscene literature," just as the Anti-Saloon League lumped together as advocates of the saloon and drunkenness all who did not endorse the 18th Amendment.

The strength of Anthony Comstock in New York City was Judge Charles L. Benedict, who was a hide-bound Presbyterian. Outside of New York, the Federal judges often ruled severely against him, but before Judge Benedict he used to boast that he had "never failed to secure a conviction." Once a jury trying an obscenity case in his court disagreed. Judge Benedict sent them back to the jury room with more stringent instructions. Still they could not arrive at a verdict. He repeated this six times, after which an agreement was reached. The fact that Benedict was to preside at Bennett's trial boded no good for the "old infidel" publisher.

Stewart L. Woodford, district attorney for the Southern District of New York, thought little of the case and did not care to prosecute it. But his assistant, W. P. Fiero, entered into it with all the zeal of a Spanish inquisitor. Bennett had been cleverly "framed."

Like the Chicago anarchists, in 1887, he was accused of one offense and tried for another. The anarchists were charged with murder, but their speeches and writings, advocating radical social and economic opinions, were placed before the jury, and on these they were convicted.

Bennett was charged with dealing in obscene literature, but the indicted matter, which no sensible person considered objectionable, was kept out of sight, while his paper and other heretical publications were flaunted before the jury to influence them to convict. The indictment did not charge that the entire **Cupid's Yokes** was pornographic. Instead, a few isolated passages were selected as obscene. Under this interpretation of the law, a publisher sending a copy of Shakespeare, or the Bible, through the mails would be subject to conviction. Bennett's lawyer was not permitted to call the attention of the jury to the connection of these isolated passages with the context. A score of literary men, publishers, and authors were subpoenaed who were ready to testify that **Cupid's Yokes** was not an obscene publication, but they were not permitted to go on the stand. There might as well have been no trial.

Yet the prosecution did not have everything its own way. Two of the jurors held out for acquittal, and finally voted for a verdict of guilty, as they stated later in the **New York Herald**, hoping a higher court would reverse some of Judge Benedict's rulings. Prominent ministers sat inside the railing to give encouragement to the prosecution, just as a Protestant minister, a Catholic priest and a rabbi recently sat beside the judge on the bench during the trial of Mary Ware Dennett on a similar charge. The difference was that while Mrs. Dennett, who, like Bennett, was advanced in years, was convicted, a higher court released her, and her publication stands vindicated. The trial

was denounced by all the New York papers. But a verdict of guilty was
the foregone conclusion, and Bennett was sentenced to 13 months at
hard labor in Albany Penitentiary. This was the first real opposition
that Comstock and his society had encountered. The case aroused
great excitement and resentment.*

In the case of E. H. Heywood President Hayes had stood nobly between the inquisitors and their victim, and the friends of Mr. Bennett
at once appealed to him. The greatest number of signatures ever af-
fixed to a petition for an executive pardon was presented to Mr. Hayes.
He had released the author of the book because he thought it not objectionable under the law. Would he now do the same for a bookseller
who had sold it? It was hoped he would, and, as was afterwards learned,
the pardon form was made out. There was this difference, however,
as the President soon found out, between the two cases. Heywood had
done nothing to offend the Churches and the ministers, hence there
was no organized section of the population demanding that he serve
his sentence. Bennett's case was different. The ministers thought he
should be locked up because he had attacked them, their Bible and
creeds, even though he had done nothing else that was reprehensible.
Comstock and the ministers became active.

Comstock went to Washington to see the President, representing
Bennett to be a bad man engaged in the publication of pernicious literature. The ministers organized, and appealed to **Mrs. Hayes**, urging
her by all means to persuade her husband to keep this bad man in
prison. The President was in a dilemma. The Churches were then powerful politically, though not so well organized to influence officials and
legislation as they are today. The friends of Mr. Bennett were not. The
Churches were rich, while Bennett's friends were poor. To do the President absolute justice, we will quote his own words, which alone will con-
demn the position he took: In his **Diary** for July 1, 1879, he writes:

> "I have heard arguments by Ingersoll and Wakeman in favor
> of pardoning D. M. Bennett, convicted of sending obscene matter
> through the mails, viz., a pamphlet of a polemical character in
> favor of free love. **While I am satisfied that Bennett ought not
> to have been convicted**, I am not satisfied that I ought to un-
> dertake to correct the mistakes of courts—constantly persisted
> in by the exercise of the pardoning power. There is great heat
> on both sides of the question. The religious world are against
> the pardon, the unbelievers are for it." (**Diary and Letters of
> R. B. Hayes**, vol. 3, p. 563.)

> "The true rule as to obscene matter is, Does it tend to excite
> the passions or inflame the sensual appetite or desires of the
> young? Does the book or pamphlet belong to that class of pub-
> lications which are sold secretly to the young? The fact that
> it is Atheistic, or Infidel or immoral in doctrine, does not make
> it obscene." (Page 567.)

> "I was never satisfied as I would wish, with the correct-
> ness of the result to which I came chiefly in deference to the
> courts. **Cupid's Yokes** was a free-love pamphlet of bad prin-
> ciples, and in bad taste, but Colonel Ingersoll had abundant
> reason for his argument that it was not, in the legal sense,
> obscene." (Vol. 5, p. 68.)

In all this, President Hayes was fair enough to point out the difference between disagreeing with a man's views, and sending him to
prison for those views. Neither Ingersoll nor Wakeman, nor even Ben-

---

*I have a stenographic report of the trial of D. M. Bennett, which was
published at the time.

nett, agreed with the opinions expressed in the prosecuted book more than did the President; but is not freedom of opinion the corner-stone of American institutions?

President Hayes, in common with the majority of other right-thinking men who had examined **Cupid's Yokes**, did not consider it objectionable under the law. No one can therefore take issue with him as to the soundness and consistency of his views. Only when we come to his acts can we criticise him. Two men had been convicted for sending this publication through the mails. In both cases it was evident that the defendants had been "railroaded." President Hayes had pardoned one of them for what he considered and stated as good and sufficient reasons. He had not changed his opinion; hence, the same reasons applied to the other, yet he refused to interfere. We can see no cause for this partiality, in which the President did not act in accordance with his own convictions, except that while no considerable number of people were interested in keeping one of these men in prison, powerful influences, of a religious, social and political nature, demanded the incarceration of the other.

The President's "deference" to the courts is hardly a good defense. Theodore Roosevelt once said: "Pardons must sometimes be given in order that the cause of justice may be served." While the pardoning power is sometimes abused, its object is to correct errors of courts and juries, which the history of the world proves not only to have been many times in error but in many cases in gross error. Charles Sumner said:

"Let me here say that I hold judges, and especially the Supreme Court of the country, in much respect; but I am too familiar with the history of judicial proceedings to regard them with any superstitious reverence. Judges are but men, and in all ages have shown a full share of human fraility. Alas! Alas! the worst crimes of history have been perpetrated under their sanction. The blood of martyrs and of patriots, crying from the ground, summons them to judgment.

"It was a judicial tribunal which condemned Socrates to drink the fatal hemlock, and which pushed the Saviour barefoot over the pavements of Jerusalem, bending beneath the cross. It was a judicial tribunal which, against the testimony and entreaties of her father, surrendered the fair Virginia as a slave; which arrested the teachings of the great apostle to the Gentiles, and sent him in bonds from Judea to Rome; which, in the name of the old religion, adjured the saints and fathers of the Christian Church to death in all its most dreadful forms, and which afterwards, in the name of the new religion, enforced the tortures of the Inquisition amidst the shrieks and agonies of its victims, while it compelled Galileo to declare, in solemn denial of the great truth he disclosed, that the earth did not revolve around the sun. Ay, sir, it was a judicial tribunal in England, surrounded by all the forms of law, which sanctioned every despotic caprice of Henry VIII, from the unjust divorce of his queen to the beheading of Sir Thomas More; which lighted the fires of persecution that glowed at Oxford and Smithfield, over the cinders of Latimer, Ridley, and John Rodgers; which, after elaborate argument, upheld the fatal tyranny of ship money against the patriotic resistance of Hampden; which, in defiance of justice and humanity, sent Sydney and Russell to the block; which persistently enforced the laws of conformity that our Puritan fathers persistently refused to obey; and which afterwards, with Jeffries on the bench, crimsoned the pages of English history with massacre and murder, even with the blood of innocent women. Ay, sir, and it was a judicial tribunal in **our** country, surrounded by all the forms of law, which hung witches at Salem, which affirmed the constitutionality of the Stamp Act, while it admonished 'jurors and people' to obey; and which now, in our day, has lent its sanction to the unutterable atrocity of the Fugitive Slave law."

After the great agitation of three years over what would have been otherwise an unknown book, D. M. Bennett, alone, left a favorable impression. After he had served his term in prison his friends raised a fund and sent him on a trip around the world, an account of which he published in a work of four volumes. Everywhere he was hailed as the victim of a biogted conspiracy. When he died, in 1882, the same friends erected an imposing monument over his grave. They felt he had been sacrificed to popular clamor and prejudice.

President Hayes' position in the case was most unfortunate. His public and private life had been beyond reproach. But he was not one of our strongest statesmen, and was wanting in courage before the enemy. He knew the right, had done the right, but was afraid to do it again, owing to a religious-political-clerical lobby operating through his wife. He once offered to appoint Robert G. Ingersoll Minister to Germany. The clergy started a vociferous opposition. Ingersoll did not particularly want it, and, to relieve the President of embarrassment, declined.

Anthony Comstock lived until 1915. Owing to his becoming at least partially incompetent, in his latter years, the management of the "Society for the Suppression of Vice" was taken out of his hands. The Society is still in existence, but retains little of its former powers and influence. The courts today in trying cases involving obscene literature base their decisions, not upon isolated passages, but upon the book, pamphlet or article as a whole.

What was the fate of the 15c-pamphlet which so perturbed Church and state in 1878 and 1879? Its author was again arrested for mailing it. At his trial, the jury disagreed, and he was never tried again. In Massachusetts, a woman was also arrested for mailing it. At her trial the judge ordered the clerk to read the entire book aloud in court. When he had finished, the judge said, "This court is strong enough to stand anything in that book," and immediately discharged the defendant. **Cupid's Yokes** was then retired to the obscurity which it deserved, and from which it never should have emerged.

CHAPTER VI

PRESIDENTS WHOSE RELIGIOUS VIEWS ARE DOUBTFUL

JAMES MADISON

**Born, March 16, 1751. Died, June 28, 1836. President,
March 4, 1809—March 4, 1817.**

We have had one President who, in his youth, was a minister, but who abandoned that profession for politics, the law and the army. This was James Abram Garfield. We have had two Presidents—John Adams and James Madison—who studied for the ministry, but never entered upon its work. Madison was one of our most solid and useful, if not one of our most brilliant, statesmen. He was the "Father of the Constitution," and has left us a report of the proceedings of the Constitutional Convention. His letters and papers were considered to be of such great value that after his death Congress appropriated $30,000 for their purchase. He was a Virginian by birth, and the homes of Madison, Jefferson and Monroe were within a radius of 30 miles from each other.

In 1768, at the age of 17, young Madison entered Princeton College. He finished his classical course, after which he took a post-graduate course in Greek, Hebrew and Christian evidences under the famous Dr. Witherspoon, intending, as all thought, to become a minister. Why he did not enter the ministry has been a puzzling question. His biographer and the editor of his **Writings**, Gaillard Hunt, says: "At any rate, after he left Princeton he never recorded any desire nor took any visible step toward consummating the logical result of his post-graduate course." (**Life of Madison**, p. 16.)

While he did not become a clergyman, James Madison played an important part in the development of the spirit of religious liberty in the United States. After graduating, in 1771, Madison returned home to his native Virginia. There, although the American Colonies were girding themselves for the struggle, that would, in a dozen years, throw off the yoke of English rule, he found the jails filled with men imprisoned for no other crime than preaching doctrines contrary to those of the Protestant Episcopal Church, the established Church of Virginia. Many of these were Baptists, who had become numerous in the Colony.

This persecution aroused all the ire of Madison's young and liberty-loving nature. In a letter written in 1774, he said:

> "If the Church of England had been the established and general religion in all the northern colonies as it has been among us here, and uninterrupted tranquillity had prevailed throughout the continent, it is clear to me that slavery and subjection might and could have been so gradually insinuated among us. Union of religious sentiment begets a surprising confidence, and ecclesiastical establishments tend to great ignorance and corruption; all of which facilitates the execution of mischievous projects."

These sentiments, coming from a young man who had just been graduated from a theological seminary, were remarkable. And Madison had himself been reared in the Protestant Episcopal Church of Virginia; his father was a vestryman; his mother, a devout member, and his second cousin, the Rt. Rev. James Madison, became the first Bishop of Virginia.

Let us look for a moment at the Episcopal Church of Virginia, that claimed the exclusive right to administer moral and spiritual instruction to the people. This Church was responsible for the "Dale Code," a series of laws against heresy, and non-conformity, which were on the statute books and in force in the Colony. Under this code, all rival Churches were excluded. The annual support of a minister was fixed "at 1,500 pounds of tobacco and sixteen barrels of corn, to be assessed at the rate of ten pounds of tobacco and one bushel of corn per head for every man and boy over 16 years old." Then he was also to receive, because of the "low rates of tobacco," "the 20th calfe, the 20th kidd of goates, and the 20th pigge."

The following list of penalties indicates the severity with which non-conformity was punished:

1. To speak impiously of the Trinity or one of the divine persons, or against the known articles of Christian faith, was punishable by death.

2. The same penalty of death was to avenge "blaspheming God's holy name."

3. To curse or "banne"—for the first offense, some severe punishment; for the second, a "bodkin should be thrust through the tongue"; if the culprit was incorrigible, he should suffer death.

4. To say or do anything "to the derision or despight of God's holy word," or in disrespect of any minister, exposed the offender to be "openly whipped three times, and to ask public forgiveness in the assembly of the congregation, three several Saboth daies."

5. Non-attendance on religious services entailed a penalty, for the first offense, of the stoppage of allowance; for the second, whipping; for the third, the galleys for six months.

6. For Sabbath-breaking the first offense brought the stoppage of allowance; the second, whipping; and the third, death.

7. Preachers and ministers were enjoined to faithfulness in the conduct of regular services on pain "of loosing their entertainment."

8. Every person in the Colony, or who should come into it, was required to repair to the minister for examination in the faith. If he was unsound he was to be instructed. If he refused to go to the minister, he should be whipped; on a second refusal, he should be whipped twice and compelled to "acknowledge his fault on Saboth day in the assembly of the congregation"; for a third refusal, he should be "whipt every day until he makes acknowledgement."

It is said that these extreme penalties were seldom enforced. Upon this point Thomas E. Watson says: "Written in London and sent over to the Colony, the Virginia laws against heresy were as savage a set as ever disgraced the books. Had the early Virginians been as much given to pious practices as the Puritan brethren of New England, there might have been a reign of religious terror South as there was North. Fortunately for humanity, the early Virginian was an easy-going, generous-tempered mortal, who never could have found luxury in whipping bare-shouldered women, pressing old men to death under piles of stone, torturing little children to extort evidence against their parents, and fattening the gallows upon the rotting bodies of witches and Quakers. . . . The Virginian code, written under the supervision of London ecclesiastics, was

bloody enough to have pleased Loyola or Torquemada, but it was treated as all Christian nations now treat the sublime moral code of Christ—all believe and none practice."*
On January 27, 1774, Madison wrote:
"That diabolical, hell-conceived principle of persecution rages among some. . . . There are at this time in the adjacent county not less than five or six well-meaning men in close jail, for publishing their religious sentiments, which in the main are very orthodox. . . . I have squabbled and scolded, abused and ridiculed so long about it, that I am without common patience. So I must beg you to pity me, and pray for liberty of conscience for all."

The moral condition of the clergy of the Episcopal Church of Virginia at the time is illustrated by the following quotation from the historian of the Church, the Rev. Dr. S. D. McConnell, who, in his **History of the American Episcopal Church** (pp. 89 and 90), says:

"A large proportion of the Southern clergy were adventurers, broken men, valets who had secured ordination from some complaisant bishop through the interest of their masters for whom they had done some questionable favor. . . . Their letters of orders were often suspicious, and their characters still more so. Commissaries Blair of Virginia and Bray of Maryland repeatedly reported to the Bishop of London that the meager support of the clergy and the slight honor in which they were held prevented them from making honorable marriages and led them into disgraceful connections. A love-letter still survives written by a Maryland clergyman to a planter's daughter, in which he argues at length that inasmuch as his suit was allowable on other grounds, the fact of his being in orders ought not to be an insuperable barrier. They provoked contempt and allowed themselves to be treated like lackeys. Governor Nicholson led one out who was drunk in the church, and caned him soundly with his own hand; clapped the hat over the eyes of another; and sent **billets-doux** to his mistress by a third.

"There were always present in these Colonies some clergy of exemplary life and high character, but neither their example nor their reproofs were able to redeem their brethren. Most of them were planters, and did priestly duty now and then to eke out their income. They hunted, played cards, drank punch and canary, turned marriages, christenings, and funerals alike into revels. One bawled out to his church warden at the holy communion, 'Here, George, this bread is not fit for a dog.' One fought a duel in his graveyard. Another, a powerful fellow, thrashed his vestrymen one by one, and the following Sunday preached before them from the text, 'And I contended with them, and cursed them, and smote certain of them, and picked off their hair.' Another dined every Sunday with his chief parishioner, and was sent home in the evening drunk, tied in his chaise."
Patrick Henry said in the famous "Parsons' Cause":
"We have heard a great deal about the benevolence and holy zeal of our reverend clergy, but how is this manifested? Do they manifest their zeal in the cause of religion and humanity by practising the mild and benevolent precepts of the gospel of Jesus? Do they feed the hungry and clothe the naked? Oh, no, gentlemen! Instead of feeding the hungry and clothing the

---

*Life of Jefferson.**

naked, these rapacious harpies would, were their powers equal
to their will, snatch from the hearth of their honest parishioner
his last hoe cake, from the widow and her orphan children their
last milch cow! the last bed, nay, the last blanket from the
lying-in woman."

The venerable pre-Civil War Bishop of the Virginia Episcopal
Church, the Rt. Rev. William Meade, says: "At no time from its first
establishment, was the moral and religious condition of the Church
in Virginia even tolerable good." (**Old Churches, Ministers and Families
of Virginia**, vol. 2, p. 351.)

It would now be considered anomalous that an institution bearing this reputation should have any part in the moral and religious
training of a people, to say nothing of its claiming a legally exclusive
right to the privilege. So great was the indignation of the people, both
with the moral character and persecutions of the clergy, that petitions
were presented in the session of the legislature of 1774 demanding relief. Three-fourths of the inhabitants of Virginia were not members
of the Church of England, but it had power in that it was supported by
the majority of the legislature, and the "first families."

In May, 1776, the legislature met again, this time to declare independence of England. It adopted a Bill of Rights. The last section,
written by George Mason, but introduced by Patrick Henry, read as
follows:

> "That religion, or the duty which we owe to our Creator,
> and the manner of discharging it, can be directed only by reason
> and conviction, and therefore all men are equally entitled to
> the free exercise of religion, according to the dictates of con-
> science; and that it is the mutual duty of all to practise Chris-
> tian forbearance, and charity toward each other."

There was another form of the resolution, but neither pleased
James Madison, who was a member of this legislature. The resolution,
as proposed, made religious freedom only a matter of grace, not of
right. It was only to be a thing of "Christian forbearance." Madison
introduced the following resolution:

> "That religion, or the duty we owe to our Creator, and the
> manner of discharging it, being under the direction of reason
> and conviction only, not of violence or compulsion, all men are
> equally entitled to the full and free exercise of it, according to
> the dictates of conscience; and that therefore no man, or class
> of men, ought, on account of religion, to be invested with pe-
> culiar emoluments or privileges, nor subjected to any penalties
> or disabilities, unless, under color of religion, the preservation of
> equal liberty and the existence of the state be manifestly en-
> dangered."

Under this resolution religious liberty became a **right**, not a **privilege**.
Both a state priesthood and a state Church would be impossible, and
no citizen could be taxed to support either without his consent. Madison's resolution was defeated, but the battle was on, and nine years
later, complete liberty was granted. Gradually the Church of England
was deprived of its emoluments. The legislature of 1776 relieved dissenters from paying church rates. In 1779, it refused to continue paying the salaries of the clergy. In 1780 the civil powers of the vestry
were abolished. During the Revolution, most of the Established clergy
took the side of England, and they, with the Methodists, were driven
from the country. At the opening of the war, there were in the State 95
parishes, with 91 ministers. At its close, 23 parishes were extinct, 34
were vacant, and only 28 of the clergy remained.

The Revolution, like all wars, was followed by a period of dishonesty, carelessness in fulfilling contracts, and general immorality. The clergy attributed this condition to the lack of organized and state-supported religion. We had the same experience at the close of the World War, when the clergy demanded laws compelling the reading of the Bible in the schools. They also proposed adjournment of schools for religious instruction; and the Fundamentalists asked for laws prohibiting teaching of Evolution. In the Virginia legislature of 1784, they were marshaled in force to demand a return of their old prerogatives. James Madison was also there.

There were two parties supporting the pretensions of the Church. First, those of the Church of England. An old Virginia aristocrat who was present said he was "for giving all a fair chance, that there were many roads to heaven, and he was in favor of letting every man take his own way; but he was sure of one thing, that no **gentleman** would choose any but the Episcopal." Then there were those who did not believe in an established Church, but who held that there should be a general tax for the support of religion, each taxpayer indicating to what Church his taxes should be applied. Those who did not wish to contribute to a Church might stipulate that it be paid into the school fund. This proposal seemed fair enough, and received the support of men like Washington, John Marshall, Patrick Henry and others equally prominent. Nearly everyone then believed that it was the duty of the state to support religion, on the alleged ground of its moral and social values, even though they did not need it for themselves. The Church of today is largely supported by men who seldom enter its doors but who think it is a necessity for other people.

Madison found the majority were against him, and that there would be a conflict. The measure to incorporate the Episcopal Church was passed, after which another was introduced and approved, incorporating all Christian religious societies. The taxing bill for the support of all the Churches passed at the second reading by a vote of 47 to 32. The outlook for religious freedom was not bright.

Madison adopted a ruse. He asked a postponement of further consideration of the bill until the next session, and his request was granted. He then entered a protest with the people. He called their attention to the question of morality, which seemed to concern the advocates of a tax for the support of religion. He told them that Pennsylvania, New York and Rhode Island, where there was no such tax, were as moral as those States which had the tax, and that the condition of religion in those States was as good, if not better. On the question of dividing the tax between the different Churches, he called attention to the fact that, in the end, the Church having the greatest political, social and financial influence would secure more money and power than the other Churches.

There was another serious question. If the people were to be taxed to support **Christian Churches**, it would be necessary for the courts to decide what are Christian Churches? Are they trinitarian, unitarian, Calvinistic, or other? Are the doctrines of hell and the virgin birth an essential part of their theology? Here was the Pandora's box which, when opened, would renew all the conflicts and persecutions under the old system.

Petitions favoring these views were widely circulated. Candidates were compelled to state whether or not they favored the church tax. When the legislature met in 1785, its attitude was completely changed. Thomas Jefferson, who had worked in harmony with Madison, though he was now absent from the country on a mission to France, had, in 1779, proposed the following religious liberty bill:

"No man shall be compelled to frequent or support any religious worship, ministry, or place whatsoever; nor shall be enforced, restrained, molested, or burdened in his body or goods;

nor shall otherwise suffer on account of his religious opinion or belief: but all men shall be free to profess, and by argument to maintain, their opinions in matters of religion; and the same shall in no wise diminish, enlarge, or affect their civil capacities."

This bill, which was both effective and comprehensive, was passed, repealing the taxation measure. It is written on Jefferson's tombstone that he was "the Author of the Statute of Virginia for Religious Freedom." He was as proud of this achievement as he was of the authorship of the Declaration of Independence. Madison was so elated that he exclaimed, "In this country is forever extinguished the ambitious hope of making laws for the human mind," but, alas, he did not dream of our modern Fundamentalists!

It must be admitted that the opposition of many to the church tax was not due to dislike of religion, but to dislike of being taxed. Nearly all in that day were anxious to go to heaven, but they did not want toll-gates along the route.

From this time on, James Madison was a vigorous opponent of all measures designed to enslave the mind. The next test came in the national Constitutional Convention, of which he was a member. While the Constitution (Article VI, section 3) states that "no religious test shall ever be required as a qualification to any office or public trust under the United States," this was as far as it went. It contained no bill of rights. Some of the delegates, for this cause, refused to ratify it. Madison pledged his word that if it was ratified he would see that the missing guarantee should be forthcoming. The first 10 Amendments began: "Congress shall make no law respecting an establishment of religion, or prohibiting the free exercise thereof; nor abridging the freedom of speech or of the press; or the right of the people peaceably to assemble and to petition the government for a redress of grievances."

Today, the question is often raised, "Can a State pass a law establishing religion?" Some persons affirm that it cannot be prevented from doing so. On December 14, 1875, James G. Blaine introduced into the House of Representatives an Amendment which read: "No State shall make any law respecting an establishment of religion, or prohibiting the free exercise thereof; and no money raised by school taxation in any State, for the support of public schools, or derived from any public fund therefor, nor any public lands devoted thereto, shall ever be divided between religious sects or denominations." This resolution passed the House by a vote of 180 to 7, but was defeated in the Senate.

Madison was a leader in the movement for the abolition of congressional chaplains. Few remember that in the past there was much opposition to them. On December 27, 1839, a heated debate was held in the House upon the subject, when a motion was made to reconsider the vote on the resolution which authorized the appointment of chaplains. Representative Cooper, of Georgia, led the opposition. He said, in part, that he believed the House had proceeded in this matter without just and proper authority. He believed the effect of the employment to be evil. Who is the chaplain? Is he an officer of this House? By what authority do you appoint him? If there was any authority, he wished to be pointed to it. What are the effects of the practice? They seemed to be evil. The resolution, to be sure, proposed to elect two chaplains of different denominations, but notwithstanding this, he objected to it, because this matter of religious denominations should not be agitated in this House. This matter of sectarianism might create no difficulty for some time, but a time might come when it would.

In 1850, Senator Underwood, of Kentucky, in presenting a petition praying Congress to abolish the office of chaplain, said: "A national chaplaincy, no less than a national Church, is considered by us emphatically as 'an establishment of religion.' " In 1839, the vote against chaplains in Congress was 12, in 1840, 21, in 1860, it had jumped to 61. Since then, the question has not been debated. James Madison did not hesitate to state his position:

"I observe with particular pleasure the view you have taken of the immunity of religion from civil jurisdiction, in every case where it does not trespass on private rights or the public peace. This has always been a favorite principle with me; and it was not with my approbation that the deviation from it took place in Congress, when they appointed chaplains, to be paid from the national treasury. It would have been a much better proof to their constituents of their pious feeling if the members had contributed for the purpose a pittance from their own pockets. As the precedent is not likely to be rescinded, the best that can now be done may be to apply to the Constitution the maxim of the law, **de minimis non curant**." (No notice is taken of trifles.) (**Madison's Writings**, vol. 3, p. 274.)

In 1806 the Baptist Church of the District of Columbia petitioned Congress for so simple a favor as an act of incorporation, as did the Protestant Episcopal and Presbyterian congregations. No notice was taken of them. Then the Baptists and Presbyterians united in an effort, and a bill for the purpose was introduced. Considerable debate took place. the opposition being on the ground that the measure tended to establish religion. It ended by the bill's being indefinitely postponed. At the next session of Congress another attempt was made with the same failure. But the Churches were persistent. They continued the fight. In 1810, the Episcopal Church introduced another bill for the same purpose. It passed the House but was defeated in the Senate on the second reading. Then a member who had voted against it was induced to change his vote, which enabled it to pass. James Madison was President, and was not afraid to do his duty. He at once vetoed it, giving the following reasons for his action:

"TO THE HOUSE OF REPRESENTATIVES OF THE
UNITED STATES:

"Having examined and considered the bill entitled 'An act incorporating the Protestant Episcopal Church in the town of Alexandria, in the District of Columbia,' I now return the bill to the House of Representatives, in which it originated, with the following objections:

"Because the bill exceeds the rightful authority to which governments are limited by the essential distinction between civil and religious functions, and violates, in particular, the article of the Constitution of the United States which declares that 'Congress shall make no law respecting an establishment of religion.'

"Because the bill vests in said incorporated church an authority to provide for the support of the poor, and the education of poor children of the same; an authority which, being altogether superfluous, if the provision is to be the result of pious charity, would be a precedent for giving to religious societies, as such, a legal agency in carrying into effect a public and civil duty.

"Feb. 21, 1811.   JAMES MADISON."

We have seen that James Madison's early ambition was to become a minister, and that he prepared himself at Princeton's theological seminary, a very orthodox institution. Did he continue to be a believer in later life? There is no evidence that he did, yet we have nothing to justify us in asserting dogmatically that he did not.

Bishop Meade, of the diocese of Virginia, in his **Old Churches, Ministers and Families of Virginia** (vol. 2, p. 100), indicates that Madison abandoned orthodoxy after he entered public life. He says:

"His religious feeling, however, seems to have been short lived. His political association with those of infidel principles, of whom there were many in his day, if they did not actually change his creed, yet subjected him to the general suspicion of it. Whatever may have been the private sentiments of Mr. Madison on the subject of religion, he was never known to declare any hostility to it. He always treated it with respect, attended worship in his neighborhood, invited ministers of religion to his house, had family prayer—though he did not kneel himself at prayer. I was never at Mr. Madison's but once, and then our conversation took such a turn—though not designed on my part—as to call forth some expressions and arguments which left the impression on my mind that his creed was not strictly regulated by the Bible."

A few facts, and some extracts from his writings may place the reader in a position to judge for himself.

In 1816, the last year of Madison's term as President, St. John's Episcopal Church, in Washington, was completed. The Vestry offered the President his choice of pews, free of charge. This generous offer Mr. Madison declined; but he did agree to accept any pew the Vestry might select for him. This incident proves nothing. John Adams, though a Unitarian, accepted an "official pew" in Christ Church, Philadelphia, while he was President. It was in the interest of the Church to offer it, and not in the interest of the President to refuse to accept.

Strange as it might appear, Mr. Madison positively refused to discuss the subject of religion, an unusual thing in his day if a man were, in fact, religious. In a letter to the Rev. Miles King, written on September 5, 1816, he says:

"The letters and communications addressed to me on religious subjects have been so numerous, and of characters so various, that it has been an established rule to decline all correspondence on them. Your reflection will, I doubt not, do justice to this rule. You may be assured that I do it fully to the pious motives which dictated your letter, and that I am very thankful for the kind solicitude you expressed for my future happiness." (**Writings**, vol. III, p. 19.)

That a man, who, as a youth, had an ambition to preach religion and save souls, should, in his later years, refuse to discuss it at all, is an enigma, unless policy was consulted, which is scarcely in accord with the supposition that he was religious himself. As we read the four large volumes of Madison's **Writings**, we find, that like Jefferson, he discusses all the great questions of his day. Why should he omit and refuse to discuss religion, which was held to be one of the most vital issues of his time? There are a score of reasons why a man who ceased to be religious should decline to talk, but we can see none for silence on the part of one who is convinced of the truth of Christianity.

A minister, one Wilson, had circulated a report that President Madison, during his first term as Secretary of State, had a habit of reading the Bible, but abandoned the practice during his second term. This statement brought from Madison the following letter in contradiction:

"The passage is a sad example of pulpit authenticity, justice and delicacy. In what relates to me there is scarcely any part wholly true in the sense intended. How such a string of misinformation could have been gathered it is not easy to imagine.

".... That of my studying the Bible on the Sabbath during
the first term, and abandoning during the second term of my
service in the Department of State, is, throughout, a sheer fabrication for the sake of the sting put into the tail of it.
"The preacher says he had spoken to me on the subject of
my faith, and that I always evaded his object. I recollect one
person only of his name (Wilson) who could have made the allusion. He was presented to me at Washington by Mr. Piper,
and perhaps other members of Congress, and called on me several times afterwards late in the evening. He was considered a
man of superior genius, and a profound erudition, for his years;
but eccentric, and subject occasionally to flights into the region
of mental derangement, of which, it was said, he gave proofs in
a sermon preached in Washington. This infirmity betrayed itself
during a visit to me with Mr. Piper, who apologized for it. In
intervals perfectly lucid, his conversation was interesting."

Twice Madison discusses religion in general, the first time in considering its influence upon conduct, particularly in its influence in the
prevention of the enactment of unjust laws. In his **Notes on the Confederacy**, written in April, 1787, he says:

"Will religion, the only remaining motive, be a restraint?
It is not pretended to be such, on men individually considered.
Will its effect be greater on them considered in an aggregate
view? Quite the reverse. The conduct of every popular assembly
acting on oath, the strongest of religious ties, proves that individuals join without remorse in acts against which their consciences would revolt if proposed to them under like sanction,
separately in their closets. When, indeed, religion is kindled into
enthusiasm, its force, like that of other passions, is increased
by the sympathy of the multitude. But enthusiasm is only a
temporary state of religion, and, while it lasts, will hardly be
seen with pleasure at the helm of Government. Besides, as religion in its coolest state is not infallible, it may become a
motive of oppression as well as a restraint from injustice."
(**Writings**, vol. IV, pp. 326-327.)

To the Rev. F. Beasley, who had sent him a tract entitled, **Proofs of
the Being and Attributes of God**, on November 20, 1825, Mr. Madison
wrote as follows:

"The finiteness of the human understanding betrays itself
on all subjects, but more especially when it contemplates such
as involve infinity. What may safely be said seems to be, that
the infinity of time and space forces itself on our conception,
a limitation of either being inconceivable; that the mind at
once prefers the idea of a self-existing cause to that of an infinite series of cause and effect, which augments, instead of
avoiding, the difficulty; and that it finds more facility in as-
senting to the self-existence of an invisible cause, possessing
infinite power, wisdom and goodness, than to the self-existence
of the Universe, visibly destitute of those attributes, and which
may be the effect of them. In this comparative facility of conception and belief, all philosophical reasoning on the subject
must, perhaps, terminate."

Here Madison is simply stating a problem as old as thought, and
which has never been settled except from the standpoint of faith. Even
in this passage he is not telling distinctly his own views. He only tells
what "the mind at once prefers." (**Works**, vol. III, p. 504.)

In a letter to Dr. C. Caldwell, written in the same year, in discussing
the question of God, he says:

"I concur with you at once in rejecting the idea maintained

by some divines, of more zeal than discretion, that there is no road from Nature up to Nature's God, and that all the knowledge of his existence and attributes which preceded the written revelation of them was derived from oral tradition."

Here he makes a positive statement of opinion, but he was at variance with all the orthodox theologians of his time.

Madison took an interest in the panaceas of social reform and the abolition of slavery, as advocated by Robert Dale Owen and Fanny Wright, which were agitated in the first quarter of the 19th Century, without taking a definite stand either for or against them.

James Madison, in an age in which the drinking customs were strenuous, was practically a total abstainer from alcoholic stimulants. He used no spirits and drank only one glass of wine at dinner.

Judge Thomas Hertell, of the Admiralty Court, of New York City, had written the first work ever published in the United States advocating total abstinence from all alcoholic drinks as the solution of the drink evil. On December 20, 1809, Mr. Madison wrote him:

"A complete suppression of every species of stimulating indulgence, if attainable at all, must be a work of peculiar difficulty, since it has to encounter not only the force of habit, but propensities in human nature. In every age and nation some exhilarating or exciting substance seems to have been sought for, as a relief from the languor of idleness, or the fatigues of labor. In the rudest state of society, whether in hot or cold climates, a passion for ardent spirits is in a manner universal. In the progress of refinement, beverages less intoxicating, but still of an exhilarating quality, have been more or less common. And where all these sources of excitement have been unknown, or been totally prohibited by a religious faith, substitutes have been found in opium, in the nut of the betel, in the root of the ginseng, or the leaf of the tobacco plant.

"It would doubtless be a great point gained for our country, and a great advantage toward the object of your publication, if ardent spirits could be made only to give way to malt liquors, to those afforded by the apple and the pear, and the lighter and cheaper varieties of wine. It is remarkable, that in the countries where the grape supplies the common beverage, habits of intoxication are rare; and in some places almost without example."

In considering the career of James Madison, we cannot overlook his wife, Dolly Madison, the "Nation's Hostess" for many years. Mrs. Madison was reared a Quakeress, but upon her marriage to Mr. Madison, in 1794, cast aside her Quaker bonnet for the gaieties of society. Not until 1845, nine years after Madison's death, when she was 77 years old, did she join the Church. Then she applied to the Rev. Smith Pyne, rector of St. John's Church, to be confirmed. (**Life and Letters of Dolly Madison**, by Clark, p. 364.)

With her niece, Miss Annie Payne, she was accordingly confirmed and became a communicant. All biographers of Mrs. Madison admit this fact. How strange that none who have written the life of James Madison have a word to say about his religious beliefs or Church relations from the time he was a very young man until his death at the age of 85?

JAMES MONROE
Born, April 28, 1758. Died, July 4, 1831. President, March 4, 1817—March 4, 1825.

Though not an orator, nor a writer as were Jefferson and Madison, James Monroe occupies a position of honor among American Presidents.

He came of Virginia cavalier stock, and served as an officer during the
Revolution. In 1776, when he was 18, he was a lieutenant in the army
of Washington, and took part in the Battles of Harlem and White
Plains and in the retreat across the Jerseys. At the Battle of Trenton
he was wounded. Later, he was in the famous Battles of Brandywine,
Germantown and Monmouth.

Leaving the army, he returned to Virginia and studied law under
Thomas Jefferson, again going into the army when the British invaded
Virginia, in 1781. He was a member of the State legislature in 1782, of
Congress from 1783 until 1786, and in 1790 was elected to the United
States Senate.

In 1794, Washington appointed him Minister to France, where he
had many delicate problems to handle. Thomas Paine had been confined in the Luxembourg Prison for a year, although he was not charged
with any crime. Paine remained in prison largely through the hostility
of Gouverneur Morris, Monroe's predecessor as Minister, who is the hero
of a biography written by Theodore Roosevelt.* The efforts of his friends
to have him released had failed, and it seemed as though he would remain there indefinitely. He had barely escaped the guillotine. Mr. Monroe claimed him as an American citizen, secured his release, and took
him to his own house.

The American government thought Monroe was too much in sympathy with the French Revolution, and in 1796 he was recalled. Upon
arriving home. he was elected Governor of Virginia, but in 1803 was
again sent to France by President Jefferson, where, with Robert R. Livingston, he negotiated the Louisiana Purchase. He served as Secretary of
State and Secretary of War under President Madison.

President Monroe is best known in history by the "Monroe Doctrine."
In the first quarter of the 19th Century the Spanish and Portuguese
colonies in the western hemisphere rebelled against their rulers. Ar-
gentina declared its independence in 1816; Mexico, in 1820; Peru. in
1821; and Brazil, in 1822. The autocratic "Holy Alliance" was formed in
Europe to crush republican forms of government. President Monroe issued a proclamation declaring any effort on the part of a European
nation to hold territory by force in the western hemisphere would be
considered an unfriendly action and would be met with resistance on
the part of the United States. From that time on, the Monroe Doctrine
has remained a fundamental principle of American foreign policy.

Little is known concerning President Monroe's religious views. We
do not know if he had any, and if he did, what they were. His biographer,
Daniel C. Gilman, says: "He was extremely reticent in his religious sentiments, at least in all that he wrote. Allusions to his belief are rarely,
if ever, to be met with in his correspondence." (Pages, 245-246.) A still
later biography by George Morgan does not say even so much as this
one by Gilman. The six volumes of his **Writings** confirm the fact of his
reticence on religious subjects.

MARTIN VAN BUREN
**Born, December 5, 1782. Died, July 24, 1862. President,
March 4, 1837—March 4, 1841.**

Martin Van Buren, born in 1782, was the first President of the
United States who did not come into this world a subject of Great
Britain. Born in the State of New York, of Dutch ancestry, he early
came under the influence of Aaron Burr, from whom he drew his in-

---

*For a detailed account of Paine's imprisonment and its causes, see
Life of Thomas Paine, by Moncure D. Conway, chapters XXX, XXXI,
XXXII, XXXIII.

spiration for political intrigue. Although in disgrace in the public eye, Burr, almost to the day of his death, was, through other men, a power 'in New York politics. Van Buren began his political career in the New York legislature and as Attorney General of the State. These were the stepping stones by which he became the political boss of New York. He was elected to the United States Senate in 1821, and later, in 1828, when he resigned to become Governor of New York.

Under the direction of Aaron Burr, Martin Van Buren had long worked to make Andrew Jackson President. Failing in 1824, he succeeded in 1828, and was appointed Jackson's Secretary of State. He resigned in 1831 to become Minister to England, taking with him his son John. The young man became a favorite of English society, and danced and drank wine with Queen Victoria, while she was yet a young princess.

Van Buren, as a reward for the friendship he had manifested for President Jackson, received the Vice-Presidential nomination in 1832, and, with Jackson as his running-mate, was elected. Jackson chose him as his successor, and in 1836 Van Buren was elected President. The administration of President Van Buren has been called the "parentheses in American history," something which could have been left out without spoiling the sense. It is remembered only because of the great financial panic of 1837. Van Buren was defeated for reelection in 1840. He was nominated for the Presidency by the Free Soil party, in 1848, when, his political career ending, he retired from public life.

In Kinderhook, the little village on the Hudson, where he was born, and where he spent his last days, Martin Van Buren attended the Dutch Reformed Church. As President, and during his other official residence in Washington, he attended "The Presidents' Church," the aristocratic St. John's Episcopal Church, which has caused some writers to call him a member of the Dutch Reformed denomination, and others, an Episcopalian. We can find no positive evidence that he was a communicant in either Church, or that he took any interest in religious subjects other than conventional adherence. It is said that in the church in Kinderhook his voice could be heard above the entire congregation in song, which seems to be the only evidence at hand of his religiosity. Once, while he was in Rome, a report was circulated that he had been converted to Roman Catholicism, which he promptly denied.

A book by Denis Tilden Lynch, **An Epoch and a Man: Martin Van Buren and His Times**, gives no evidence of piety on the part of the subject. In 1920, the United States government published his **Autobiography**, edited by John C. Fitzpatrick. In this he makes no profession of religion, but he does criticise the ministers for interfering in political affairs. His funeral was conducted by Bishop Alonzo Potter, of the Episcopal Church, and by the Rev. Benjamin Van Zandt, of the Dutch Reformed faith.

JOHN TYLER
Born, March 29, 1790. Died, January 18, 1862. President,
April 4, 1841—March 4, 1845.

John Tyler was the first Vice President to succeed to the Presidency. He came of an old Virginia family, prominent in the affairs of the State, his father having been Governor, and United States District Judge. John Tyler himself rose rapidly in politics. He was a member of the legislature; in 1816, he was elected to Congress, where he remained until 1821. In 1823 he returned to the legislature, and from 1825 until 1827 was Governor of the State.

Tyler was then chosen to succeed John Randolph, of Roanoke, as U.S. Senator, and he supported President Jackson in the battle against nullification, but opposed him in his fight against the United States Bank. Sometimes he was with the Democrats and at other times with the Whigs. He had been both an advocate and an opponent of the United

States Bank, but in 1840 he was elected Vice President on the Whig
ticket, with General Harrison, on a platform advocating the recharter-
ing of the bank. General Harrison lived but a month after his inauguration, and when Tyler took his place it was expected that he would sign
a bill re-establishing the bank. Instead, he vetoed it, to the great disgust of the Whigs who had elected him. Henceforth, like Grover Cleveland, he was for the rest of his life a man without a party. His last
public activities were as a delegate to the "Peace Conference," held in
Washington in February, 1861, in an effort to prevent secession, and
later as a member of the Confederate Congress in Richmond.

   While President Tyler's career as a statesman was not brilliant, he
left his mark on the social life of the White House. He was a lover of
music, an accomplished violinist himself, and was the first to institute
Saturday afternoon concerts on the White House lawn. His first wife
died while he was President, and before his term was over he took another, Miss Julia Gardner, of New York. The second Mrs. Tyler was a
beautiful woman, and her portrait still adorns the walls of the Executive Mansion.

   Henry A. Wise, who was one of John Tyler's personal friends, said
of him: "He was a firm believer in the atonement of the son of God,
and in the efficacy of his blood to wash away every stain of mortal
sin. He was by faith and heirship a member of the Episcopal Church,
and never doubted divine revelation." This is a sweeping assertion, and
is not borne out by corroborative evidence, particularly in any statement of President Tyler himself.

   In 1826, shortly after the death of John Adams and Thomas Jefferson, he delivered a eulogy upon Jefferson, whom he praised for his
work for the separation of Church and state in Virginia. In this oration
he speaks of "our Redeemer." In 1855, the year Sprague's **Annals of the
American Pulpit** was compiled, Mr. Tyler furnished for this work his
recollections of Bishop James Madison, under whom he had studied at
William and Mary. He eulogizes Bishop Madison, but says nothing that
would indicate his own religious views. Bishop Johns, of the Diocese of
Virginia, who conducted President Tyler's funeral service, is not as
positive as was Henry A. Wise. In his discourse he said:

   "It is comforting to know that the great work of eternity
   had not been neglected. His gifted mind held fast as a foundation of its faith and hope to the oracles of God. He was long
   accustomed to meditate on the things of eternity; and when,
   a few years ago, he was prostrated by illness and impressed by
   the idea of approaching dissolution, the testimony of the pastor
   whose service he was so fond of attending in the Church he had
   so reverently joined, shows the brightness of the faith in which
   he died."

   The Bishop, it would appear, was talking under a strain. Deathbed
religion is always under suspicion. If a man is really religious, he makes
it known before he dies, and should he wait until the time of dissolution, his testimony is of little value. Then if a man is really religious,
some one besides the minister usually knows it. When this had happened,
"a few years ago," Tyler did not die, but recovered.

   A detailed account of his last illness is given by Mrs. Tyler in **Letters and Times of the Tylers**, vol. 2, pp. 670, 671 and 672. Here nothing
is said of "faith and hope in the oracles of God," or "the things of
eternity," or "the brightness of faith." "The idea of approaching dissolution" does not arise, nor was there any "testimony of the pastor,"
for none was present. Henry A. Wise appears to know all about President Tyler's religious views and church affiliations. Bishop Johns, an
ecclesiastic of the Episcopal Church, seems to know much less; while

his wife, who was in a position to know more than either, seems to know nothing, as she says nothing. And, if he were such a devout member of the Episcopal Church, and as he was an ex-President of the United States, why, with so many priests of that Church in the city of Richmond, was none of them called in to administer to him the last sacrament? As with the others in this chapter, evidence is lacking.

ZACHARY TAYLOR
Born, September 24, 1784. Died, July 9, 1850. President, March 4, 1849—July 9, 1850.

This soldier-President, prior to his election, had spent nearly all his adult life in military service. In the War of 1812, he had defended Fort Harrison, in the territory of Indiana, against the Indians, and defeated them with great slaughter. In the Black Hawk War, of 1832, he received the surrender of the Indian chief from whom the war took its name. Abraham Lincoln and Jefferson Davis both served in this campaign. Davis was then a young officer, fresh from West Point. He fell in love with General Taylor's daughter, and married her without her father's consent. Shortly after the wedding, she became ill, and died. Later, General Taylor fought the Seminole Indians in Florida, defeated them, and was made a brigadier general.

General Taylor played a leading role in the War with Mexico, and his victories over greatly superior numbers made him the hero of the hour. The Democratic party, in whose interest the war was started, was not successful in developing from it a hero. General Taylor was a Whig, and in 1848 that party made him its candidate for President. He was elected, defeating his Democratic opponent, General Lewis Cass.

General Taylor's administration proved to be one of great excitement, and he died 16 months after his inauguration. On July 4, 1850, he became overheated during the celebration of the national holiday, was taken sick, and died on the ninth. His last words were, "I am ready to die. I have faithfully endeavored to do my duty."

In Montgomery's **Life of Taylor**, it is stated that during the President's illness a minister was called to his bedside and offered prayer, after which the sick man felt relieved and asked for a glass of water. Ministers are always looking for such opportunities, and where could there have been a more welcome one than to be called to pray with a President of the United States? The result of the visit could not have been gratifying, since the President only "felt relieved" and asked for water. Many a man in health has felt relieved when a minister stopped praying.

In the above-mentioned biography, Humphrey Marshall writes seven pages on the character of General Taylor. Here was a splendid opportunity to say something about the President's religion, if he had any, but Marshall is silent on the subject. Montgomery says: "In the secret communion of his own heart with heaven, who can say he did not die a Christian?" This is an admission that no one knew anything about his religious belief.

This is confirmed by the funeral sermon of the Rev. Dr. Pyne, rector of St. John's Church. The discourse was both eloquent and lengthy, but the reverend doctor said nothing about President Taylor's religion, and very little else of a personal character. It is said that, prior to his nomination for the Presidency, General Taylor had taken so little interest in politics that he never went to the polls. For all we know to the contrary, he took so little interest in religion that he never went to church.

CHESTER ALAN ARTHUR
**Born, October 5, 1830. Died, November 18. 1886. President,
September 20, 1881—March 4, 1885.**

Chester Alan Arthur, who, as Vice President, became President after the death of Garfield, was a native of Vermont. He had been a teacher, a lawyer and Quartermaster-General of New York State during the Civil War. President Grant appointed him collector of the port of New York, from which position he was removed by President Hayes for failing to carry out certain reform measures.

Above all, Arthur was a politician, and an adherent of Roscoe Conkling, in opposition to James G. Blaine. A resident of New York City, he was the first "city man" to occupy the White House, all former Presidents having come from small towns or the country. His political record in New York State was not to his credit, yet as President his administration was satisfactory, and there was some sentiment in favor of his nomination for a second term, in 1884.

Nothing is known of President Arthur's personal religious views. Mrs. Arthur, who died before he became President, was an Episcopalian. While living in Washington, Arthur attended St. John's Church, the "State Church," or the "President's Church." He has never, so far as is known, been claimed as a communicant, or as having more than a conventional respect for religion. People who knew him in New York City have told me that he was much of a "sport," loving his Scotch highballs and convivial society.

CHAPTER VII

THOMAS JEFFERSON, FREETHINKER
Born, April 13, 1743. Died. July 4. 1826. President, March 4, 1801—March 4, 1809.

As a thinker, Thomas Jefferson was probably the greatest of our Presidents. He took an interest in science and philosophy as well as in government and politics. He gave more attention to the subject of religion than did any of our other Presidents, and while, like other public men of the past and present, he did not publicly express his views, in his letters to his friends he did so without reserve. Hence, except among his ultra-religious admirers, there has been no controversy over his religious opinions, as there has been in the cases of Washington and Lincoln.

Washington was not speculative. His mind always turned upon practical things. Lincoln often expressed himself in private conversation with his friends, upon whom we are very largely dependent for a knowledge of what his views were.

Jefferson's most voluminous biographer, Henry J. Randall (vol. 3, pp. 553-562), insists upon calling him a "Christian," a word which is subject to many qualifications. Yet Mr. Randall admits that Jefferson disbelieved in all strictly orthodox dogmas, and was a Unitarian. Unitarians, like Deists, were considered to be as much "Infidels" in Jefferson's day as an Atheist is now. But in his own day, Jefferson could scarcely have claimed to be a Unitarian, since in the first half of the 19th Century that Church was supernaturalistic and far from being as broad as it is at the present time.

Jefferson himself defined the word "Christian" as he wanted it applied to himself, in these words: "I am a Christian in the only sense in which he [Jesus] wished any one to be; sincerely attached to his doctrines in preference to all others; ascribing to himself every **human** excellence; and believing he never claimed any other." (Morse's **Jefferson**, American Statesmen Series, p. 304.)

Morse also says:

"Jefferson's religious opinions, both during his life time and since his death, have given rise to much controversy. His opponents constantly charged him with 'Infidelity'; his friends as vigorously denied the charge. The discussion annoyed and irritated him; but he would not aid in establishing an inquisition of conscience. His grandson says that even his own family knew no more than the rest of the world concerning his religious opinions. One cannot but think that, had he been a firm believer in Christianity, he would probably not have regarded such reticence as justifiable, but would have felt it his duty to give to the faith the weight of his influence, which he well knew to be considerable. Nearly all the evidence which has been collected falls into the same scale, going to show that he was not a Christian in any strict sense of that word. It is true that the phrase bears widely different meanings to different persons; but probably the most liberal admissable interpretations would hardly make it apply to Jefferson." (Pages 338-340.)

"He compared Christ with Socrates and Epictetus, and says that when he [Christ] died at about 33 years of age, his reason had 'not yet attained the maximum of its energy, nor the course of his preaching, which was but of three years at most, presented occasions for developing a complete system of morals. Hence the doctrines which he really delivered were defective as a whole; and fragments only of what he did deliver have come to us multilated, misstated, and often unintelligible.' This hardly describes the Christian notion of God's revelation. After such language it was not worth while to add the saving clause, that 'the question of his being a member of the Godhead, or in direct communication with it—is foreign to the present view!'

"To my mind, it is very clear that Jefferson never believed that Christ was other than a human moralist, having no peculiar inspiration or divine connection, and differing from other moralists only as Shakespeare differs from other dramatists, namely, as greatly their superior in ability and fitness for his function. But those admirers of Jefferson, who themselves believe in the divinity of Christ, will probably refuse to accept this view, though they find themselves without sufficient evidence conclusively to confute it." (Pages 340-341.)

James Parton, one of the standard biographers of Jefferson, says:

"His religious tone was also that of most healthy English souls before religion became intense and opinionative. The Jeffersons appear to have been of that good-tempered and sensible class who escaped the anguish and narrowness of the Puritan period, equally incapable of fighting a bishop or stoning a Quaker. To such, religion was never a system or a salvation. It was the supreme decency, the highest etiquette, with the addition of bell-ringing and Merry Christmas. That Jefferson was able to attain to a rational and comfortable tone of mind on this distracted subject, without any severe internal conflict, was a happiness he owed to the well-tempered mind of his father, and to the healthy race from which he sprang." (**Life of Jefferson**, p. 738.)

Richard Hildreth, the historian, in speaking of Jefferson's religious opinions, says:

"Jefferson's relations to the religious opinions of his country were somewhat peculiar. He believed, like Paine, in a personal God and a future life, but, like him, regarded Christianity, in the supernatural view of it, as a popular fable, an instrument for deluding, misgoverning and plundering mankind; and these opinions he entertained, as he did most others, with little regard to any qualifying considerations, and with an energy approaching to fanaticism. But he was no more inclined than were the New England Rationalists to become a martyr to the propagation of unpopular ideas. That he left to Paine and others of less discretion or more courage than himself." (**History of the United States**, vol. 5, p. 458.)

"Jefferson seems to have considered himself excessively ill-treated by the clergy, who were constantly twitting him with his Infidel opinions." (Ibid, p. 461.)

That Jefferson did not want to become a martyr, only places him in the same category as most other men. Paine was the vicarious atonement offered in behalf of heresy in the United States, and though he wore the crown of thorns, received the stripes, and was hanged on the cross of bigotry, orthodoxy was never satisfied. Jefferson was not anxious to be another victim, and why should he? After 140 years, Paine has been vindicated.

Jefferson was justified in resenting the clerical abuse showered upon him because of his "Infidel" opinions. He no doubt wondered why, in a country where Church and state were separate, and where freedom of conscience was incorporated in the Constitution, the clergy of any particular Church or religion should presume to exercise control over a citizen's opinion.

Mr. Randall persists in calling Jefferson a Christian, regardless of the fact that by his own admission he did not believe in the doctrines that distinguish a Christian from other religionists. Mr. Hildreth did not like Jefferson, therefore he made all he could out of his unpopular opinions, that he might discredit him. Mr. Parton, considered Jefferson's liberal views to be a credit to him, and to the English-speaking world. Mr. Morse merely told the truth.

Most important of all is the evidence of Thomas Jefferson's own words as to what he believed. The following quotation, from a letter (Aug. 10, 1787) which he wrote to his young nephew and ward, Peter Carr, sheds much light on Jefferson's religious opinions:

> "Religion. In the first place, divest yourself of all bias in favor of novelty and singularity of opinion. Indulge them on any other subject rather than that of religion. On the other hand, shake off all the fears and servile prejudices under which weak minds are servilely crouched. Fix Reason firmly in her seat, and call to her tribunal every fact, every opinion. Question with boldness even the existence of a God; because, if there be one, he must more approve of the homage of Reason than of blindfolded fear. You will naturally examine, first, the religion of your own country. Read the Bible, then, as you would Livy or Tacitus. For example, in the book of Joshua we are told the sun stood for several hours. Were we to read that fact in Livy or Tacitus, we should class it with their showers of blood, speaking of statues, beasts, etc. But it is said that the writer of that book was inspired. Examine, therefore, candidly, what evidence there is of his having been inspired. The pretension is entitled to your inquiry, because millions believe it. On the other hand, you are astronomer enough to know how contrary it is to the laws of Nature. You will next read the New Testament. It is the history of a personage called Jesus. Keep in your eye the opposite pretensions: 1, Of those who say he was begotten by God, born of a virgin, suspended and reversed the laws of Nature at will, and ascended bodily into heaven; and, 2, Of those who say he was a man of illegitimate birth, of a benevolent heart, enthusiastic mind, who set out with pretensions to divinity; ended in believing them, and was punished capitally for sedition, by being gibbeted, according to the Roman law, which punished the first commission of that offense by whipping, and the second by exile, or death in fures. . . . Do not be frightened from this inquiry by any fear of consequences. If it ends in a belief that there is no God, you will find incitements to virtue in the comfort and pleasantness you will feel in its exercise, and the love of others which it will procure you. If you find reason to believe there is a God, a consciousness that you are acting under his eye, and that he approves you, will be a vast additional incitement: if that Jesus was also a God, you will be comforted by a belief of his aid and love. Your own reason is the only oracle given you by heaven; and you are answerable, not for the rightness, but uprightness, of the decision." (Parton's **Life of Jefferson**, pp. 338 339.)

Morse comments:

"On August 10, 1787, in a letter of advice to his young ward,

Peter Carr, he dealt with religion at much length, telling Carr to examine the question independently. He added instructions so colorless that they resemble the charge of a painfully impartial judge to a jury. But in this especial matter labored impartially usually signifies a negative prejudice. At least Jefferson showed that he did not regard Christianity as so established a truth that it was to be asserted dogmatically, and though he so carefully seeks to conceal his own bias, yet one instinctively feels that this letter was not written by a believer. Had he **believed**, in the proper sense of the word, he would have been unable to place a very young man midway between the two doors of belief and unbelief, setting both wide open, and furnishing no indication as to which led to error." (**Life of Jefferson**, pp. 45 and 46.)

Jefferson abhorred intolerance, and regarding it he uses the following strong language:

"It does me no injury for my neighbor to say there are 20 gods, or no God. It neither picks my pocket nor breaks my leg. . . . It is error alone which needs the support of government. Truth can stand by itself. Subject opinion to coercion, and whom will you make your inquisitors? Fallible men, governed by bad passions, by private as well as public reasons. And why subject it to coercion? Difference of opinion is advantageous to religion. The several sects perform the office of **censor morum** over each other. Is uniformity attainable? Millions of men, women and children, since the introduction of Christianity, have been burned, tortured, fined, imprisoned; yet we have not advanced one inch toward uniformity. What has been the effect of coercion? To make one half the world fools, and the other half hypocrites; to support roguery and error all over the earth." (Parton's **Life of Jefferson**, pp. 211, 212.)

The following quotations are taken from the **Writings of Thomas Jefferson**, published by G. P. Putnam's Sons, in 1894. Of the trinity he says:

"It is too late in the day for men of sincerity to pretend they believe in the Platonic mysticism that three are one and one is three, and yet, that the one is not three, and the three are not one. . . . But this constitutes the craft, the power, and profits of the priests. Sweep away their gossamer fabrics of fictitious religion, and they would catch no more flies." (Vol. 9, pp. 412, 413.)

Writing to John Adams, on July 5, 1814, he again refers to the same subject:

"The Christian priesthood, finding the doctrines of Christ leveled to every understanding, and too plain to need explanation, saw in the mysticisms of Plato materials with which they might build up an artificial system, which might, from its indistinctness, admit everlasting controversy, give employment for their order and introduce it to profit, power and preeminence." (Ibid, p. 463.)

For Presbyterianism he had no use, and on November 2, 1822, he wrote the following letter to Dr. Cooper:

"I had no idea, however, that in Pennsylvania, the cradle of toleration and freedom of religion, it (fanaticism) could have arisen to the height you describe. This must be owing to the growth of Presbyterianism. The blasphemy of the five points of Calvinism, and the impossibility of defending them, render their advocates impatient of reasoning, irritable, and prone to denunciation." (Vol. 10, p. 242.)

"It is not so in the districts where Presbyterianism prevails undividedly. Their ambition and tyranny would tolerate no rival if they had power. Systematical in grasping an ascendancy over all other sects, they aim, like the Jesuits, at engrossing the education of the country, are hostile to every institution they do not direct, and jealous at seeing others begin to attend at all to that object." (Ibid, p. 243.)

Speaking of religious fanaticism in Richmond, the capital of Virginia, he said, in a letter to Dr. Cooper:

"In our Richmond there is much fanaticism, but chiefly among the women. They have their night meetings and praying parties, where, attended by their priests, and sometimes by a hen-pecked husband, they pour forth the effusions of their love to Jesus in terms as amatory and carnal as their modesty would permit to a merely earthly lover." (Ibid, p. 242.)

"The Presbyterian clergy are the loudest, the most intolerant of all sects; the most tyrannical and ambitious, ready at the word of the law-giver, if such a word could now be obtained, to put their torch to the pile, and to rekindle in this virgin hemisphere the flame in which their oracle, Calvin, consumed the poor Servetus, because he could not subscribe to the proposition of Calvin, that magistrates have a right to exterminate all heretics to the Calvinistic creed! They pant to be reestablished by law as the holy inquisition which they can now only infuse into public opinion." (**Works**, 1829 edition, vol. 4, p. 322.)

"His (Calvin's) religion was demonism. If ever man worshiped a false God, he did. The being described in his five points is . . . a demon of malignant spirit. It would be more pardonable to believe in no God at all, than to blaspheme him by the atrocious attributes of Calvin." (Ibid, p. 363.)

"I should as soon undertake to bring the crazy skulls of Bedlam to sound understanding, as inculcate reason into that of an Athanasian." (Ibid, p. 353.)

Speaking of the eucharist, he refers to the orthodox clergy as "cannibal priests." (Ibid, p. 205.)

It is interesting to see the opinion of Jefferson upon the orthodox idea of Jesus:

"The day will come when the mystical generation of Jesus, by the Supreme Being as his father, in the womb of a virgin, will be classed with the fable of the generation of Minerva in the brain of Jupiter." (Vol. 4, p. 365.)

"If we could believe that he (Jesus) really countenanced the follies, the falsehoods, and the charlatanisms which his biographers (Matthew, Mark, Luke and John) father on him, and admit the misconstructions, interpolations, and theorizations of the fathers of the early, and the fanatics of the latter, ages, the conclusion would be irresistible by every sound mind that he was an imposter."

On the same page, he speaks of the gospel story of Jesus as "a ground work of vulgar ignorance, of things impossible, of superstitions, fanaticisms, and fabrications." (Ibid. p. 325.)

Jefferson, however, did not regard Jesus as an imposter. He believed that the stories that made him appear to be one were written in after years. He says:

"Among the sayings and discourses imputed to him by his

biographers, I find many passages of fine imagination, correct morality, and of the most lovely benevolence; and others, again, of so much ignorance, of such absurdity, so much untruth and imposture, as to pronounce it impossible that such contradictions should have proceeded from the same being. I separate, therefore, the gold from the dross, restore to him the former, and leave the latter to the stupidity of some and the roguery of others of his disciples." (Ibid, p. 320.)

In regard to Jesus's believing himself to be inspired, he said: "This belief carried no more personal imputation than the belief of Socrates that he was under the care and admonition of a guardian demon. And how many of our wisest men still believe in the reality of these inspirations while perfectly sane on all other subjects?" (Ibid, p. 327.)

When the Church was disestablished in New England, Jefferson wrote the following words to John Adams: "I join you, therefore, in sincere congratulations that this den of the priesthood is at length broken up, and that a Protestant Popedom is no longer to disgrace the American history and character." (Works, vol. 4, p. 301.)

In a letter to Dr. Woods, he said: "I have recently been examining all the known superstitions of the world, and do not find in our particular superstition (Christianity) one redeeming feature. They are all alike, founded upon fables and mythology."

In a letter to James Smith, Jefferson says: "The hocus pocus phantasm of a God, like another Cerberus, with one body and three heads, had its birth and growth in the blood of thousands and thousands of martyrs." (Ibid, p. 360.) Of Paul he said: "Of this band of dupes and imposters, Paul was the great Corypheus, the first corrupter of the doctrines of Jesus." (Ibid, p. 327.) We might triple these quotations from Jefferson's writings did space permit.

Some may ask, "Did not Jefferson prepare a Bible, known as the 'Jefferson Bible'?" He did, but it consisted of only the moral teachings of Jesus which he admired, and omitted those he disliked. All supernaturalism was eliminated. Early in this century this "Bible" was published by an act of Congress at the government printing office. Some, who knew nothing of its nature, hoped to find evidence that Jefferson was a believer. The clergy, however, knew better, and made a protest against the publication of the book, which they said fostered "Infidelity." It has since been republished.

Jefferson had no use for the priesthood. Writing from Paris he said: "If anybody thinks that kings, nobles and priests, are good conservators of the public happiness, send him here (Paris). It is the best school in the Universe to cure him of his folly. He will see here with his own eyes that these descriptions of men are an abandoned confederacy against the happiness of the mass of the people."

That Jefferson was often denounced by the clergy and others for his anti-religious views is well known. The Rev. John S. C. Abbott, the clerical historian, referring to Jefferson's part in the establishment of the University of Virginia, says:

"He devoted much attention to the establishment of the University at Charlottesville. Having no religious faith which he was willing to avow, he was not willing that any religious faith whatever should be taught in the University as a part of its course of instruction. This establishment, in a Christian land, of an institution for the education of youth, where the relation existing between man and his maker was entirely ignored, raised a general cry of disapproval throughout the whole country. It left a stigma upon the reputation of Mr. Jefferson,

in the minds of Christian people, which can never be effaced."
(**Lives of the Presidents**, p. 142.)

The Rev. Dr. Wilson, in his famous sermon on "The Religion of the
Presidents," says:

"I believe the influence of his example and name has done
more for the extension of Infidelity than that of any other
man. Since his death, and the publication of Randolph (his
works, edited by his grandson), there remains not a shadow
of doubt of his Infidel principles. If any man thinks there is,
let him look at the book itself. I do not recommend the purchase of it to any man, for it is one of the most wicked and
dangerous books extant."

The **New American Encyclopedia**, in the edition of 1874, says: "He
carried the rule of subjecting everything to the test of abstract reason
into matters of religion, venerating the character of Christ, but refusing belief in his divine mission."

Benson J. Lossing, in his **Lives of the Signers of the Declaration of
Independence** (p. 183), says: "In religion he was a Freethinker; in morals, pure and unspotted."

Timothy Dwight, President of Yale University, says: "It cannot be
necessary to adopt any train of reasoning to show that a man who dis-
believes the inspiration and divine authority of the Scriptures—who not
only denies the divinity of our Savour, but reduces him to the grade of
an uneducated, ignorant and erring man—who calls the God of Abraham (The Jehovah of the Bible) a cruel and remorseless being, cannot
be a Christian." George Bancroft, in his **History of the United States**
(vol. 5, p. 323), states: "He was not only a hater of priestcraft and
superstition and bigotry and intolerance; he was thought to be indifferent to religion."

The **New York Observer**, a Presbyterian journal, gave Jefferson's
works, when they were first published, the following notice: "Mr. Jefferson, it is well known, was never suspected of being very friendly
to the orthodox religion, but these volumes prove not only that he was
a disbeliever, but a scoffer of the very lowest class."

The **Chicago Tribune** once said: "A question has been raised as to
Thomas Jefferson's religious views. There need be no question, for he
has settled that himself. He was an Infidel, or, as he chose to term it,
a Materialist. By his own account he was as heterodox as Colonel
Ingersoll, and in some respects more so."

Tucker, in his biography of Jefferson, says: "It is very certain that
he did not believe at all in the divine origin of Christianity, and of
course not in the inspiration of the Scriptures; even of the New Testament."

During the eight years that Thomas Jefferson was President, he
refused to issue a Thanksgiving proclamation*. In a letter to the Rev.
Mr. Miller, he gave his reasons for refusing:

"I consider the Government of the United States as inter-
dicted by the Constitution of the United States from meddling
with religious institutions, their doctrines, discipline, or exercises. . . . But it is only proposed that I should recommend, not
prescribe, a day of fasting and praying. That is, I should indirectly assume to the United States an authority over religious
exercises, which the Constitution has directly precluded them
from. . . . Every one must act according to the dictates of his

*Presidents Jackson and Taylor also refused to issue Thanksgiving
proclamations. See Appendix V.

own reason and mine tells me that civil powers alone have been given to the President of the United States, and no authority to direct the religious exercises of his constitutents."

Jefferson denied that Christianity was a part of the common law, either of England or of the United States. He went into the subject historically, and gave the following scholarly account of how, by fraud, this statement had gained currency:

"In **quare impedit**, in Common Bench (Year Book), 34th year Henry VI, folio 38 (anno 1458), the defendant, Bishop of Lincoln, pleads that the church of the plaintiff became void by the death of the incumbent; that the plaintiff and I. S., each pretending a right, presented two several clerks; that the church being thus rendered litigious, he was not obliged, by the ecclesiastical law, to admit either, until an inquisition **de jure patronatus**, in the ecclesiastical court; that, by the same law, this inquisition was to be at the suit of either claimant, and was not **ex officio** to be instituted by the Bishop, and at his proper costs; that neither party had desired such an inquisition; that six months passed; whereupon it belonged to him of right to present as on a lapse, which he had done. The plaintiff demurred.

"A question was. How far the ecclesiastical law was to be respected in this matter by the common law court. And Prisot, chapter 5, in the course of his argument uses this expression: 'A tiel leis qu'ils de seint eglise ont en **ancien scripture**, covient a nous a donner credence' (To such laws as those of holy church had in ancient writing, it is proper for us to give credence).

"Finch mistakes this in the following manner: 'To such laws of the church as have warrant in **Holy Scripture**, our law giveth credence' and cites the above case, and the words of Prisot in the margin. Finch's law, book 1, chapter 3, published in 1613. Here we find 'ancien scripture' (**ancient writing**) converted into 'Holy Scripture,' whereas it can only mean the **ancient written** laws of the church.

"With such a license, we might reverse the sixth commandment into 'Thou shalt not omit murder.' It would be the more extraordinary in this case, when the mistranslation was to effect the adoption of the whole code of the Jewish and Christian laws into the texts of our statutes, to convert religious offenses into temporal crimes, to make the breach of every religious precept a subject of indictment.

"It cannot mean the Scriptures—First, because the term 'ancien scripture' must then be understood as meaning the Old Testament in contradiction to the New, and to the exclusion of that; which would be absurd and contrary to the wish of those who cite this passage to prove that the Scriptures, or Christianity, is a part of the common law. Second, because Prisot says: 'Ceo (est) common ley sur quel touts manners leis sont fondes' (It is common law, on which all manners of law are founded). Now it is true that the ecclesiastical law, so far as admitted in England, derives its authority from the common law. But it would not be true that the Scriptures so derive their authority."

Jefferson produces a long list of authorities who have made the claim that Christianity is a part of the common law, but shows that all of them hang on the same hook—the perverted expression of Prisot. Then he deals with the question historically:

"Authorities for what is common law may, therefore, be as well cited, as for any part of the **lex scripta**; and there is no better

instance of the necessity of holding judges and writers to a
declaration of their authorities than the present, where we de-
tect them endeavoring **to make law where they found none,** and
to submit to us, at one stroke, a whole system, no particle of
which has its foundation in the common law, or has received
the 'esto' of the legislator. For we know that the common law
is that system of law which was introduced by the Saxons on
their settlement in England, and altered, from time to time, by
proper legislative authority, from that time to the date of the
Magna Charta, which terminates the period of the common law,
or **lex non scripta,** and commences that of the statute law, or
lex scripta. This settlement took place about the middle of the
Fifth Century, but Christianity was not introduced until the
Seventh Century; the conversion of the first Christian king of
the Heptarchy having taken place about the year 598, and that
of the last about 686. Here, then, was a space of about 200 years,
during which the common law was in existence, and Christianity
no part of it. If it ever, therefore, was adopted into the common law, it must have been between the introduction of Christianity and the date of the Magna Charta. But of the laws of
that period we have a tolerable collection by Lambard and
Wilkins, probably not perfect; but neither very defective; and
if any one chooses to build a doctrine of that period, supposed
to have been lost, it is incumbent on him to prove it to have
existed, and what were its contents. These were so far al-
ternations of the common law, and became themselves a part
of it, but none of these adopt Christianity as a part of the common law. If, therefore, from the settlement of the Saxons to
the introduction of Christianity among them, that system of
religion could not be a part of the common law, because they
were not yet Christians, and if, having their laws from that
period to the close of the common law, we are able to find
among them no such act of adoption, we may safely affirm
(though contradicted by all the judges and writers on earth)
**that Christianity neither is, nor ever was, a part of the com-
mon law.** Another cogent proof of this truth is drawn from the
silence of certain writers on the common law. Bracton gives us
a very complete and scientific treatise of the whole body of the
common law. He wrote this about the close of the reign of
Henry III, a few years after the date of the Magna Charta.
We consider this book as the more valuable, as it was written
about the time which divides the common and statute law, and
therefore gives us the former in its ultimate state .Bracton,
too, was an ecclesiastic, and would certainly not have failed to
inform us of the adoption of Christianity as a part of the common law, had any such adoption ever taken place. But no word
of his, which intimates any thing like it, has ever been cited."

After citing other authorities to the same effect, Jefferson adds:
"It was reserved for Fitch, 500 years after, in the time of Charles **II,**
by a falsification of a phrase in the Year Book, to open this new doctrine, and for his successors to join full-mouthed in the cry, and give
to the fiction the sound of fact."

He calls attention to the fact that the first judicial declaration of
this claim was made by Sir Matthew Hale, in 1662, in justification for
hanging Rose Cullender and Amy Duny, two old women, for witch-
craft. In conclusion, he says:

"In truth. the alliance between Church and state in England
**has ever made their judges accomplices in the frauds of the
clergy,** and even bolder than they are; for instead of being con-

tented with the surreptitious introduction of these four chapters of Exodus, they have taken the whole leap, and declared at once that the whole Bible and Testament, in a lump, make a part of the common law of the land; the first judicial declaration of which was by this Sir Matthew Hale."

The foregoing is an appendix to **Reports of Cases Determined in the General Court of Virginia, from 1730 to 1740 and from 1768 to 1772,** by Thomas Jefferson. In a letter to Edward Everett, written in 1824, Jefferson says:

"I do not remember the occasion which led me to take up this subject, while a practitioner of the law. But I know I went into it with all the research in which a very copious law library enabled me to indulge; and I fear not for the accuracy of my quotations. The doctrine might be disproved by many other and different topics of reasoning; but having satisfied myself of the origin of the forgery, and found how, like a rolling snowball, it had gathered volume, I leave its further pursuit to those who need further proof." (**Jefferson's Works,** vol. VII, p. 383.)

We have later data, however, than these of Jefferson. Some years ago, in England, a Mr. Bowman made a will leaving 10,000 pounds to the National Secular Society. The heirs contested the will on the plea that the N.S.S. was an anti-Christian organization and therefore contrary to the law of the land. The old "common law" plea was used. The case went through all the courts of England, and was finally decided in the House of Lords. There the will was sustained, the House of Lords holding that the statement that "Christianity is a part of the law of the land is more rhetoric than fact."

That the question has been a mooted one is apparent by the fact that two State supreme courts in the United States have decided that this common law is a part of the law of the United States—Arkansas, in 1850 and Missouri, in 1854; while the supreme courts of Ohio and California have declared that it is not.

When Thomas Paine was marooned in France, Jefferson generously offered him passage in a federal man-of-war. This greatly offended the clergy. Paine visited the President at the White House, and often walked arm in arm with him on the street. In a letter to Francis Eppes, Jefferson said: "You ask my opinion of Lord Bolingbroke and Thomas Paine. They were alike in making bitter enemies of the priests and Pharisees of their day. Both were honest men; both advocates for human liberty."

The great sorrow of Jefferson's life was the death of Mrs. Jefferson, which occurred in 1782. When the wife of his old friend, John Adams, passed away in 1818, he wrote the following letter to Adams:

"The public papers, my dear friend, announce the fatal event, of which your letter of October 20 had given me ominous foreboding. Tried myself in the school of affliction, by the loss of every form of connection which can rive the human heart, I know well, and feel what you have lost, what you have suffered, are suffering, and have yet to endure. The same trials have taught me that, for ills so immeasurable, time and silence are the only medicines. I will not, therefore, by useless condolences open afresh the sluices of your grief, nor, though mingling sincerely my tears with yours, will I say a word more where words are vain; but that it is of some comfort to us both that the time is not very distant, at which we are to deposit in the same cerement, our sorrows and suffering bodies, and to ascend in essence to an ecstatic meeting with the friends we have loved and lost, and whom we shall still love and never lose again.

God bless you and support you under your heavy affliction."
Jefferson, like Paine, believed in a God, and hoped for happiness
beyond this life, though of the two men, Paine was the more religious.
As Jefferson approached old age, Dr. William Ellery Channing, the
noted Unitarian divine, was attaining distinction. Jefferson admired
him and said, in 1822:

> "I rejoice that in this blessed country of free inquiry and
> belief, which has surrendered its creed and conscience neither
> to kings nor priests, the genuine doctrine of the only true God
> is reviving; and I trust there is not a young man now living in
> the United States who will not die a Unitarian."

Yet, in contradistinction to Spiritualism, Jefferson called himself
a Materialist. In a letter to John Adams, written a short time before
he died, he said:

> "On the basis of sensation, we may erect the fabric of all
> the certainties we can have or need. I can conceive thought to
> be an action of matter or magnetism or loadstone. When he
> who denies to the Creator the power of endowing matter with
> the mode of motion called thinking shall show how he could
> endow the sun with the mode of action called attraction, which
> reins the planets in their orbits, or how an absence of matter
> can have a will, and by that will put matter into motion, then
> the Materialist may be lawfully required to explain the process
> by which matter exercises the faculty of thinking. When once
> we quit the basis of sensation, all is in the mind. To talk of im-
> material existences, is to talk of nothings. To say that the human
> soul, angels, God, are immaterial, is to say they are nothings,
> or that there is no God, no angels, no soul. I cannot reason
> otherwise. But I believe that I am supported in my creed of
> Materialism by the Lockes, the Tracys, and the Stewarts."

Jefferson was a model husband and father. He was a temperance
advocate, like Madison, drinking but little wine and no strong spirits.
He was an advocate of peace. His object in the enactment of the em-
bargo of 1807 was, to use his own words, "to introduce between nations
another umpire than arms." Like Washington, Jefferson supported the
Church in his own neighborhood, thinking it of value as a social institution, as, for this reason only, many men support the Church today.
But above all, he was the champion of education and the founder of
the University of Virginia. His mind was sanguine, as Parton says,
within nine days of his death, when he wrote with a trembling hand:

> "All eyes are opened, or opening, to the rights of man. The
> general spread of the light of science has already laid open to
> every view the palpable truth, that the mass of mankind have
> not been born with saddles on their backs, nor a favored few
> booted and spurred, ready to ride them legitimately by the grace
> of God."

Once when he thought the parish clergyman was in the room he
said, "I have no objection to see him as a good and kind neighbor," but
he did not want to see him in his professional capacity. At 20 minutes
until one, on the afternoon, of July 4, 1826, he breathed his last. In
the evening of the same day, his old friend and co-worker, John Adams,
passed away in Quincy, Mass. The great achievements of Jefferson's
life are engraved on his tombstone:

> "HERE WAS BURIED THOMAS JEFFERSON, AUTHOR OF
> THE DECLARATION OF INDEPENDENCE, OF THE STATUTE
> OF VIRGINIA FOR RELIGIOUS FREEDOM, AND FATHER OF
> THE UNIVERSITY OF VIRGINIA."

CHAPTER VIII

ABRAHAM LINCOLN, DEIST, AND ADMIRER OF THOMAS PAINE
Born, February 12, 1809. Died, April 15, 1865. President, March 4, 1861—April 15, 1865.

In 1865, following the assassination of Lincoln, a number of histories of his career were published. From a literary standpoint, the best of these was written by Dr. Josiah G. Holland, then a widely read American author, and afterwards, and until his death, the editor of Scribner's Monthly. Concerning Lincoln's religious views, Dr. Holland made the following comments:

"He was a religious man. The fact may be stated without any reservation—with only an explanation. He believed in God, and in his own personal supervision of the affairs of men. He believed himself to be under his control and guidance. He believed in the power and ultimate triumph of the right, through his belief in God. This unwavering faith in a Divine Providence began at his mother's knee, and ran like a thread of gold through all the experiences of his life. His constant sense of human duty was one of the forms by which his faith manifested itself. His conscience took a broader grasp than the simple apprehension of right and wrong. He recognized an immediate relation between God and himself, in all the actions and passions of his life. He was not professedly a Christian—that is, he subscribed to no creed—joined no organization of Christian disciples. He spoke little then, perhaps less than he did afterwards, and always sparingly, of his religious belief and experiences; but that he had a deep religious life, sometimes imbued with superstition, there is no doubt. We guess at a mountain of marble by the outcropping ledges that hide their whiteness among the ferns." (Pages 61, 62.)

"Moderate, frank, truthful, gentle, forgiving, loving, just, Mr. Lincoln will always be remembered as a Christian President; and the almost immeasurably great results which he had the privilege of achieving, were due to the fact that he was a Christian President." (Page 542.)

"Mr. Newton Bateman, Superintendent of Public Instruction for the State of Illinois, occupied a room adjoining and opening into the Executive Chamber. Frequently this door was open during Mr. Lincoln's receptions; and throughout the seven months or more of his occupation Mr. Bateman saw him nearly every day. Often when Mr. Lincoln was tired, he closed this door against all intrusion, and called Mr. Bateman into his room for a quiet talk. On one of these occasions Mr. Lincoln took up a book containing a careful canvass of the city of Springfield, in which he lived, showing the candidate for whom each citizen had declared it his intention to vote in the approaching election. Mr. Lincoln's friends had, doubtless at his own request, placed the result of the canvass in his hands. This was toward the close of October, and only a few days before the election. Calling Mr. Bateman to a seat by his side, having previously locked all the doors, he said: 'Let us look over this book. I wish particularly to see how the ministers of Springfield are going to vote.' The leaves were turned, one by one, and as the names were examined Mr. Lincoln frequently asked if this one or that one were not a minister, or an elder, or the member of such and such a Church, and received an affirmative answer. In that manner they went through the book, and then he closed it and sat silently and for some minutes regarding a memorandum in pencil which lay before him. At length he turned to Mr. Bateman with a face full of sadness, and said: 'Here are 23 ministers, of different denominations, and all of them are against me but three; and here are a great many prominent members of the Churches, a very large majority of whom are against me. Mr. Bateman, I am not a Christian— God knows I would be one—but I have carefully read the Bible, and I do not understand this book'; and he drew from his bosom a pocket New Testament. 'These men well know,' he continued, 'that I am for freedom in the territories, freedom everywhere as far as the Constitution and the laws will permit, and that my opponents are for slavery. They know this, and yet, with this book in their hands, in the light of which human bondage cannot live a moment, they are going to vote against me. I do not understand it at all.'

"It was one of the peculiarities of Mr. Lincoln to hide these religious experiences from the world. In the same State House where this conversation occurred, there were men who imagined —who really believed—who freely said—that Mr. Lincoln had probably revealed himself with less restraint to them than to others—men who thought they knew him as they knew their bosom companions—who had never in their whole lives heard from his own lips one word of all these religious convictions and experiences. They did not regard him as a religious man. All this department of his life he had kept carefully hidden from them. Why he should say that he was obliged to appear differently to others does not appear; but the fact is a matter of history that he never exposed his own religious life to those who had no sympathy with it. It is doubtful whether the clergymen of Springfield knew anything of these experiences."

At present, I have no comments to make on these statements of Dr. Holland, and will permit the reader to form his own opinions.* A few unquestioned facts will not be out of place in explanation. When Dr. Holland's book reached Springfield, Ill., where Lincoln had lived and practiced law, all his old neighbors and friends were surprised to read these passages, and many of them smiled. There it was well known that Abraham Lincoln did not profess religion, though he occasionally accompanied Mrs. Lincoln to the First Presbyterian Church, of which she was a member. It was well known among his intimate friends that he was a Deist, after the manner of Thomas Paine, and that in early life he had written a pamphlet criticising the Bible and orthodoxy. This, while yet in manuscript, was thrown in the fire by one of his friends, who feared it would injure him professionally and politically. In those days he was outspoken in his unbelief. Later he became more cautious.

In 1846, when he was a candidate for Congress against a Methodist minister, the Rev. Peter Cartwright, his opponent openly accused him of being an unbeliever, and Lincoln never denied it. A story is told of Mr. Cartwright's holding a revival meeting while the campaign was in progress, during which Lincoln stepped into one of his meetings.

---

*See Appendix III for comments on Dr. Holland's statements.

When Cartwright asked the audience, "Will all who want to go to heaven stand up?" all arose except Lincoln. When he asked, "Now, will all who want to go to hell stand up?" Lincoln still remained in his seat. Mr. Cartwright then said, "All have stood up for one place or the other except Mr. Lincoln, and we would like to know where he expects to go." Lincoln arose and quietly said, "I am going to Congress," and there he went.

On March 26, 1843, at the time Lincoln was attempting to obtain the nomination for Congress, he wrote to Martin M. Morris, of Petersburg, Ill.:

> "There was the strangest combination of church influence against me. Baker is a Campbellite; and therefore, as I suppose with few exceptions, got all of that Church. My wife had some relations in the Presbyterian churches, and some in the Episcopal churches; and therefore, wherever it would tell, I was set down as either one or the other, while it was everywhere contended that no Christian ought to vote for me because I belonged to no Church, was suspected of being a Deist and had talked about fighting a duel." (**Complete Works of Abraham Lincoln**, Nicolay & Hay edition, vol. 1, p. 80.)

It is only fair to say that Dr. Holland had never had any personal knowledge of Lincoln. In preparing his **Biography**, he had visited Springfield, where he spent two weeks among Lincoln's old friends, collecting information. Chief of those he had consulted was William H. Herndon, who had been the great Emancipator's law partner for 22 years, and was in that relationship to Lincoln at the time of the assassination. When Dr. Holland asked Mr. Herndon about his partner's religious convictions, Mr. Herndon replied that he had none, and the less he said on that subject the better. "Oh well," replied Dr. Holland, "I'll fix that."

After the "Bateman interview" had been read by Herndon, he walked over to the Capitol, where Bateman, as Superintendent of Public Instruction, had his office, and held a conversation with him. He refused to either affirm or deny the accuracy of the interview. Later he told Herndon something in confidence, which has never been revealed. He did go so far, however, as to admit that he and Mr. Lincoln were talking politics and not religion.

Throughout this work it has been my object to state facts and avoid argument as much as possible. Yet I must give an account of the controversy, one of the most bitter in American history, which raged over the question of Lincoln's position in regard to religion. Personal, religious and political animosity, almost resulting in libel suits, was involved.

In 1872, Colonel Ward H. Lamon published his **Life of Abraham Lincoln.** Colonel Lamon had the advantage over Dr. Holland of being Lincoln's friend and acquaintance of years. When the President-elect started for Washington, Colonel Lamon had charge of the arrangements. Lincoln appointed him Marshal of the District of Columbia. When the body of the martyred President was carried back to Springfield, Colonel Lamon was in charge of the funeral train. In addition to being qualified by knowledge to write the life of his chief and friend, he had another advantage. He had the benefit of the collection of manuscripts pertaining to Lincoln gathered by William H. Herndon, who knew the real Lincoln better than any other man. Lamon was not so brilliant a writer as Dr. Holland, but he knew his subject, and he waited seven years to publish his book, giving great attention to accuracy.

Colonel Lamon tells what he personally knew of Lincoln's religious belief, and reinforces his own statements by the testimony of the 10 following witnesses, who knew Lincoln equally well: William H. Herndon,* Judge David Davis, Colonel James H. Matheny, John T Stuart, Dr. C. H. Ray, Wm. H. Hannah, James W. Keyes, Jessie W. Fell, Colonel John G. Nicolay, and Mrs. Mary Todd Lincoln. Mr. Lamon was himself a religious man, and tells what he does about Lincoln as a matter of truthful history, though he did not agree with his views.

Colonel Lamon says:

"Any analysis of Lincoln's character would be defective that did not include his religious opinions. On such matters he thought deeply, and his opinions were positive. But perhaps no phase of his character has been more persistently misrepresented and variously misunderstood, than this of his religious belief. Not that the conclusive testimony of many of his intimate associates relative to his frequent expressions on such subjects has ever been wanting; but his great prominence in the world's history, and his identification with some of the great questions of our time, which, by their moral import, were held to be eminently religious in their character, have led many people to trace in his motives and actions similar convictions to those held by themselves. His extremely general expressions of religious faith called forth by the grave exigencies of his public life, or indulged in on occasions of private condolence, have often been distorted out of relation to their real significance or meaning to suit the opinions or tickle the fancies of individuals or parties.

"Mr. Lincoln was never a member of any Church, nor did he believe in the divinity of Christ, or the inspiration of the Scriptures in the sense understood by evangelical Christians." **(Life of Lincoln, p. 486.)**

"When a boy, he showed no sign of that piety which his many biographers ascribe to his manhood. When he went to church at all, he went to mock, and came away to mimic." (Ibid, pp. 486, 487.)

"When he came to New Salem, he consorted with Freethinkers, joined with them in deriding the gospel story of Jesus, read Volney and Paine, and then wrote a deliberate and labored essay, wherein he reached conclusions similar to theirs. The essay was burned, but he never regretted nor denied its composition. On the contrary, he made it the subject of free and frequent conversations with his friends at Springfield, and stated, with much particularity and precision, the origin, arguments, and objects of the work." (Ibid, p. 487.)

"The community in which he lived was preeminently a community of Freethinkers in matters of religion; and it was no secret, nor has it been a secret since, that Mr. Lincoln agreed with the majority of his associates in denying the authority of divine revelation. It was his honest belief, a belief which it was no reproach to hold in New Salem, Anno Domino, 1834, and one which he never thought of concealing. It was no distinction, either good or bad, no honor, and no shame. But he had made himself thoroughly familiar with the writings of Paine and Volney—the **Ruins** by the one, and **The Age of Reason** by the other. His mind was full of the subject, and he felt an itching to write. He did write, and the result was a little book. It was probably merely an extended essay, but it is ambitiously spoken of as 'a book' by himself and by the persons who were made acquainted with its contents. In this work he intended to demonstrate—

" 'First, that the Bible is not God's revelation.

" 'Second, that Jesus was not the son of God.'

"No leaf of this volume has survived. Mr. Lincoln carried it in manuscript to the store of Samuel Hill, where it was read and discussed. Hill was himself an unbeliever, but his son considered his book 'in-

---

*For Herndon's testimony, see Appendix IV.

famous.' It is more than probable that Hill, being a warm personal friend of Lincoln, feared that the publication of the essay would some day interfere with the political advancement of his favorite. At all events, he snatched it out of his hand, and threw it into the fire, from which not a shred escaped." (Ibid, pp. 157, 158.)

"As he grew older, he grew more cautious; and as his New Salem associates, and the aggressive Deists with whom he originally united at Springfield, gradually dispersed, or fell away from his side, he appreciated more and more keenly the violence and extent of the religious prejudice which freedom in discussion from his standpoint would be sure to arouse against him. He saw the immense and augmenting power of the Churches, and in times past had practically felt it. The imputation of Infidelity had seriously injured him in several of his earlier political contests; and, sobered by age and experience, he was resolved that the same imputation should injure him no more. Aspiring to lead religious communities, he foresaw that he must not appear as an enemy within their gates; aspiring to public honors under the auspices of a political party which persistently summoned religious people to assist in the extirpation of that which it denounced as the 'nation's sin,' he foresaw that he could not ask their suffrages whilst aspersing their faith. He perceived no reason for changing his convictions, but he did perceive many good and cogent reasons for not making them public." (Ibid, pp. 497, 498.)

"But he never told anyone that he accepted Jesus as the Christ, or performed a single one of the acts which necessarily follow upon such a conviction. At Springfield and at Washington he was beset on the one hand by political priests, and on the other by honest and prayerful Christians. He despised the former, respected the latter, and had use for both. He said with characteristic irreverence that he would not undertake to 'run the Churches by military authority'; but he was, nevertheless, alive to the importance of letting the Churches 'run' themselves in the interest of his party. Indefinite expressions about 'Divine Providence,' the 'Justice of God,' and 'the favor of the Most High,' were easy and not inconsistent with his religious notions. In this, accordingly, he indulged freely; but never in all that time did he let fall from his lips or his pen an expression which remotely implied the slightest faith in Jesus as the son of God and the Saviour of men." (Ibid, p. 502.)

Speaking of Lincoln's letter to his dying father, Colonel Lamon says:
"If ever there was a moment when Mr. Lincoln might have been expected to express his faith in the Atonement, his trust in the merits of a Living Redeemer, it was when he undertook to send a composing and comforting message to a dying man. But he omitted it wholly. He did not even mention the name of Jesus, or intimate the most distant suspicion of the existence of a Christ." (Ibid, p. 497.)

Speaking of Lincoln's mental characteristics, Lamon says:
"Mr. Lincoln was by no means free from a kind of belief in the supernatural. . . He lived constantly in the serious conviction that he was himself the subject of a special decree, made by some unknown and mysterious power, for which he had no name." (Ibid, p. 503.)

"His mind was filled with gloomy forebodings and strong apprehensions of impending evil, mingled with extravagant visions of personal grandeur and power. His imagination painted a scene just beyond the veil of the immediate future, gilded with glory yet tarnished with blood. It was his 'destiny'—splendid but dreadful, fascinating, but terrible. His case bore little resemblance to those of religious enthusiasts like Bunyan, Cowper

and others. His was more like the fatalist conscious of his
star." (Ibid, p. 475.)

After giving his own testimony, Colonel Lamon gives that of John
T. Stuart. Mr. Stuart, who was at one time a member of Congress from
Illinois, and Lincoln's first law partner, says:

"Lincoln went further against Christian beliefs and doctrines and principles than any man I ever heard: he shocked
me. I don't remember the exact line of his argument—suppose
it was against the inherent defects, so called, of the Bible, and
on grounds of reason. Lincoln always denied that Jesus was
the Christ of God, as understood and maintained by the Christian Church. The Rev. Dr. Smith, who wrote a letter, tried to
convert Lincoln from Infidelity so late as 1858, and couldn't
do it." (Lamon's **Life of Lincoln**, p. 488.)

The next witness quoted by Colonel Lamon was Colonel James H.
Matheny, who was not only a friend of Lincoln, but for a while his
political manager. He said:

"I knew Lincoln as early as 1834-7; knew he was an Infidel.
He and W. D. Herndon used to talk Infidelity in the Clerk's
office in this city, about the years 1837-40. Lincoln attacked the
Bible and the New Testament on two grounds: first, from the
inherent or apparent contradictions under its lids; second, from
the grounds of reason. Sometimes he ridiculed the Bible and
the New Testament, sometimes seemed to scoff at it, though I
shall not use that word in its full and literal sense. I never
heard that Lincoln changed his views, though his personal and
political friend from 1834 to 1860. Sometimes Lincoln bordered
on Atheism. He went far that way and shocked me. I was then
a young man, and believed what my good mother taught me.
Stuart and Lincoln's law office was in what is called Hoffman's
Row, on North Fifth Street, near the public square. It was in
the same building as the Clerk's office, and on the same floor.
Lincoln would come into the Clerk's office, where I and some
young men—Evan Butler, Newton Francis and others—were
writing or staying, and would bring the Bible with him; would
read a chapter, argue against it. Lincoln then had a smattering
of geology, if I recollect it. Lincoln often, if not wholly, was an
Atheist; at least bordered on it. Lincoln was enthusiastic in
his Infidelity. As he grew older he grew more discreet, didn't
talk much before strangers about his religion; but to friends,
close and bosom ones, he was always open and avowed, fair and
honest; but to strangers, he held them off from policy. Lincoln
used to quote Burns. Burns helped Lincoln to be an Infidel, as
I think; at least he found in Burns a like thinker and feeler.

"From what I know of Mr. Lincoln and his views of Christianity, and from what I know as honest, well-founded rumor;
from what I have heard his best friends say and regret for
years; from what he never denied when accused, and from
what Lincoln has hinted and intimated, to say no more, he
did write a book on Infidelity, at or near New Salem, in Menard
County, about the year 1834 or 1835. I have stated these things
to you often. Judge Logan, John T. Stuart, yourself, know what
I know, and some of you more.

"Mr. Herndon, you insist on knowing which you know I
possess, and got as a secret, and that is, about Lincoln's little
book on Infidelity. Mr. Lincoln **did** tell me that he **did write a
little book on Infidelity.** This statement I have avoided hereto-
fore; but, as you strongly insist upon it—probably to defend

yourself against charges of misrepresentation—I give it to you as I got it from Lincoln's mouth." (Lamon's **Lincoln**, pp. 487, 488.)

The next witness is Dr. C. H. Ray, a personal friend of Lincoln, and at one time editor of the **Chicago Tribune**. Dr. Ray says:

"You knew Lincoln far better than I did, though I knew him well; and you have served up his leading characteristics in a way that I should despair of doing, if I should try. I have only one thing to ask: that you do not give Calvinistic theology a chance to claim him as one of its saints and martyrs. He went to the old school church; but, in spite of that outward assent to the horrible doctrines of the sect, I have reason from himself to know that his 'vital purity,' if that means belief in the impossible, was of the negative sort."* (Lamon's **Lincoln**, pp. 489, 490.)

Next there follows the testimony of William H. Hannah, a member of the Bloomington, Ill., bar, and a man of high standing, to whom Lincoln expressed his view of eternal punishment:

"Since 1856, Mr. Lincoln told me that he was a kind of an immortalist; but that he could never bring himself to believe in eternal punishment; that man lived but a little while here, and that, if eternal punishment were man's doom, he should spend that little life in vigilant and ceaseless preparation by never ending prayer." (**Life of Lincoln, p. 489.**)

James W. Keyes, an old resident of Springfield, who knew Lincoln from the time he moved to Springfield, and who talked to him on the question of religion, says:

"As to the Christian theory, that Christ is God, and equal to the Creator, he said that it had better be taken for granted; for, by the test of reason, we might become Infidels on that subject, for evidence of Christ's divinity came to us in a somewhat doubtful shape." (**Life of Lincoln, p. 490.**)

Jesse W. Fell was Secretary of the Illinois Republican State Central Committee in the Lincoln-Douglas campaign, and was instrumental in bringing Lincoln forward as a candidate for President in 1860. It was for him that Lincoln wrote the well-known biographical sketch which formed the basis of his campaign biographies. Mr. Fell himself was a Unitarian and had talked with Lincoln many times on the subject of religion. This is what he wrote to Colonel Lamon:

"Though everything relating to the character of this extraordinary personage is of interest, and should be fairly stated to the world, I enter upon the performance of this duty—for so I regard it—with some reluctance, arising from the fact that, in stating my convictions on the subject, I must necessarily place myself in opposition to quite a number who have written on this topic before me, and whose views largely preoccupy the public mind. This latter fact, whilst contributing to my embarrassment on this subject, is, perhaps, the strongest reason, however, why the truth in this matter should be fully disclosed; and I therefore yield to your request. If there were any traits of character that stood out in bold relief in the person of Mr. Lincoln, they were those of truth and candor. He was utterly incapable of insincerity, or professing views on this or any other subject he did not entertain. Knowing this to be his true character, that insincerity, much less du-

---

*Beveridge shows (vol. 1, p. 505) that Lincoln was not a regular attendant at church, though he went at times with Mrs. Lincoln.

plicity, were traits wholly foreign to his nature, many of his old friends were not a little surprised at finding, in some of the biographies of this great man, statements concerning his religious opinions so utterly at variance with his known sentiments. True, he may have changed or modified those sentiments after his removal from among us, though this is hardly reconcilable with the history of the man, and his entire devotion to public matters during his four years residence at the national capital. It is possible, however, that this may be the proper solution of this conflict of opinions; or, it may be, that, with no intention on the part of any one to mislead the public mind, those who have represented him as believing in the popular theological views of the times may have misapprehended him, as experience shows to be quite common where no special effort has been made to attain critical accuracy on a subject of this nature. This is more probable from the well-known fact that Mr. Lincoln seldom communicated to anyone his views on this subject. But, be this as it may, I have no hesitation whatever in saying that, whilst he held many opinions in common with the great mass of Christian believers, he did not believe in what are regarded as the orthodox or evangelical views of Christianity.

"On the innate depravity of man, the character and office of the great head of the Church, the Atonement, the infallibility of the written revelation, the performance of miracles, the nature and design of present and future rewards and punishments (as they are popularly called) and many other subjects, he held opinions utterly at variance with what are usually taught in the Church. I should say that his expressed views on these and kindred subjects were such as, in the estimation of most believers, would place him entirely outside the Christian pale. Yet to my mind, such was not the true position, since his principles and practices and the spirit of his whole life were of the very kind we universally agree to call Christian; and I think this conclusion is in no wise affected by the circumstance that he never attached himself to any religious society whatever.*

"His religious views were eminently practical, and are summed up, as I think, in these two propositions: 'the fatherhood of God, and the brotherhood of man.' He fully believed in a superintending and overruling Providence that guides and controls the operations of the world, but maintained that law and order, not their violation or suspension, are the appointed means by which this Providence is exercised.

"I will not attempt any specification of either his belief or disbelief on various religious topics, as derived from conversations with him at different times during a considerable period; but as conveying a general view of his religious or theological opinions, will state the following facts: Some eight or 10 years prior to his death, in conversing with him on this subject, the writer took occasion to refer, in terms of approbation to the sermons and writings generally of Dr. W. E. Channing; and, finding he was considerably interested in the statement I made of the opinions held by that author, I proposed to present him a copy of Channing's entire works, which I soon after did. Subsequently the contents of these volumes, together with the writings of Theodore Parker, furnished him, as he informed me, by his friend and law-partner, became naturally the topics of conversation with us; and though far from believing there was an entire harmony

---

*In other words, Mr. Fell considers Lincoln to have been a very good Christian from the Unitarian standpoint, which professes no creed and insists upon no theological belief; but a poor Christian from the standpoint of orthodoxy, which strongly insists upon both.

of views on his part with either of these authors, yet they were generally much admired and approved by him.

"No religious views with him seemed to find any favor, except of the practical and rationalistic order; and if, from my recollections on this subject, I was called upon to designate an author whose views most nearly represented Mr. Lincoln's on this subject, I would say that author was Theodore Parker.

"As you have asked from me a candid statement of my recollections on this topic, I have thus briefly given them, with the hope that they may be of some service in rightly settling a question about which—as I have good reason to believe—the public mind has been misled. Not doubting that they will accord, substantially, with your own recollections, and that of his other intimate and confidential friends, and with the popular verdict after this matter shall have been properly canvassed, I submit them." (**Life of Lincoln**, pp. 490-492.)

Colonel John G. Nicolay, who was Lincoln's private secretary while President, and who knew him also in Illinois, makes the following statement in which he denies that Lincoln changed his religious views after he went to Washington:

"Mr. Lincoln did not, to my knowledge, in any way, change his religious ideas, opinions or beliefs, from the time he left Springfield till the day of his death. I do not know just what they were, never having heard him explain them in detail, but I am very sure he gave no outward indication of his mind having undergone any change in that regard while here." (**Life of Lincoln, p. 492.**)

The most important of all the witnesses cited by Colonel Lamon is David Davis, a judge of the Eighth Judicial Circuit of Illinois, afterwards a United States Senator, and finally a Justice of the U.S. Supreme Court. He and Lincoln traveled over the same circuit, rode in the same vehicle and often slept in the same bed. Judge Davis says:

"I enjoyed for over 20 years the personal friendship of Mr. Lincoln. We were admitted to the bar at about the same time, and traveled for many years what is known in Illinois as the Eighth Judicial Circuit. In 1848, when I first went to the bench, the circuit embraced 14 counties, and Mr. Lincoln went with the Court to every county. . . . He [Lincoln] had no faith, in the Christian sense of the term—had faith in laws, principles, causes and effects—philosophically. . . . The idea that Lincoln talked to a stranger about his religion or religious views, or made such speeches, remarks, etc., about it as are published, is to me absurd. I knew the man too well. He was the most reticent, secretive man I ever saw, or expect to see." (**Life of Lincoln, p. 489.**)

The last witness quoted by Colonel Lamon is Mrs. Mary Todd Lincoln, wife of the martyred President. She says of her husband's religious views: "Mr. Lincoln had no hope, and no faith, in the usual acceptation of those words." (**Life of Lincoln, p. 489.**) She also made the following statement to Mr. Herndon: "Mr. Lincoln's maxim and philosophy were: 'What is to be, will be, and no prayers of ours can arrest the decree.' He never joined any Church. He was a religious man always, I think, but was not a technical Christian." (Herndon, **Religion of Lincoln.**)

When Holland's **Life of Lincoln**, representing him as a staunch Christian believer, made its appearance it caused no controversy. The Christian people were pleased, while those who had known Lincoln and knew that what Holland said was not true, only smiled and acted indifferently. When Lamon's **Life** appeared, in 1872, the situation was

different. It has been the habit of Christian advocates to declare that
all great and good men have been believers in Christianity. Lincoln
was a great and good man. That following Holland's **Life**, another
should appear asserting that Lincoln was an "Infidel," was considered
an insult by the pious. They felt that their idol had been shattered. A
storm arose. Dr. Holland, in the magazine he edited, **Scribner's Monthly**,
made a fierce, almost savage attack on Lamon's book. The basis of Holland's animosity was that it was a rival of his book, and that it
directly contradicted his own statements. He called Lincoln's Freethought friends, "heathens," "barbarians," "savages," and said the
book was an "outrage on decency."

Another who was greatly perturbed was the Rev. J. A. Reed,
minister of the First Presbyterian Church, of Springfield, Ill. His first
maneuver was an attempt to induce Lamon's 10 witnesses to Lincoln's
religious views to retract their statements. He partially succeeded with
two of them, John T. Stuart, and Colonel James Matheny. But the
manner of the retraction was hardly creditable either to these gentlemen or to the Rev. Mr. Reed. Neither Mr. Stuart nor Colonel Matheny
denied one statement of fact they had made in the book. Both, however, said they had never written a word of the testimony quoted. This
was a quibble, as no one claimed that they did. They dictated their
testimony to Mr. Herndon, who **wrote** it down, and both gentlemen
signed it. The other eight witnesses, all of whom were approached by
the Rev. Mr. Reed with a request that they retract or modify their
evidence, stood firm.

Then the Rev. Mr. Reed delivered in Springfield a lecture entitled,
"The Later Life and Religious Experience of Abraham Lincoln," which
Dr. Holland published in **Scribner's Monthly**. Mr. Herndon replied, and
the reply was published in the Springfield **Register**. The Rev. Mr. Reed
then began a personal attack on Mr. Herndon, for, as in other controversies involving religion, "mud slinging" was brought into requisi-
tion. The battle extended from the prairies of Illinois to the Atlantic
Coast, where the New York **World**, in the interest, as it believed, of
truth and justice, summed up the merits of the case as follows:

"Mr. Ward H. Lamon is the author of one **Life of Lincoln**,
and Dr. J. G. Holland is the author of another. Mr. Lamon was
the intimate personal and political friend of Lincoln, trusting
and trusted, from the time of their joint practice in the Illinois
Quarter Sessions to the moment of Mr. Lincoln's death in Washington. Dr. Holland was nothing to Mr. Lincoln, neither known
nor knowing. Dr. Holland rushed his **Life** from the press before
the disfigured corpse was fairly out of sight, while the public
mind lingered with horror over the details of the tragedy, and,
excited by morbid curiosity, was willing to pay for its gratification. Mr. Lamon waited many years, until all adventitious interest had subsided, and then with incredible labor and pains
produced a volume founded upon materials which for their full-
ness, variety, and seeming authenticity are unrivaled in the
history of biographies. Dr. Holland's single volume professed to
cover the whole of Mr. Lincoln's career. Mr. Lamon's single
volume was modestly confined to part of it. Dr. Holland's was
an easy, graceful, off-hand performance, having but the one
slight demerit of being in all essential particulars untrue from
beginning to end. Mr. Lamon's was a labored, cautious, and
carefully verified narrative which seems to have been accepted by disinterested critics as entirely authentic.

"Dr. Holland would probably be very much shocked if anybody should ask him to bear false witness in favor of his neighbor in a court of justice, but he takes up his pen to make a

record which he hopes and intends shall endure forever, and
in that record deliberately bears false witness in favor of a
public man whom he happens to admire, with no kind of of·
fense to his serene and 'cultured' conscience. If this were all—
if Dr. Holland merely asserted his own right to compose and
publish elaborate fictions on historical subjects—we might
comfort ourselves with the reflection that such literature is
likely to be as evanescent as it is dishonest, and let him pass
in silence. But this is not all. He maintains that it is everybody's duty to help him to deceive the public and to write down
his more conscientious competitor. He turns up the nose of
'culture,' and curls the lip of 'art' at Mr. Lamon's homely narrative of facts, and gravely insists that all other noses and all
other lips shall be turned up and curled because his are. He
implores the public, which he insulted and gulled with his own
book, to damn Mr. Lamon's, and he puts his request on the
very ground that Mr. Lamon has stupidly gone and narrated
undeniable truths, whereby he has demolished an empty shrine
that was profitable to many, and broken a painted idol that
might have served for a god.

"The names of Lamon and Holland are not of themselves
and by themselves illustrious; but starting from the title pages
of the two lives of Lincoln, and representing, as they do, the
two schools of biographical writers, the one stands for a principle and the other for the want of it."

The **World** then takes into consideration Messrs. Reed, Stuart and
Matheny:

"This individual testimony is clear and overwhelming, without the documentary and other evidence scattered profusely
through the rest of the book. How does Mr. Reed undertake to
refute it? In the first place, firstly, he pronounces it a 'libel,'
and in the second place, secondly, he is 'amazed to find'—and
he says he has found—that the principal witnesses take exception to Mr. Lamon's report of their evidence. This might have
been true of any or all of Mr. Lamon's witnesses without exciting the wonder of a rational man. Few persons, indeed, are
willing to endure reproach merely for the truth's sake, and
popular opinion in the Republican party of Springfield, Ill., is
probably very much against Mr. Lamon. It would, therefore, be
quite in the natural order if some of his witnesses who find
themselves unexpectedly in print should succumb to the social
and political terrorism of their time and place, and attempt to
modify or explain their testimony. They zealously assisted Mr.
Herndon in ascertaining the truth, and while they wanted him
to tell it in full they were prudently resolved to keep their own
names snugly out of sight. But Mr. Reed's statement is not
true, and his amazement is entirely simulated. Two only out of
the 10 witnesses have gratified him by inditing, at his request,
weak and guarded complaints of unfair treatment. These were
John T. Stuart, a relative of the Lincolns and Edwardses, and
Jim Matheny, both of Springfield, whom Mr. Lincoln taught his
peculiar doctrines, but who may by this time be deacons in
Mr. Reed's church. Neither of them helps Mr. Reed's case a
particle. Their epistles open, as if by concert, in form and
words almost identical. They say they did not **write** the
language attributed to them. The denial is wholly unnecessary,
for nobody affirms that they did write it. They talked and Mr.
Herndon wrote. His notes were made when the conversation

occurred, and probably in their presence. At all events, they are both so conscious of the general accuracy of his report that they do not venture to deny a single word of it, but content themselves with lamenting that something else, which they did not say, was excluded from it. They both, however, in these very letters, repeat emphatically the material part of the statements made by them to Mr. Herndon, namely, that Mr. Lincoln was to their certain knowledge, until a very late period of his life, an 'Infidel,' and neither of them is able to tell when he ceased to be an infidel and when he became a Christian. And this is all Mr. Reed makes of his re-examination of the two persons whom he is pleased to exalt as Mr. Lamon's 'principal witnesses.' They are but two out of the 10. What of the other eight? They have no doubt been plied and tried by Mr. Reed and his friends to no purpose: they stand fast by the record. But Mr. Reed is to be shamed neither by their speech nor their silence."

Mr. Remsburg describes the characteristics of Holland's and Lamon's books in the following language:

"In Lamon's work, Lincoln's character is a rugged oak, towering above its fellows and clothed in nature's livery; in Holland's work, it is a dead tree with the bark taken off, the knots planed down, and varnished." (**Abraham Lincoln: Was He a Christian?** p. 146.)

Was Abraham Lincoln Converted? One thing this controversy had made manifest—that Lincoln had been an "Infidel" in Illinois up to the time he went to Washington. It would be a waste of time to present further evidence. The testimony of eight of Lamon's witnesses has not been impugned, while the other two, Messrs. Stuart and Matheny, did not alter their testimony in any material point. Dr. Holland, the only one who ever denied it, was obliged to admit his error and retreat from his position. (See **Scribner's Monthly**, vol. 4, p. 506.)

One thing only remained for those who maintained Lincoln's orthodoxy. It was to admit these well-known facts, to which any number of people who knew Lincoln could testify; then to assert that he was afterwards converted. As this has been said of every well-known Freethinker from Paine and Voltire to Ingersoll, and proved to be untrue in nearly all cases, it would not look otherwise than suspicious. A prominent Presbyterian journal has been obliged to admit the untruth of this general statement made of Infidels, so far as Paine and Voltaire were concerned, although an offer of one thousand dollars was made it if it proved the truth of the statement.*

In the case of Ingersoll, his family has many times denied the allegation that he changed his views, yet the story is periodically revived by ministers in the rural districts.

The Rev. J. A. Reed, who was at all times ready to leap into any breach in behalf of Lincoln's orthodoxy, bravely undertook the task of proving that he was converted. True, he had no knowledge of the alleged conversion himself, but he was better at finding witnesses than was Dr. Holland. It is a well-recognized principle of law, that where a certain condition of affairs is known to have once existed, it is supposed to continue to exist, unless, by a preponderance of evidence, it can be proved that a change has occurred. Then, to establish any fact, the time and place of its occurrence must be proved. Lincoln was once an "Infidel." If he changed his views and became orthodox, it must be established by his own testimony, or the unquestioned testimony of

*New York Observer, in 1877.

those who knew of it. And the time and place where it occurred must likewise be substantiated.

Mr. Reed summons as witnesses, the Rev. Dr. James Smith, his predecessor as pastor of the First Presbyterian Church of Springfield, Niniam W. Edward, a brother-in-law of Lincoln, Thomas Lewis, a deacon in Dr. Smith's church, Noah Brooks, then somewhat known as a writer, the Rev. Dr. Sunderland, the noted Presbyterian minister, of Washington, D. C., the Rev. Dr. Miner, a Universalist clergyman of Boston, and the Rev. Dr. Gurley, minister of the Presbyterian church in the Capital, where Lincoln and his wife sometimes attended. The Rev. Dr. Smith claims to be the minister who converted Lincoln, snatched him as a brand from the burning, convinced him that his objections to the Bible were groundless, and made of him a stern Presbyterian. He was one of the three Springfield ministers who supported Lincoln for the Presidency in 1860, and was rewarded by receiving the consulship at Dundee, Scotland.

Dr. Smith says:

"It is a very easy matter to prove that while I was pastor of the First Presbyterian Church of Springfield, Mr. Lincoln did avow his belief in the divine authority and inspiration of the scriptures, and I hold that it is a matter of the last importance not only to the present, but all future generations of the great Republic, and to all advocates of civil and religious liberty throughout the world, that this avowal on his part, and the circumstances attending it, together with very interesting incidents illustrative of his character, in my possession, should be made known to the public. . . . It was to my honor to place before Mr. Lincoln arguments designed to prove the divine authority and inspiration of the scriptures accompanied by arguments of Infidel objectors in their own language. To the arguments on both sides, Mr. Lincoln gave a most patient, impartial and searching investigation. To use his own language, he examined the arguments as a lawyer who is anxious to reach the truth investigates testimony. The result was the announcement by himself that the argument in favor of the divine authority and inspiration of the Scriptures was unanswerable."

Next comes the testimony of Mr. Edwards:

"A short time after the Rev. Dr. Smith became pastor of the First Presbyterian Church of this city, Mr. Lincoln said to me, 'I have been reading a work of Dr. Smith on the evidence of Christianity, and have heard him preach and converse on the subject, and I am now convinced of the truth of Christianity."

Thomas Lewis testifies as follows:

"Not long after Dr. Smith came to Springfield, and I think very near the time of his son's death, Mr. Lincoln said to me, that when on a visit somewhere, he had seen and partially read a work of Dr. Smith on the evidences of Christianity which had led him to change his views about the Christian religion; that he would like to get that work to finish the reading of it, and also to make the acquaintance of Dr. Smith. I was an elder in Dr. Smith's church, and took Dr. Smith to Mr. Lincoln's office and introduced him; and Dr. Smith gave Mr. Lincoln a copy of his book, as I know, at his own request."

Mr. Brooks writes Mr. Reed from New York City, on December 31, 1872, as follows:

"In addition to what has appeared from my pen, I will state that I have had many conversations with Mr. Lincoln, which were more or less of a religious character, and while I never tried to draw anything like a statement of his views from him, yet he freely expressed himself as having 'a hope of blessed immortality through Jesus Christ.' . . . Once or twice, speaking to me of the change which had come upon him, he said, while he could not fix any definite time, yet it was after he came here, and I am positive that in his own mind he identified it with about the time of Willie's death. . . . In many conversations with him, I absorbed the firm conviction that Mr. Lincoln was at heart a Christian man, believed in the Saviour, and was seriously considering the step which would formally connect him with the visible Church on earth."*

The next witness is the Rev. Byron Sunderland, D. D.:

"After some conversation, in which he seemed to have his joke and fun, he settled down to a serious consideration of the subject before his mind, and for one half hour poured forth a volume of the deepest Christian philosophy I ever heard."

The Rev. Dr. Miner:

"All that was said during that memorable afternoon I spent alone with that great and good man is engraven too deeply on my memory ever to be effaced. I felt certain of this fact, that if Mr. Lincoln was not really an experimental Christian, he was acting like one. He was doing his duty manfully, and looking to God for help in time of need; and, like the immortal Washington, he believed in the efficacy of prayer, and it was his custom to read the Bible and pray himself."

The last of Mr. Reed's witnesses, the Rev. Dr. Gurley, states:

"I have had frequent and intimate conversations with him on the subject of the Bible and the Christian religion. when he could have no motive to deceive me, and I considered him not only sound on the truth of the Christian religion but on all its fundamental doctrines and teachings. And more than that, in the latter days of his chastened and weary life, after the death of his son, Willie, and his visit to the battlefield of Gettysburg, he said, with tears in his eyes, that he had lost confidence in everything but God, and that he now believed his heart was changed, and that he loved the Saviour, and, if he was not deceived in himself, it was his intention soon to make a profession of religion."*

Had Mr. Reed been a lawyer, instead of a clergyman, it is possible that he might have observed the contradictory character of the testimony of his witnesses. Not being one. he takes all these statements seriously, and does not perceive the lack of harmony that pervades them. When Dr. Smith said "It is very easy to prove" that under his influence Lincoln "did avow his belief in the divine authority and inspiration of the scriptures." he states what is not apparent from the facts and circumstances in the case.

If it were "a very easy matter to prove," how does it happen that Mr. Reed could only find, with great effort in a city of nearly 10.000 people, but two witnesses to the alleged fact, Mr. Edwards and Mr.

*Mr. Brooks had written a book entitled **Washington in Lincoln's Time,** in which he said much about Lincoln, but nothing about his conversion. It seems strange that none of Mr. Reed's witnesses ever expressed themselves upon the subject until he was in a position to need their evidence.

*All the testimony of Reed's witnesses will be found in **Scribner's Monthly** for July, 1873, as well as in Remsburg's book.

Lewis? Then in a city of this size every one would have heard of Lincoln's conversion had it been a fact. The letter he received from Edwards was dated, December 24, 1872. On January 8, 1873, Lewis wrote his letter, so after securing one witness it required two weeks to find another, to a fact which Dr. Smith said was well known and easy to prove. Then, when Dr. Holland came to Springfield in 1865, combing the city to obtain evidence of Lincoln's orthodoxy, no one ever heard that Dr. Smith had converted him, and all Mr. Holland could obtain was the shady "Bateman interview."

A few pertinent questions may be properly asked. If Dr. Smith convinced Mr. Lincoln of the truth of the Bible and the Christian religion, why did he never announce the fact to the world during Lincoln's life time? Why was it that Lincoln never announced it himself? How does it happen that none of Lincoln's friends, for instance, Mr. Herndon, Mr. Speed, Colonel Lamon, and Mrs. Lincoln, ever heard of it? Why, for perhaps 20 years, was it sealed up in the brains of Mr. Edwards and Mr. Lewis? Why did not Mr. Lincoln join Dr. Smith's church? It is a queer coincidence that no one knew of it until after Lincoln's death, and when the Rev. Reed had occasion to make use of it.

When did Dr. Smith convert Lincoln? Edwards and Lewis say it was soon after Dr. Smith came to Springfield, and after the death of Lincoln's little boy, Willie. Both of these events occurred in 1848. Dr. Smith does not in his statement give any date, only saving that it happened "while I was pastor of the First Presbyterian Church of Springfield." This might mean any time between 1848 and 1861. On another occasion he has stated that it was in 1858. If this were true, the statements of both Lewis and Edwards contradict him. In 1848, Lincoln was a member of Congress, and taking an active part in the Presidential campaign. In 1858, he was a candidate for the United States Senate, and holding debates with Douglas. It is not likely that during either of these years when he was immersed in politics did he have any time to study theological problems.

Lewis claims the honor of bringing Dr. Smith and Lincoln together, when the reverend doctor gave Lincoln the book which they say converted him. Stuart, in his attempted disclaimer of his evidence, says that Dr. Smith's first visit to Lincoln was "at the suggestion of a lady friend." Then, what has become of this book? Any work which would cause the conversion of a man of the type of Lincoln would have lived, and been made use of to convert other "Infidels." It is now unknown.

Amidst all these contradictions there is but one thing which we may truthfully say happened—Dr. Smith visited Lincoln and presented him with a book, or pamphlet, dealing with the evidences of Christianity. Dr. Smith says Lincoln read it and was convinced. Mr. Herndon says: "No one of Lincoln's old acquaintances in this city ever heard of his conversion to Christianity by Dr. Smith or anyone else. It was never suggested nor thought of here until after his death. . . . I never saw him read a second of time in Dr. Smith's book on Infidelity. He threw it down upon our table—spit upon it as it were—and never opened it to my knowledge."

As Lincoln was, during this decade, 1850 to 1860, deeply in politics, a candidate for the United States Senate twice, and already suggested for the Presidency, he did not want to get into any controversy with the preachers. He therefore possibly said something complimentary of Dr. Smith's book, but had the reading of it converted him, we would have heard more of it from Dr. Smith himself, as well as by Lincoln and many others.

I believe that Carl Sandburg, in his **Abraham Lincoln: The Prairie**

Years, vol. 1, pp. 413-414, tells the exact truth about this alleged "conversion" of Lincoln by the Rev. James Smith, D. D.:

> "The Lincoln's rented a pew in the church. Mrs. Lincoln took the sacrament, and joined in membership. (She had formerly been an Episcopalian.) The Rev. Mr. Smith presented Lincoln with a copy of his book, **The Christian's Defense,** a reply to Infidels and Atheists; it argued that the creation of the world, as told in the book of Genesis, the fall of man in the Garden of Eden, the flood which ended with Noah's ark on Mount Ararat were true events, that the books of the Old Testament are not forgeries, that a number of profane authors testify to the truth of the New Testament evangels, that only an Atheist can deny divine inspiration; the divine authority of the Scriptures is proved from prophecy and its fulfilment.
>
> "Lincoln read **The Christian's Defense,** said he was interested, later attended revival meetings held in the First Presbyterian Church. But when asked to join the Church, he said he 'couldn't quite see it.' "

Colonel Lamon correctly diagnosed Dr. Smith's case when he said of him:

> "The abilities of this gentleman to discuss such a topic to the edification of a man like Mr. Lincoln seem to have been rather slender; but the chance of converting so distinguished a person inspired him with a zeal which he might not have felt for the salvation of an obscurer soul. Mr. Lincoln listened to his exhortations in silence, apparently respectful, and occasionally sat out his sermons in church with as much patience as other people." **(Life of Lincoln,** p. 498.)

Mr. Reed does not realize that the testimony of Mr. Brooks nullifies that of Dr. Smith. Mr. Brooks makes the date of Lincoln's conversion, as "after he came here (Washington) and I am positive that in his own mind he identified it with about the time of Willie's death." Willie died in 1862. If Brooks is right, the alleged conversion of Lincoln by Dr. Smith collapses. Lewis and Edwards both say the conversion occurred about 1848, Smith, about 1858, Brooks, in 1862. Then others have said it took place in 1863, when Lincoln visited the battlefield of Gettysburg. Altogether they have assigned five dates for this event. Therefore it must be admitted that the time, a very necessary legal point, has not been established. Neither is the place established, for some say, Illinois, while others the City of Washington.

As to Thomas Lewis, his reputation for truth and veracity in Springfield was under a cloud. Mr. Herndon, in his reply to Mr. Reed, published in the Springfield **Register,** thus speaks of the gentleman:

> "Mr. Lewis's veracity and integrity in this community need no comment. I have heard good men say they would not believe his word under any circumstances, especially were he interested. I hate to state this of Tom, but if he will obtrude himself in this discussion, I cannot help but say a word in self-defense. Mr. Lincoln detested this man, I know. The idea that Mr. Lincoln would go to Tom Lewis and reveal to him his religious convictions, is to me, and to all who know Mr. Lincoln and Tom Lewis, too absurd."

The Rev. Dr. Sunderland says that in his hearing Mr. Lincoln "poured forth a volume of the deepest Christian philosophy I ever heard." As we read what Dr. Sunderland says Lincoln said, in the July, 1873, **Scribner's Monthly,** we are tempted to remark that the reverend doctor wrote this out 10 years after he had talked with President Lincoln, and we must make allowances for lapses of memory. But let it stand as written, because it contains nothing which commits Lincoln to a belief in orthodox Christianity, and only makes him say what any Deist or Unitarian might say without doing violence to his principles.

The Rev. Dr. Miner nowhere gives a report of what Lincoln said on "that memorable afternoon," and he seems to be uncertain as to whether Lincoln was "an experimental Christian," or some other kind. That he believed in the efficacy of prayer, in the orthodox sense, or that he prayed himself, or that Washington prayed, are well-known myths for which there has never been any good evidence.

The Rev. Dr. Gurley considered Lincoln "sound not only on the truth of the Christian religion but on all its fundamental doctrines and teachings." This means that Lincoln was a Presbyterian and a Calvinist, something none of his intimate friends ever knew him to be. He gives aid to Mr. Brooks in putting to the discard the story of the Rev. Dr. Smith. Dr. Gurley officiated at the Lincoln obsequies in Washington, and assisted Bishop Simpson at the obsequies at Springfield, but on neither occasion did either of these clergymen assert that Lincoln was a believer, something ministers never fail to do if it is a fact, and sometimes when it is not. Bishop Simpson never claimed him as a believer, nor did Dr. Gurley until the Rev. J. A. Reed was caught in a tight place, and called on him for help. The plain, common man will ask Mr. Brooks and Dr. Gurley why, if Lincoln had the love for Jesus they both say he had, and the faith in immortality, why, in all his letters and writings, he never mentions the names **Jesus** or **Christ**, and only once the word **immortality**?

We are impressed by the manner in which the Rev. Mr. Reed's witnesses not only nullify each other, but nullify themselves. We are reminded of the saying of Napoleon Bonaparte that history consists "of lies agreed upon," but agreement is not all. There should be also good memories.

The New York **World**, in commenting on the Rev. Reed's attempt to refute Lamon's witnesses, said:

"It is admitted by Mr. Reed and everybody else that Mr. Lincoln was a working Infidel up to a very late period of his life, that he wrote a book and labored earnestly to make proselytes to his own views, that he never publicly recanted, and that he never joined the Church. Upon those who, in the face of these tremendous facts, allege that he was nevertheless a Christian lies the burden of proof. Let them produce it or forever hold their peace. In the meantime it is a sad and puerile subterfuge to argue that he **would** have been a Christian if he had lived long enough, and to lament that he was not 'spared' for that purpose. He **had** been spared 56 years and surrounded by every circumstance that might soften his heart and every influence that might elevate his faith. If he was at that late, that fatal, hour standing gloomily without the pale, what reason have we to suppose that he intended ever to enter?"

The controversy engendered by the publication of Colonel Lamon's book caused it to be a failure financially. The religious world boycotted it. Today it is hard to buy a copy, and few are available, even in libraries. Those in existence were no doubt destroyed.

When Herndon, in 1889, published the first edition of his **Life of Lincoln**, most copies were bought up to keep them out of circulation. After 60 years have passed, Herndon's work is acknowledged to be the best on Lincoln's personal career, while no writer today of any standing will affirm that Abraham Lincoln was an orthodox Christian. Hol-

land's book, so popular in the day in which it was written, is now considered to be on a par with Weems' **Life of Washington**, a book notorious for its mythical character.

It now having been established that Lincoln was an "Infidel"
in Illinois—the two individuals most interested in this controversy,
the Rev. J. A. Reed and Dr. Holland, having admitted this fact and the
same persons and their friends having asserted that he was converted
to orthodoxy after he moved to Washington—we will, in the interest
of impartiality, consider more evidence from those who say he was
there converted.

The **Western Christian Advocate**, shortly after the close of the
Civil War, published the following comment, which is quoted in Raymond's **Life of Lincoln**, p. 735:

"On the day of the receipt of the capitulation of Lee, we
learned from a friend intimate with the late President, the
cabinet meeting was held an hour earlier than usual. Neither
the President nor any member was able, for a time, to give
utterance to his feelings. At the suggestion of Mr. Lincoln, all
dropped on their knees, and offered, in silence and tears, their
humble and heartfelt acknowledgement to the Almighty for the
triumph he had granted to the national cause."

In 1891, Hugh McCullough, who was Secretary of the Treasury,
and who attended every cabinet meeting, firmly denied this. (For Mr.
McCullough's statement, see the first chapter of this book, "George
Washington, the Vestryman who was not a Communicant.")

Frank B. Carpenter, the artist, who painted the picture of "The
Signing of the Emancipation Proclamation," spent six months at the
White House for that purpose, and while there he was in constant
touch with the President. He says:

"There is a very natural and proper desire, at this time,
to know something of the religious experience of the late President. Two or three stories have been published in this connection, which I have never yet been able to trace to a reliable
source, and I feel impelled to say here, that I believe the facts
in the case—if there were such—have been added unto, or un-
warrantably embellished. . . Mr. Lincoln could scarcely be
called a **religious** man, in the common acceptance of the term,
and yet a sincerer **Christian**, I believe, never lived. A constitutional tendency to dwell upon sacred things; an emotional
nature which finds ready expression in religious conversation
and revival meetings; the culture and development of the devotional element till the expression of religious thought and
experience becomes almost habitual, were not among his
characteristics."

This is in direct contradiction to what those who say he was converted in Washington would have us believe. Mr. Carpenter considered
Lincoln not as a **religious** man, but a sincere **Christian**. He makes the
common mistake of confusing the three words, **religion, Christianity**
and **morality**. He did not stop to realize that a man may be religious
without being a Christian, and that he might be moral without being
either religious or Christian. Since Carpenter knew that Lincoln was
a good man, he thought he must be a Christian, though he here admits
the fact that Lincoln was not a Christian in any conventional or doc-
trinal sense of the word. Here Carpenter disagrees with all the other
witnesses who have declared that Lincoln was converted while in
Washington.

Dr. Holland abandoned his first claim that Lincoln was always a
believer, but attempted to prove, in **Scribner's Monthly** for July, 1873,

that he became one after he moved to Washington. Dr. Holland wrote:

"What Abraham Lincoln was when he lived in New Salem and wrote an anti-Christian tract (which the friend to whom he showed it somewhat violently but most judiciously put in the fire) is one thing, and it may be necessary for an impartial historian to record it. What he was when he died at Washington with those most Christian words of the Second Inaugural on his lips, and the most Christian record of five years of patient tenderness and charity behind him, is quite another thing."

It may have been difficult for Dr. Holland to understand that "patient tenderness and charity," as well as other virtues, are not the property of any particular form of religious belief or disbelief.

Turning to the Second Inaugural, in which Dr. Holland finds evidence that Lincoln changed his views and was converted, we find nothing that justifies the supposition, but rather the reverse. In this document there are references to God, and the Bible, but not such as an orthodox Christian would make. In referring to the two parties engaged in the war he said:

"Both read the same Bible and pray to the same God, and each invokes his aid against the other. It may seem strange that any men should dare to ask a just God's assistance in wringing their bread from the sweat of other men's faces, but let us judge not that we be not judged."

He was particular to say, "Both read the same **Bible**," not, "Both read the same **Word of God**." He mentally took note of the fact that there are many different Bibles, of which the Christian Bible is but one. His reference to both sides praying to the same God to help them defeat the other side is the best of sarcasm.

"Shall we discern there any departure from those divine attributes which the believers in a living God always ascribe to him?" Of course, Lincoln does not express an opinion, but he has plainly in mind his own idea of God, which was fate, and he does not state his own opinion, but what the "**believers** in a living God ascribe to him." And when he said, "as was said 3,000 years ago," he does not say that God said it, nor that any particular person said it. He was careful not to commit himself. He was a student of the Bible, like all other great Freethinkers, such as Paine, Voltaire, Bradlaugh and Ingersoll, and he knew how to quote it with effect, but nowhere does he imply belief in its divine inspiration, or that he accepts its authority any more than he accepts the authority of any other book.

Bishop Matthew Simpson, of the Methodist Church, has been often quoted as saying that Abraham Lincoln was a believer after he went to Washington, but as most of these quotations are garbled, and the context is not given, I shall quote the bishop from the original source, his funeral address over Lincoln at Springfield. The entire sermon was published in the New York **Christian Advocate**, exactly as Bishop Simpson delivered it, immediately after the funeral. In its issue of February 11, 1904, the **Advocate** reprinted this address exactly as it appeared in 1865. I was at that time living in New York City, where I visited the **Advocate** office and purchased a copy. Here is what Bishop Simpson said:

"Abraham Lincoln was a good man. He was known as an honest, temperate, forgiving man, a just man, a man of noble heart in every way; as to his religious experience I cannot speak definitely, because I was not privileged to know much of his private sentiments. My acquaintance with him did not give me the opportunity to hear him speak on this topic. I know, however, he read the Bible frequently; loved it for its great truths and for its profound teachings; and he tried to be guided by its precepts. He believed in Christ, the Saviour of sinners, and I think he was sincerely trying to bring his life into the principles of revealed religion. Certainly if there ever was a man who illustrated some of the principles of pure religion, that man was our departed President. Look over all his speeches. Listen to his utterances. He never spoke unkindly to any man; even to the rebels no words of anger from him, and his last day illustrated in a remarkable manner his favorite disposition. A dispatch had been received that afternoon that Thompson and Tucker were trying to make their escape through Maine, and it was proposed to arrest them. Mr. Lincoln, however, preferred rather to let them quietly escape and this morning we read the proclamation offering $25,000 for the arrest of these men as aiders and abetters of his assassination. Thus, in his last expiring acts he was saying, 'Father, forgive them; they know not what they do.'

"As a rule I doubt if any President has ever shown such trust in God, or in the public documents so frequently referred to divine aid. Often did he remark to his friends and to delegations that his hope for our success rested in his conviction that God would bless our efforts because we were trying to do right. To the address of a large body he replied, 'Thanks be unto God, who in our national trials has given us the Churches.' To a minister who said he hoped the Lord was on his side, he replied that it gave him no concern whether the Lord was on our side or not, for, he said, 'I know the Lord is always on the side of the right'; and with deep feeling he added, 'But God is my witness and it is my constant anxiety and prayer that both myself and this nation should be on the Lord's side.' "

None will contend with Bishop Simpson in his eloquent eulogy of President Lincoln's virtues, yet we might say, as we have said before, that these virtues are the property of all religions, and not the monopoly of any one. That Lincoln read the Bible there is no doubt. He also read Burns, Byron and Shakespeare. He took them all for just what they were worth. That he believed in Christ must be taken with a qualification. We can believe in Christ in a dozen different ways, without accepting any orthodox view. Many Infidels, including Paine, Ingersoll and Rousseau, have admired some of Christ's teachings, but none of them believed in his divinity or supernatural character.

But the most important part of Bishop Simpson's testimony is his admission that he did not know what Lincoln's "religious experience" had been, and could not "speak definitely," because he "was not privileged to know much of his private sentiments"; and his "acquaintance with him did not give me the opportunity to hear him speak on the topic." It is well known, as the **National Encyclopedia** says, that Bishop Simpson "was a close friend of President Lincoln." Then, if he did not know what his religious sentiments were, how did some other ministers who happened to find their way into the White House for a few minutes, learn all about them? We are inclined to think that of all of them, Bishop Simpson was the only honest one.

Many years ago I heard the very eloquent Baptist preacher, the Rev. Dr. George C. Lorimer, say from the platform of Carnegie Hall:

"Biographies by preachers are of no value. If they admire a man they always make him a saint, while if they dislike one, they always make him a demon."

As Lincoln was a close friend of Bishop Simpson, and did not tell him what he believed, it is only additional evidence that he was not in the habit of unbosoming hmself even to his friends, to say nothing of strangers. When Lincoln said, as quoted by the bishop, that instead of asking the Lord to be on his side, he preferred to be on the Lord's side, he only confirms Lincoln's idea of God, which was that God had his own purposes, and did not swerve from them through any prayers. This I will later prove.

While Bishop Simpson, a Methodist, did not claim that Lincoln was an orthodox Christian, the Methodist Church was not to be outdone by the Presbyterian in asserting that it had converted him. At one time, the Rev. James F. Jacques, D.D., was pastor of the First Methodist Church, of Springfield, Ill. He was later the colonel of the 73rd Regiment, Illinois Volunteer Infantry. Toward the close of the war he made a trip to Richmond on his own initiative to urge Jefferson Davis to stop fighting. The Rev. Ervin Chapman, D.D., gives us Colonel Jacques' statement in his book, **Latest Light on Abraham Lincoln**, pp. 396, 387:

"One beautiful Sunday morning in May, I was standing in the front door of the parsonage when a little boy came up to me and said: 'Mr. Lincoln sent me around to see if you was going to preach today.' Now, I had met Mr. Lincoln, but I never thought any more of 'Abe' Lincoln that I did of any one else. I said to the boy, 'You go back and tell Mr. Lincoln that if he will come to church he will see whether I am going to preach or not.' The little fellow stood working his fingers and finally said, 'Mr. Lincoln told me he would give me a quarter if I would find out whether you are going to preach.' I did not want to rob the little fellow of his income, so I told him to tell Mr. Lincoln that I was going to try to preach.

"The church was filled that morning. It was a good-sized church, but on that day all the seats were filled. I had chosen for my text the words, 'Ye must be born again,' and during the course of my sermon I laid particular stress on the word 'must.' Mr. Lincoln came into the church after the services had commenced, and there being no vacant seats, chairs were put in the altar in front of the pulpit, and Mr. Lincoln and Governor French and wife sat in the altar during the entire services, Mr. Lincoln on my left and Governor French on my right, and I noticed that Mr. Lincoln appeared to be deeply interested in the sermon. A few days after that Sunday, Mr. Lincoln called on me and informed me that he had been greatly impressed with my remarks on Sunday and that he had come to talk with me further on the matter.

"I invited him in, and my wife talked and prayed with him for hours. Now, I have seen many persons converted; I have seen hundreds brought to Christ, and if ever a person was converted, Abraham Lincoln was converted that night in my house."

Strange to say, the world never heard of this conversion until September 28-29, 1897, when Colonel Jacques told it at the reunion of the 73rd Regiment, held in Springfield. Then few, if any, were alive who could contradict it. No one among all of Lincoln's friends ever heard of it, which causes us to wonder why it was that Lincoln was continuously converted, and all appear to be ignorant of the alleged facts except the ministers who did the work? When one is really converted, he stands up before the church and acknowledges Christ. Why, in all of these alleged conversions, did not Lincoln do the same?

Another who endeavored, with a qualification however, to make

Lincoln a believer was Isaac N. Arnold, at one time a member of Congress from Chicago, and the author of a **Life of Lincoln**, published in 1885. He says:

"No more reverent Christian than he ever sat in the executive chair, not excepting Washington. He was by nature religious; full of religious sentiment. The veil between him and the supernatural was very thin. **It is not claimed that he was orthodox.** For creeds and dogmas he cared little. But in the great fundamental principles of religion, of the Christian religion, he was a firm believer. Belief in the existence of God, in the immortality of the soul, in the Bible as the revelation of God to man, in the efficacy and duty of prayer, in reverence toward the Almighty, and in love and charity to men, was the basis of his religion." (**Life of Lincoln**, p. 446.)

"His reply to the Negroes of Baltimore when they, in 1864, presented him with a magnificent Bible, ought to silence forever those who charge him with unbelief. He said: 'In regard to the great book I have only to say that it is the best gift which God has given to man. All the good from the Saviour of the world is communicated through this book.' "

"His faith in a Divine Providence began at his mother's knee, and ran through all the changes of his life. Not orthodox, not a man of creeds, he was a man of simple trust in God."

Here, Mr. Arnold has the distinction of being at variance with all the other witnesses to the conversion of Lincoln. All of them have staked their reputations upon the statement that he was "orthodox," and "a man of creeds." If he was not, all the conversion stories would be like the play of Hamlet with Hamlet left out. The Rev. Dr. Gurley, who never claimed Lincoln as a believer while he lived—not even at his funeral—in order to help out the Rev. J. A. Reed, in 1873, said: "I considered him sound not only on the truth of the Christian religion, but on all its fundamental doctrines and teachings."

According to all the other statements we have quoted, he was converted to orthodoxy, or he was not converted at all. He always did believe in God, being a Deist. On this point, which no one ever denied, the conversion advocates exhaust all their strength, taking it for granted that because he did believe in God, he therefore accepted all the other dogmas of the orthodox Church.

Mr. Arnold's citing the speech to the Baltimore Negroes, when they presented Lincoln with a Bible, is unfortunate, but he cautiously omitted one sentence in the speech which is not creditable to Lincoln. In Raymond's **Life of Lincoln**, page 617, where the speech is reported, the following line occurs: "**But for that book we could not know right from wrong.**" Sometimes this statement is made, but always by ignorant people. Lincoln was not an ignorant man.

No one will accuse Lincoln of being so ignorant that he thought the ancient Greeks and Romans, the ancient Egyptians and Babylonians, to say nothing of the followers of Buddha, in India, and of Confucius, in China, did not know right from wrong. Evidently, when Arnold omitted quoting this line, he had some regard for Lincoln's intellectual reputation.

There are several versions of this speech, but the one from which Arnold quotes says, in conclusion: "All the good from the Saviour of the world is communicated through this book." Another version has it: "All those things desirable to man are contained in it." Whoever reported or originated the first version was not very familiar with the Scriptures, which say: "And there are also many other things which Jesus did, the which, if they should be written every one, I suppose that even the world itself could not contain the books that should be written." (John, 21:25.)

This speech was supposed to have been delivered in 1864. While the papers mentioned the gift of the Bible, this alleged address was not published until two months afterwards. Of Lincoln's impromptu speeches, there are many versions. The one he delivered in Springfield before departing for Washington is a case in point. No two reports are alike.

Another who maintained that Lincoln was converted while in Washington, was the well-known Presbyterian clergyman, the Rev. J. W. Barrows, D.D. He said:

"In the anxious uncertainties of the great war, he gradually rose to the heights where Jehovah became to him the sublimest of realities, the ruler of nations. When he wrote his immortal Proclamation, he invoked upon it not only 'the considerate judgment of mankind,' but the 'gracious favor of Almighty God.' When darkness gathered over the brave armies fighting for the nation's life, this strong man in the early morning knelt and wrestled in prayer with Him who holds the fate of empires. When the clouds lifted above the carnage of Gettysburg, he gave his heart to the Lord Jesus Christ. When he pronounced his matchless oration on the chief battlefield of the war, he gave expression to the resolve that 'this nation, under God, should have a new birth of freedom.' And when he wrote his last Inaugural Address, he gave it the lofty religious tone of an old Hebrew psalm." (**Lincoln Memorial Album**, p. 508.)

Mr. Barrows' statement is simply an expression of his own personal opinion. Only two of the more than 200 contributors to the **Lincoln Memorial Album** claim that Lincoln was orthodox. Dr. Barrows is only repeating what he had heard others say. Later we will examine the Emancipation Proclamation, the first draft of which does not mention God. Neither was the Deity mentioned in the first draft of the Gettysburg Address. "A Pious Nurse," name not known, tells of Lincoln's alleged belief on orthodoxy, as does "An Illinois Clergyman," also unknown. The Rev. Francis Vinton, a clergyman from New York City, and a stranger, tells how, when he visited Lincoln, the President "fell upon his neck and wept like a child," and that Lincoln asked him to send a copy of a sermon he had preached.

That Lincoln would make confidants of strangers, wear his heart on his sleeve, or tell them his private affairs, is considered ridiculous by all who knew him well. Except Mr. Herndon, his law-partner, no one knew him better than Judge David Davis, who said:

"The idea that Lincoln talked to a stranger about his religion or religious views, or made such speeches, remarks, etc., about it as published, is to me absurd. I knew the man too well. He was the most reticent, secretive man I ever saw, or expect to see." (Lamon's **Lincoln**, p. 489.)

What would we think of any man who had one set of opinions and a way of speaking for one class of people, and another for another class? Yet, this is exactly the type of man these people, by implication, if not in words, say Abraham Lincoln was. They make of him either a hypocrite or a fool, and Abraham Lincoln was neither.

To know the position of Lincoln toward the Churches while he was President, we must first appreciate the gigantic task he had before him. At his inauguration he found the Union split asunder. The South had seceded, and its people, except in certain localities, were united for rebellion. The North was divided. For three years the result of the conflict was uncertain, and at times Lincoln himself despaired of the re-

sult. His first duty was to unite all the people of every political and
religious persuasion, in defense of the flag. After 75 years have passed,
we, today, see how well he did his duty.

Why have so many books been written about Lincoln? Because, as
the decades rolled on, we see more of his excellencies—his shrewdness
as a politician, his tact in managing men, his moderation, his manner
of appealing to the people and bringing them over to his side.

One of the strongest forces in the molding of opinion in Lincoln's
day were the Churches and ministers. They were by no means all for
the Union. In the South, they openly preached rebellion. In the North,
they were divided. When Lincoln was a candidate, 20 of the 23 ministers
of his home-town, Springfield, were against him. Lincoln immediately
perceived that the Churches must be won over on his side. Hating
slavery as he did, he would not jeopardize the Union by prematurely
abolishing it, yet as soon as he saw that the destruction of the hated
institution would save the Union, he issued the Emancipation Proclamation.

However, his delay in taking this step offended some of his friends,
the radical Abolitionists. As a matter of policy, Lincoln held out the
olive branch to the Churches and the ministers. He appealed to their
patriotism, and thus kept them in line. While he was deferential to the
clerics and sometimes flattered them, he at no time manifested any
sympathy for their theological teachings. The fact that Lincoln asked
the ministers to pray for him is of little significance. Primarily, prayer
is a wish, a desire for something.

He knew when a man prayed for him, that man was on his side,
and on the side of the Union. The efficacy of the prayer in moving God
was another matter. In this, Lincoln did not believe. When he once
said to a delegation of Methodist ministers, "God bless the Methodist
Church. God bless all the Churches, and blessed be God, who in this
hour of our need has given us the Churches," he was not endorsing
their creeds. He complimented them because he saw the value of their
support in reuniting the nation. A ruler in a Buddhist or a Mohammedan country, whatever might have been his private opinions, could
scarcely have done otherwise.

To those who have said, and there have been many, that he was
not candid, even was not honest in using such tactics, we answer that
hundreds of other men for the good of the country have done the same.
For the salvation of the Union Lincoln was willing to abandon for himself two of the dearest of American principles, Freethought and Free
Speech.

In the alleged conversion of Lincoln, even the Spiritualists have
put in a claim. Shortly after the death of his son Willie, in 1862, at the
request of Mrs. Lincoln, a Spiritualist medium was invited to the
White House. An account of the "messages" and "manifestations" is to
be found in **Abraham Lincoln**, by William E. Curtis, pp. 377-378.

President Lincoln received the medium in his usual kindly way.
He gave attention to the performance. The spirits of an Indian, of
General Knox, of the Revolutionary War, of Lafayette, Napoleon,
Franklin, and his old opponent Douglas "manifested" themselves. Lincoln did not appear to take the manifestations seriously, as he made
jokes while the spirits were talking. After he had heard the message
from Douglas' spirit he said: "I believe that, whether it comes from
spirit or human. It needs not a ghost from the bourne from which no
traveler returns to tell that."

This was a real "Lincolnism." The seance seemed to be more of an
entertainment than a serious gathering. Yet Spiritualists have published
a book in which it is maintained that Abraham Lincoln was a Spiritual-

ist, and with about as much truth as the assertion that he was a
Methodist or Presbyterian.

**Testimony of those who say Lincoln did not change his views in
Washington.** We will now examine the testimony of those who knew
Lincoln well in Washington, and who say they had no knowledge of his
being converted or changing his religious views while there. The first
witness, his private secretary, Colonel John G. Nicolay, in a letter written just six weeks after Lincoln's death, on May 27, 1865, says:

"Mr. Lincoln did not, to my knowledge, in any way change
his religious ideas, opinions or beliefs, from the time he left
Springfield till the day of his death. I do not know just what
they were, never having heard him explain them in detail, but
I am very sure he gave no outward indications of his mind
having undergone any change in that regard while here."
(Lamon's **Life of Lincoln**, p. 492.)

He gives us, as quoted in William E. Curtis' **Abraham Lincoln**, Lincoln's views as he had heard him tell them:

"I do not remember ever having discussed religion with Mr.
Lincoln, nor do I know of any authorized statement of his views
in existence. He sometimes talked freely, and never made any
concealment of his belief or unbelief in any dogma or doctrine,
but never provoked religious controversy." (P. 385.)

"At the same time, he did not believe in some of the dogmas
of the orthodox Churches. I have heard him argue against the
doctrine of atonement, for example. He considered it illogical
and unjust and a premium upon evil-doing if a man who had
been wicked all his life could make up for it by a few words or
prayers at the hour of death; and he had no faith in deathbed repentances. He did not believe in several other articles of
the creeds of the orthodox Churches. He believed in the Bible,
however. He was a constant reader of the Bible, and had great
faith in it, but he did not believe that its entire contents were
inspired. He used to consider it the greatest of all text-books
of morals and ethics, and that there was nothing to compare
with it in all literature; but at the same time, I have heard him
say that God had too much to do and more important things
to attend to than to inspire such insignificant writers as had
written some passages in the good book.

"Nor did he believe in miracles. He believed in inexorable
laws of Nature, and I have heard him say that the wisdom and
glory and greatness of the Almighty were demonstrated by order
and method and not by the violation of Nature's laws." (P.
386.)

"He had no sympathy with theology, and often said that
in a man's relation with his Maker he couldn't give a power
of attorney." (P. 387.)

The next witness is Colonel Ward H. Lamon, who says in his **Life of
Lincoln**, p. 502:

"But he never told anyone that he accepted Jesus as the
Christ, or performed a single one of the acts which necessarily
follow such a conviction. . . Indefinite expressions about 'Divine
Providence,' the 'Justice of God,' 'the favor of the Most High,'
were easy, and not inconsistent with his religious notions. In
this, accordingly, he indulged freely; but never in all that time
did he let fall from his lips or his pen an expression which remotely implied the slightest faith in Jesus as the son of God
and the Saviour of men."

One would think that the testimony of these gentlemen, one his

private secretary, who was with him daily, and the other, an old friend
from Illinois, whom he had given an appointment as Marshal of the
District of Columbia, ought to be sufficient. What they have said is
certainly of more value than the word of migratory ministers, whose
chief object was to be able to say they had talked with him, and to
assume that they had had the glory of converting him, merely because he had talked with them, and treated them with courtesy and
respect.

Yet, we will quote some additional witnesses. The first will be
George W. Julian, a prominent member of Congress from Indiana, one
of the founders of the Republican party, and an anti-slavery candidate
for Vice President in 1852. He was intimate with Lincoln in Washington. In a private letter to Mr. Remsburg, written from Santa Fe, N.
Mex., on March 13, 1888, he says:

"I knew him (Lincoln) well, and I know he was not a
Christian in any old-fashioned orthodox sense of the word,
but only a religious Theist. He was, substantially, such a Christian as Jefferson, Franklin, Washington and John Adams;
and it is perfectly idle to assert the contrary."

John B. Alley, who was a member of Congress during the time
that Lincoln was President, says:

"In his religious views Mr. Lincoln was very nearly what
we call a Freethinker. While he reflected a great deal upon
religious subjects he communicated his thoughts to a very few.
He had little faith in the popular religion of the times. He
had a broad conception of the goodness and power of an overruling Providence, and said to me one day that he felt sure
the Author of our being, whether called God or Nature, it
mattered not which, would deal very mercifully with poor,
erring humanity in the other, and he hoped a better, world.
He was free as possible from all sectarian thought, feeling or
sentiment. No man was more tolerant of the opinions and feelings of others in the direction of religious sentiment or had
less faith in religious dogmas. . . While Mr. Lincoln was perfectly honest and upright and led a blameless life, he was in
no sense what might be considered a religious man." (**Reminiscences of Lincoln,** pp. 590-591.)

Schuyler Colfax, Speaker of the House of Representatives while
Lincoln was President, says that a delegation of ministers from Chicago
had waited upon Lincoln, early in September, 1862, urging him to issue
the Emancipation Proclamation at once. He did issue it on September
22, but it was not to go into effect until January 1, 1863. The ministers
were impatient, and demanded that the slaves be freed at once. Mr.
Colfax says:

"One of these ministers felt it was his duty to make a more
searching appeal to the President's conscience. Just as they
were retiring, he turned, and said to Mr. Lincoln: 'What you
have said to us, Mr. President, compels me to say to you in
reply, that it is a message to you from our Divine Master,
through me, commanding you, sir, to open the doors of bondage that the slave may go free!' Mr. Lincoln replied instantly:
'That may be, sir, for I have studied this question, by day and
by night for weeks and for months, but if it is, as you say, a
message from your Divine Master, is it not odd that the only
channel he could send it by was that round-about route by that
awfully wicked city of Chicago?' " (**Reminiscences of Lincoln,**
pp. 334-335.)

William D. Kelley was for 30 years a member of Congress from

Pennsylvania, and one of the committee that notified Lincoln of his nomination. He relates a similar anecdote. A Quaker preacher, a woman, called on the President on the same errand as the delegation of Chicago ministers. She illustrated her argument by citing the history of Deborah, as told in the Bible. (Judges, Chapter 4.) Mr. Kelley says:

"Having elaborated this Biblical example, the speaker assumed that the President was, as Deborah had been, the appointed minister of the Lord, and proceeded to tell him that it was his duty to follow the example of Deborah, and forthwith abolish slavery, and establish freedom throughout the land, as our Lord had appointed him to do.

" 'Has the Friend finished?' said the President, as she ceased to speak Having received an affirmative answer, he said: 'I have neither time nor disposition to enter into discussion with the Friend, and end this occasion by suggesting for her consideration the question whether, if it be true that the Lord has appointed me to do the work she has indicated, it is not probable that he would have communicated knowledge of the fact to me as well as to her.' " (**Reminiscences of Lincoln,** pp. 284-285.)

Much has been made of the fact that the name of God appears in the Emancipation Proclamation. The truth about this great document should be told. The first draft did not mention the Deity. We are told that Lincoln made a "solemn vow to God" that if Lee were defeated at Antietam, the Proclamation would be immediately forthcoming. Yet he completed the first draft on Sunday, without mentioning God. George S. Boutwell, in **Reminiscences of Lincoln,*** p. 126, gives Lincoln's exact words concerning the issuance of the Proclamation:

"The truth is just this: When Lee came over the river, I made a resolution that if McClellan drove him back I would send the Proclamation after him. The Battle of Antietam was fought on Wednesday, and until Saturday I could not find out whether we had gained a victory or lost a battle. It was then too late to issue the Proclamation that day, and the fact is, **I fixed it up a little on Sunday,** and on Monday I let them have it."

The New York **Tribune** of February 22, 1893, carried an article by Mrs. Janet Chase Hoyt, a daughter of Salmon P. Chase, who was Lincoln's first Secretary of the Treasury, and later Chief Justice of the U.S. Supreme Court. Mrs. Hoyt quotes from a letter she received from her father, in 1867, in which the complete facts about the writing of the Proclamation are given:

"Looking over old papers, I found many of my memoranda, etc., of the war, and among them my draft of a proclamation of emancipation submitted to Mr. Lincoln the day before his own was issued. He asked all of us for suggestions in regard to its form and I submitted mine in writing, and among other sentences the close as it now stands, which he adopted from my draft, with a modification. It may be interesting to you to see precisely what I said, and I copy it. You must remember that in the original draft there was no reference whatever to Divine or human sanction of the act. What I said, was this. at the conclusion of my letter: 'Finally, I respectfully suggest that on an occasion of such interest there can be no imputation of af-

---

*In the same work, Judge Usher, a member of the Cabinet, confirms what both Mr. Boutwell and Judge Chase here say. (Pages 91-92.)

fectation against a solemn recognition of responsibility before
men and before God, and that some such close as this would
be proper: "And upon this act, sincerely believed to be an act
of justice warranted by the Constitution (and of duty demanded
by the circumstances of the country), I invoke the considerate
judgment of mankind and the gracious favor of Almighty
God."' Mr. Lincoln adopted this close, substituting only for the
words inclosed in parentheses these words: 'upon military necessity,' which I think was not an improvement."

If we recall that this was the time when Lincoln is said to have been
converted, was telling his troubles to ministers and weeping over their
necks, we cannot think it was other than an anomaly that on the
same occasion he should forget God.

Another witness who refutes the story of Lincoln's conversion is
Maunsell B. Field, who says that "Mr. Lincoln was entirely deficient
in what the phrenologists call reverence (veneration)."

"I was once in Mr. Lincoln's company when a sectarian
controversy arose. He himself looked very grave, and made no
observation until all the others had finished what they had
to say. Then with a twinkle of the eye he remarked that he
preferred the Episcopalians to every other sect, because they
are equally indifferent to a man's religion and his politics."
(**Memories of Many Men.**)

William H. Seward, Secretary of State during the Civil War,
recalls the following story often told by Lincoln to illustrate his disdain
for the doctrine of eternal punishment:

"I recall President Lincoln's story of the intrusion of the
Universalists into the town of Springfield.

"The several orthodox Churches agreed that their pastors
should preach down the heresy. One of them began his discourse with these emphatic words: 'My brethren, there is a
dangerous doctrine creeping in among us. There are those who
are teaching that all men will be saved; but, my dear brethren,
we hope for better things." (**Travels Around the World**, p. 513.)

In the **Lincoln Memorial Album**, pp. 336-337, it is related that Mr.
Lincoln gave a Universalist minister an appointment as chaplain,
notwithstanding that a delegation of the orthodox waited upon him to
protest against the appointment.

The well-known lawyer, soldier and journalist, Donn Piatt, knew
Lincoln both in Illinois and in Washington. Here is what he says about
his religious opinions:

"I soon discovered that this strange and strangely gifted
man, while not at all cynical, was a skeptic. His view of human
nature was low, but good-natured. I could not call it suspicious,
but he believed only what he saw." (**Reminiscences of Lincoln**,
p. 400.)*

---

*It would be well at this point to say something about the **Reminscences
of Lincoln**, and **The Lincoln Memorial Album**, from which I have frequently quoted. The first is a series of articles published in **The North
American Review**, early in the 1880's, and afterwards published in
book form, and edited by the editor of the **Review**, Allen Thorndyke
Rice. The second is a book of similar type, edited by O. H. Oldroydt,
once curator of the Lincoln home in Springfield, and later, and until
his death in 1930, of the Peterson house in Washington, where Lincoln
died. In both of these very valuable works, noted men of the time, who
were contemporaries and friends of the great war President, give their
recollections of him.

A. J. Grover, a reformer and old-time Abolitionist, in a private letter to Mr. Remsburg, confirms what the witnesses previously quoted have said:

"I knew Mr. Lincoln in Illinois and in Washington. I was in the war office, for a time, in a department which had charge of the President's books, so-called. I met him in passing between the White House and the buildings then occupied by the War Department, almost every day. I often had to go to Mr. Stanton's office, and have often seen Mr. Lincoln there. I frequently had to go to the White House to see him. It was known to all of his acquaintances that he was a Liberal or Rationalist."

One of Lincoln's most intimate friends was Leonard Swett. They both traveled the same circuit, were often engaged in trying the same cases, and it was Swett who placed Lincoln's name before the Republican National Convention in Chicago, in 1860. In a letter, written in 1866, in answer to an inquiry as to whether Lincoln had changed his religious views, Swett said:

"I think not. As he became involved in matters of the greatest importance, full of great responsibility and great doubt, a feeling of religious reverence, a belief in God and his justice, and overruling providence increased with him. He was always full of natural religion. He believed in God as much as the most approved church member, yet he judged of him by the same system of generalization as he judged everything else. He had little faith in ceremonies or forms. In fact, he cared nothing for the form of anything. . . If his religion were to be judged by the lines and rules of creeds, he would fall far short of the standard."

Judge James M. Nelson, a native of Kentucky, resided for years in Illinois, where he knew Lincoln, and had an intimate acquaintance with him in Washington. Judge Nelson's great-grandfather was a signer of the Declaration of Independence. In the Louisville **Times**, in 1887, he gave his recollections of Lincoln. He says, in reference to his religious opinions:

"In religion, Mr. Lincoln was about of the same opinion as Bob Ingersoll, and there is no account of his ever having changed. He went to church a few times with his family while he was President, but so far as I have been able to find out, he remained an unbeliever. Mr. Lincoln in his younger days wrote a book, in which he endeavored to prove the fallacy of the plan of salvation and the divinity of Christ. . . ."

In 1864, Lincoln issued a fervent Thanksgiving Proclamation. Of this, Judge Nelson says: "I once asked him about his fervent Thanksgiving Message and twitted him with being an unbeliever in what was published. 'Oh,' said he, 'that is some of Seward's nonsense, and it pleases the fools.' "

The Opinions of Independent Investigators. The New York **World** (about 1875), in summing up the facts concerning Lincoln's religious beliefs, said:

"While it may be fairly said that Mr. Lincoln entertained many Christian sentiments, it cannot be said that he was himself a Christian in faith or practice. He was no disciple of Jesus of Nazareth. He did not believe in his divinity and was not a member of his Church.

"He was at first a writing Infidel of the school of Paine and Volney, and afterwards a talking Infidel of the school of Parker and Channing."

The **World** then refers to Lincoln's friendly attitude toward the Churches during the war:

"If the Churches had grown cold—if the Christians had taken a stand aloof—that instant the Union would have perished. Mr. Lincoln regulated his religious manifestations accordingly. He declared frequently that he would do **anything** to save the Union, and among the many things he did was the partial concealment of his individual religious opinions. Is this a blot upon his fame? Or shall we all agree that it was a conscientious and patriotic sacrifice?"

As evidence of Lincoln's piety, we are often referred to the picture of himself and his family in a reverential group. Lincoln has a Bible before him, and his son Tad is at his side. The Boston **Globe** said:

"The pretty little story about the picture of President Lincoln and his son Tad reading the Bible is now corrected for the one-hundredth time. The Bible was Photographer Brady's picture album, which the President was examining with his son while some ladies stood by. The artist begged the President to remain quiet, and the picture was taken. The truth is better than fiction, even if its recital conflicts with a pleasing theory."

Manford's Magazine (January, 1869), a religious periodical, published in Chicago, made the following comment:

"That Mr. Lincoln was a believer in the Christian religion, as understood by the so-called orthodox sects of the day, I am compelled most emphatically to deny; that is, if I put faith in the statements of his most intimate friends in this city (Springfield). All of them with whom I have conversed on this subject agree in endorsing the statement of Mr. Herndon. Indeed, many of them unreservedly call him an Infidel."

The **Herald and Review**, a Seventh Day Adventist journal, said, in 1890:

"The testimony seems conclusive. . . The majority of the great men of the world have always rejected Christ, and, according to the Scriptures, always will; and the efforts of Christians to make it appear that certain great men who never professed Christianity were in reality Christians, is simply saying that Christianity cannot stand on its own merits, but must have the support of great names to entitle it to favorable consideration."

Alden's American edition of **Chambers' Encyclopedia**, the well-known work of reference, says:

"He [Lincoln] was never a member of a Church; he is believed to have had philosophical doubts of the divinity of Christ, and of the inspiration of the Scriptures, as these are commonly stated in the system of doctrines called evangelical. In early life he read Paine and Volney, and wrote an essay in which he agreed with their conclusions. Of modern thinkers he was thought to agree nearest with Theodore Parker." (Art., "Abraham Lincoln.")

An old edition of the **Encyclopedia Britannica** says: "His [Lincoln's] nature was deeply religious, but he belonged to no denomination; he had faith in the eternal justice and boundless mercy of Providence; and made the Golden Rule of Christ his practical creed." The 14th edition of this great Encyclopedia speaks more precisely:

"The measure of his difference from most of the men who surrounded him is best gauged by his attitude toward the fundamentals of religion. For all his devotion to his cause he did not allow himself to believe that he knew the mind of God with regard to it. He was never so much the mystic as in his later days and never so far removed from the dogmatist. Here was the final flowering of that mood which appears to have lain at the back of his mind from the beginning—his complete conviction of a reality of a supernatural world joined with a belief that it was too deep for man to fathom. **His refusal to accept the 'complicated' statement of doctrines which he rejected, carried with it a refusal to predicate the purpose of the Almighty.** Again, that singular characteristic, his power to devote himself wholly to a cause and yet to do so in such a detached, unviolent way that one is tempted to call it passionless. **He retained nothing of the tribal forms of religion and was silent when they raged about him with a thousand tongues.**" (Art., "Abraham Lincoln.")

Most important of all, is the view of his biographers, Nicolay and Hay, who were his private secretaries during the war. While Herndon's biography is considered the best from the standpoint of Lincoln's personality, this work by his secretaries is the best in the telling of his public life. It was first published, serially, in the **Century Magazine,** and now appears in 10 large volumes. They were careful not to tell in too strong language that he was an unbeliever. They deny that he was an Atheist, which no one claims he was, but they also deny that he was orthodox.

"We have no purpose of attempting to formulate his creed; we question if he himself ever did so. There have been swift witnesses who, judging from expressions uttered in his callow youth, have called him an Atheist, and others, who, with the most laudable intentions, have remembered improbable conversations which they bring forward to prove at once his orthodoxy and their own intimacy with him." (Chapter on "Lincoln and the Churches.")

It is more than strange that Nicolay and Hay, who were constantly with him, knew nothing of the alleged "conversions."

The Peoples' Library of Information, an old-time work of reference, makes the following statement:

"Lincoln attended service once a day. He seemed to be in agony while in church. . . His pastor, Dr. Gurley, had the 'gift of continuance,' and the President writhed and squirmed and gave unmistakable evidence of the torture he endured."

The Every-Day Life of Lincoln, by Francis F. Brown, confirms Salmon P. Chase's account of the changes in the Emancipation Proclamation. General M. M. Trumbull, a well-known publicist, states, in the **Open Court** for December 3, 1891:

"The religion that begs the patronage of Presidents doubts its own theology, for the true God needs not the favor of men. . . Some of his [Lincoln's] tributes to Deity are merely rhetorical emphasis, but others were not. Cicero often swore 'By Hercules,' as in the oration against Cataline, although he believed no more in Hercules than Abraham Lincoln believed in any church-made God."

The Rev. David Swing, once a popular minister of Chicago, in a sermon on "Washington and Lincoln," has judged the issue in these words:

"It is often lamented by the churchmen that Washington and Lincoln possessed little religion except that found in the

word 'God.' All that can here be affirmed is that what the religion of those two men lacked in theological details it made up
in greatness. Their minds were born with a love of great principles. . . There are few instances in which a mind great enough
to reach great principles in politics has been satisfied with a
fanatical religion. . . It must not be asked for Washington and
Lincoln that, having reached greatness in political principles,
they should have loved littleness in piety."

Another Chicago clergyman, the Rev. Jenkin Lloyd Jones, in a sermon delivered in All Souls Church, on December 9, 1888, said:

"Are there not thousands who have loved virtue who did
not accept Jesus Christ in any supernatural or miraculous
fashion, who, if they knew of him at all, knew of him only as
the Nazarene peasant—the man Jesus. Such was Abraham Lincoln, the tender prophet of the gospel of good will upon earth."

The Rev. John W. Chadwick, the well-known Unitarian minister,
of Brooklyn, N.Y., in an address delivered in Tremont Temple, Boston,
in 1872, upon the proposed "Christian Amendment" to the Constitution,
recognizing the Bible, God, and making Christianity the state religion,
said:

"Of the six men who have done most to make America the
wonder and the joy she is to all of us, not one could be the
citizen of a government so constituted; for Washington, Jefferson and Franklin, certainly the mightiest leaders in our early
history, were heretics in their day, Deists, as men called them;
and Garrison, Lincoln and Sumner, certainly the mightiest in
these later times, would all be disfranchised by the proposed
amendment. . . Lincoln could not have taken the oath of office
had such a clause been in the Constitution."

During February, 1892, the Chicago **Herald** published an editorial
on Lincoln's religion. It is too lengthy to reproduce in full, but I quote
the most important points:

"He was without faith in the Bible or its teachings. On this
point the testimony is so overwhelming that there is no basis
for doubt. In his early life Lincoln exhibited a powerful tendency to aggressive Infidelity. But when he grew to be a politician
he became secretive and non-committal in his religious belief.
He was shrewd enough to realize the necessity of reticence
with the convictions he possessed if he hoped to succeed in
politics."

"So it must be accepted as final by every reasonable mind
that in religion Mr. Lincoln was a skeptic. But above all things
he was not a hypocrite or pretender. He was a plain man,
rugged and earnest, and he pretended to be nothing more. He
believed in humanity, and he was incapable of Phariseeism.
He had great respect for the feelings and convictions of others,
but he was not a sniveler. He was honest and he was sincere,
and taking him simply for what he was, we are not likely soon
to see his like again."

In the **Westminster Review** for September, 1891, Mr. Theodore
Stanton discussed the moral character and religious beliefs of Abraham
Lincoln, and of his religious belief said:

"If Lincoln had lived and died an obscure Springfield
lawyer and politician, he would unquestionably have been
classed by his neighbors among Freethinkers. But, as is cus-
tomary with the Church, whether Roman Catholic or Protestant, when Lincoln became one of the great of the world an

attempt was made to claim him. In trying to arrive at a correct comprehension of Lincoln's theology, this fact should be borne in mind in sifting the testimony. Another very important warping influence which should not be lost sight of was Lincoln's early ambition for political preferment. Now, the shrewd American politician with an elastic conscience joins some Church, and is always seen on Sunday in the front pews. But the shrewd politician who has not an elastic conscience—and this was Lincoln's case—simply keeps mum on his religious views, or, when he must touch on the subject, deals only in platitudes."

In the **Lincoln Memorial Album** there are 200 tributes to Lincoln, most of them from men who were religious. But only two of them undertake to claim him as a Christian believer. In the **Reminiscences of Lincoln** there are 33 articles, all of which are from the pens of distinguished men who knew him. Of these, not one claims him as a believer. In none of the eulogies delivered at the time of his death is it so claimed. The reader may therefore judge for himself.

Abraham Lincoln's Religious Belief as Stated by Himself. Unfortunately, Lincoln, like Washington, neither in speech nor in writing, made a statement of what he believed, nor did he authorize anyone else to do so for him. We are almost entirely dependent upon reports of conversations with his intimate friends, his secretaries and professional associates. If he never made a statement saying that he was a Liberal, a Freethinker, or, as some prefer, an "Infidel," he likewise never made one announcing that he was orthodox, a believer in the divine inspiration of the Bible, and the divinity of Christ. If he were the latter, there is no reason why he should not say so; while if he were the former, he had many reasons for keeping silent, as the majority who hold such views do.

Yet, we can discern in Lincoln's speeches, writings, and conversations, certain sentiments, which would indicate his opinions, the same as a weather-cock tells us the direction the wind is blowing—or, to borrow a phrase from our old friend, Dr. Holland—"We guess at a mountain of marble by the outcropping ledges that hide their whiteness among the ferns." Then, what he did not say, has as important a bearing as what he said. For instance, he never mentions the name of Jesus or Christ, and only once the word immortality, proving that these subjects were not to his mind important. A reader of the Bible, and often quoting it, he never lets slip a word that would cause us to think he believed it to be the word of God. In all well-authenticated conversations with ministers, he is very cautious in his language, and two prominent ministers who knew him, Bishop Simpson and Henry Ward Beecher, do not vouch for his orthodoxy.

Amidst all the verbiage and subterranean reasoning of Dr. Holland, especially in his "Bateman Interview," above all things there stands out the words of Lincoln, "I AM NOT A CHRISTIAN." Then the writer makes him say, "God knows I would be one." Why was he not a Christian, and why could he not "be one"? There can be no answer other than the fact that he did not believe in Christianity's fundamental doctrines.

In 1842, Mr. Lincoln delivered a temperance speech in Springfield, before the Washingtonian Temperance Society.* Mr. Herndon listened to this speech, and comments as follows:

---

*This speech is to be found in full in Nicolay and Hay's collection of Lincoln's writings and speeches.

"In 1842, I heard Mr. Lincoln deliver a speech before the Washingtonian Temperance Society, of this city. . . . He scored the Christians for the position they had taken. He said in that lecture this, 'If they [the Christians] believe, **as they profess**, that Omnipotence condescended to take on himself the form of sinful man,' etc. This was spoken with energy. He scornfully and contemptuously emphasized the words, **as they profess**. The rebuke was as much in the manner of utterance as in the substance of what was said. I heard the criticisms of some of the Christians that night. They said the speech was an outrage."

Here he would not commit himself to a belief in the Atonement. In the same speech, he proved that he did not believe in future rewards and punishments, by the utterance of these words:

"Pleasures to be enjoyed, or pains to be endured, after we are dead and gone, are but little regarded. . . . There is something so ludicrous, in promises of good, or threats of evil, a great way off, as to render the whole subject with which they are connected, easily turned into ridicule. 'Better lay down that spade you are stealing, Paddy, if you don't, you will pay for it at the day of judgment.' 'Be the powers, if ye'll credit me so long I'll just take another.'" **(Lincoln Memorial Album, p. 91.)**

Lincoln was a fatalist. He believed that what must be will be, and no prayers can change it. "I have all my life been a fatalist, What is to be will be; or rather, I have found all my life, as Hamlet says:

'There's a divinity that shapes our ends,
Rough-hew them how we may.'"
(Everyday Life of Lincoln, p. 198.)

Regarding eternal punishment, he said: "If God be a just God, all will be saved or none." **(Manford's Magazine.)** In this connection he was fond of repeating the epitaph on the Kickapoo Indian, Johnnie Kongapod:

"Here lies poor Johnnie Kongapod;
Have mercy on him, gracious God,
As he would do if he were God
And you were Johnnie Kongapod."

In a speech delivered in Kansas, in 1856, he gave his views on Providence: "Friends, I agree with you in Providence; but I believe in the Providence of the most men, the largest purse, and the longest cannon." **(Lincoln's Speeches, p. 140.)**

Regarding the Churches he said: "The United States government must not undertake to run the Churches. When an individual, in the Church or out of it, becomes dangerous to the public interest he must be checked." In an order relating to a church in Memphis, Tennessee, issued on May 13, 1864, he said: "If there is no military need for the building, leave it alone, neither putting anyone in or out of it, except on finding some one preaching or practicing treason, in which case lay hands on him, just as if he were doing the same thing in any other building." (Nicolay and Hay, Chapter on "Lincoln and the Churches.")

In the same chapter Nicolay and Hay state that in order to prevent treasonable preaching, Secretary Stanton appointed Bishop Ames, of the Methodist Church, to be supervisor of all the Churches in a certain southern district. President Lincoln at once countermanded the order.

In a speech at Springfield, in 1857, Lincoln gave the Churches a thrust, in speaking of the Negro: "All the powers of the earth seem rapidly combining against him. Mammon is after him. . . . and the theology of the day is fast joining in the cry." (**Lincoln Memorial Album**, p. 100.)

In a letter (quoted at the beginning of this chapter) Lincoln wrote to Martin M. Morris, on March 26, 1843, he said he had been accused of not belonging to any Church, of being a Deist, and that people ought not to vote for him for these reasons, and that he never denied the charge. We have noted his reply to the delegation of Chicago ministers, and to the woman Quaker preacher (all of whom came to him with a message from God), in which he said he wondered why, if God had a message for him, the message was not delivered to him personally, instead of by an intermediary.

In his famous temperance address, Lincoln used the following language: "Happy day, when, all appetites controlled, all passions subdued, all matter subjugated, mind, all conquering mind, shall live and move, the monarch of the world! Glorious consummation! Hail, fall of fury! Reign of Reason, all hail!" (**Lincoln Memorial Album**, p. 96.)

Curtis says:

> "Abraham Lincoln's belief was clear and fixed so far as it went, but he rejected important dogmas which are essential to salvation by some of the evangelical denominations. 'Whenever any Church will inscribe over its altar as a qualification for membership the Saviour's statement of the substance of the law and the gospel, "Thou shalt love the Lord thy God with all thy heart, and with all thy soul, and with all thy mind, and thy neighbor as thyself," that Church will I join with all my heart and soul.'" (**Abraham Lincoln**, p. 375.)

Most important of all was Lincoln's statement of his idea of God and his manner of ruling the Universe, made in 1862, and intended for no eye but his own. It is to be found in the 14th edition of the **Encyclopedia Britannica**, article, "Abraham Lincoln," and in Curtis' work, p. 375:

> "The will of God prevails. In great contests each party claims to act in accordance with the will of God. Both may be, and one must be, wrong. God cannot be for and against the same thing at the same time. In the present civil war it is quite possible that God's purpose is something different from the purpose of either party; and yet, the human instrumentalities, working just as they do, are the best adaptations to effect his purposes. I am almost ready to say that this is probably true; that God wills this contest, and wills that it shall not end yet. By his mere great power in the minds of the now contestants, he could have either saved or destroyed the Union without a human contest. Yet the contest began. And having begun, he could give the final victory to either side any day. Yet the contest continues."

Herndon said he had often heard Lincoln remark that his creed was the same as that of an old man in Indiana, who, in experience meetings, made the following profession of faith: "When I do good, I feel good, and when I do bad I feel bad; and that's my religion." Mrs. Lincoln quotes him as saying: "What is to be will be, and no prayers of ours can arrest the decree." In **Manford's Magazine**, he is quoted as saying, with a twinkle in his eye: "It will not do to investigate the subject of religion too closely, as it is apt to lead to Infidelity."

Dr. C. H. Ray, at one time editor of the **Chicago Tribune**, said that Lincoln held substantially the same religious views as Theodore Parker.

Jesse W. Fell said: "No religious views with him seemed to find any favor, except of the practical and rationalistic order; and if, from my recollections on this subject, I was called upon to designate an author whose views nearly represented Mr. Lincoln's on this subject, I would say that author was Theodore Parker."

Herndon said that Lincoln's favorites were Parker and Thomas Paine. The Rev. Dr. Collyer said that Lincoln, seeing a copy of Parker's sermons on a table, remarked: "I think I stand where that man stands." The views of Theodore Parker are represented by the following extracts from his writings and sermons:

"To obtain a knowledge of duty, a man is not sent away, outside of himself, to ancient documents; for the only rule of faith and practice, the Word, is very nigh him, even in his heart, and by this word he is to try all documents."

"There is no intercessor, angel, mediator, between man and God; for man can speak and God hear, each for himself. He requires no advocates to plead for men."

"Manly natural religion—it is not joining the Church; it is not to believe in a creed, Hebrew, Protestant, Catholic, Trinitarian, Unitarian, Nothingarian. It is not to keep Sunday idle; to attend meetings; to be wet with water; to read the Bible; to offer prayers in words; to take bread and wine in the meeting house; love a scape-goat Jesus, or any other theological clap-trap."

Or in the words of another whose writings Lincoln loved—Thomas Paine: "The world was his country, to do good was his religion."

Had Abraham Lincoln died as an obscure Springfield lawyer and politician; had he advanced no further in political preferment than his one term in Congress, nothing would have ever been said about his being a believer in orthodox religion. But when a man becomes prominent and reaches the highest place in the gift of the nation, and in addition becomes a hero and a martyr, he is idealized. His virtues are exaggerated and his faults extenuated. Regardless of his real religious views, the ministers laud him as an orthodox believer and shining exemplar of Christianity. In time this passes as history, unless it is vigorously contradicted. If a man is a good man, they hold that he must have been a Christian. They likewise say that no bad man can possibly be one.

A possibly parallel case is that of Robert G. Ingersoll Had this great orator kept his agnostic views under a bushel, never delivered a Freethought lecture, and, like Lincoln, never talked upon the subject except to his intimate friends; had he attended church occasionally, as did Lincoln, flattered the ministers and contributed to the funds for the support of the church, he probably would have been President of the United States. Then, an orthodox minister would have preached his funeral sermon and those ministers who so vociferously denounced him as an "Infidel" would, with great pride and gusto, have exalted him as a Christian, just as they have Lincoln. They would have said, as they have said of Lincoln, that it was impossible that he could have been an "Infidel." Public opinion would have sustained them from the fact that it was well known that Ingersoll practiced all the virtues that ministers ascribe to Christianity. While there was some difference in the beliefs of these two great men, the truth is that Lincoln was no more an orthodox Christian than was Ingersoll.

I have given the facts about Lincoln's beliefs and the controversy that grew out of them. The amount of space devoted to Washington and Lincoln in this work is a natural result of their importance and of my desire to give a complete, fair, and accurate summary of their religious beliefs, in contrast to the distorted and mythical account, fostered by the clergy, which erroneously claims these two great Americans as orthodox Christians.

CHAPTER IX

JAMES ABRAM GARFIELD, THE PREACHER PRESIDENT

Born, November 19, 1831. Died, September 19, 1881. President, March 4, 1881—September 19, 1881.

Not many persons remember that we have had a "preacher President," and many writers do not mention the fact that James A. Garfield, the 20th chief executive, preached the gospel when he was a young man. This, perhaps, is due not only to his abandonment of the ministry, but to a large extent the doctrines of the Church in which he preached.

His parents, Abram and Eliza Garfield, were members of the "Disciples," or, as they insisted upon calling themselves, "The Christian Church." This organization was established during the first quarter of the 19th Century by Thomas and Alexander Campbell, father and son, who had emigrated to western Pennsylvania from Ireland, having been originally Presbyterians. This occasioned their followers to be called "Campbellites" by their enemies.

The new Church proclaimed among its chief tenets, "No Creed but the Bible," and baptism exclusively by immersion; but they little thought that in setting forth these two principal doctrines they were in fact setting up a new creed themselves. The members of this Church declaimed strongly against sectarianism, which was the basis of their indictment of the other Churches; yet, in taking the positions they occupied, and holding that none was a real Christian who did not accept their interpretation of the Bible, they themselves became a sect.

Today, the Disciples Church embraces a variety of theological opinions. Among its ministers in the Northern States are many modernists, who accept the conclusions of science and modern Biblical criticism. In the South, they are, for the most part, Fundamentalists, and their "creed" is the Bible as interpreted by the late William Jennings Bryan. In October, 1930, "The Churches of Christ" held a "World Convention," in Washington, D.C., where James A. Garfield's one-time connection with the denomination was extensively exploited and publicised.

President Garfield's parents were farmers. The death of his father, in 1833, made it necessary for the future President to begin work at an early age. He was successful in his ambition to obtain an education, and he began his career as a school teacher. Being converted, he also began to preach. The Disciples Church had no ordained ministry in the same sense as have the other denominations. Any man of ability and character whom the brethren cared to listen to, was permitted to point out the way of salvation. Garfield was very popular as a minister, and his relatives and friends hoped that he would become a famous preacher.

Garfield had attended Hiram College, located in a town of the same name in northeastern Ohio, but had not completed his education. He thought of finishing at Bethany College, in Virginia, the leading institution of the Church and presided over by its founder, Alexander Campbell. Upon paying it a visit, he decided otherwise. The locality was pro-slavery, and Mr. Campbell was a defender of slavery on Biblical grounds. Garfield decided to attend Williams College, located at Williamstown, Mass., where, after spending two years, he was graduated, in 1856.

He returned to Hiram, and was made the president of Hiram College. Here occurred the turning point of his career, which included his abandonment of the ministry. A "Campbellite" minister was looked upon as out of his element unless he was in a dispute with some other cleric and Garfield had held a number of discussions on mooted theological questions. In the neighborhood were a large number of Spiritualists. A noted Spiritualist lecturer of that time was William Denton (not John Denton, as Garfield's biographer, Theodore Clark Smith, says). An Englishman, he had been in America about nine years, was not only a Spiritualist, but a lecturer upon geology and other departments of science.

From December 27 to 31, 1858, Professors Garfield and Denton debated, in Chagrin Falls, Ohio, this proposition, of which the first took the negative and the second the affirmative: "Man, animals and vegetables came into existence by the operation of spontaneous generation, and progressive development, and there is no evidence that there was any exertion of direct creative power on this planet." The year following this debate (1859), Charles Darwin published **The Origin of Species**, a book that sustained the position of Prof. Denton; Mr. Garfield gave up the ministry, became a lawyer, for which career he had long been preparing himself, entered politics, and was elected to the Ohio State senate. In the debate with Denton, he had alarmed his friends by admitting that the earth had existed "for millions of years," quite contrary to the then almost universally accepted doctrine of creation as taught in the Bible.

The debate was a means of further stimulating Garfield's interest in geology, as well as in the other sciences, and when he took his seat in the senate of Ohio he drew up with his own hand a committee report upon the geology of the State. Ridpath says: "It is a state document of high order, revealing a scientific knowledge and a power to group statistics and render them effective, which would be looked at with wide-eyed wonder by the modern state legislator."

Garfield's opponent, Professor Denton, became distinguished as a geological writer and lecturer, and for many years he was employed by railroads and mining companies in the United States and Canada, at large salaries. He outlived Garfield by almost two years, dying of fever while on an exploring expedition in New Guinea, on August 26, 1883.

While he was at Williams College, it appears that Garfield definitely decided to quit the ministry. (See Smith's **Life and Letters of James A. Garfield**, pp. 102-103.) Ridpath quotes him as saying, in 1859:

"The desire of brethren to have me preach and teach for them, a desire to do good in all ways I could, and to earn in noble callings, something to pay my way through a course of study, and to discharge debts, and the discipline and cultivation of mind in preaching and teaching, and the exalted topics for investigation in preaching and teaching, have led me into both callings. I have never intended to devote my life to either or both; although lately Providence seemed to be hedging my way and crowding me into the ministry. I have always intended to be a lawyer, and perhaps to enter political life. Such has been my secret ambition ever since I thought of such things. I have been reading law for some time." (**Life and Work of Garfield**, p. 82.)

He became dissatisfied with his Church while at Williams College, and wrote from there: "I think our brethren are proverbial for their lack of spirituality, and personal piety, and I am somewhat almost

discouraged in regard to the Reformation, and doubt whether there
has much been gained by it." (Smith, pp. 101-102.)

The **Program** of the "World Convention," p. 12, makes this statement concerning Garfield:

"Faith in Christ and the eternal God was the central fact
of his life. Not as a politician or statesman or soldier did he
influence his nation most but as a Chrstian. He has been the
only Preacher President the United States has ever had. Interesting stories are told of his faithfulness to the services in
the humble frame meeting house while living in Washington."

This, as well as a number of other assertions in the **Program**, seems
to be more for effect than as a statement of fact, at least after President Garfield reached middle life. Smith says (vol. 2, p. 773):

"In 1872, he read James Freeman Clarke's **Ten Great Religions** and said of it: 'It is admirably written in a liberal and
philosophical spirit and I am sure it will interest you. What I
have read of it leads me to believe that we have taken too
narrow a view of religion. The absolute truths of religion of
course must be as old as the race, and such books as this of
Clarke's widen our horizon and make us more liberal.' "

On February 29, 1876, he went to a Unitarian church and heard a
sermon by Mr. Clarke. He commented, "I have not been so much instructed by a sermon in a long time. It was so free from cant and
hypercriticism and was was full of instruction." (Smith, p. 775.) It was
a long mental journey from the teachings of Alexander Campbell, in
which Garfield had been reared, and which in youth he preached himself, to Unitarianism, even as preached by so conservative a Unitarian
minister as James Freeman Clarke.

The "First World Convention Churches of Christ" **Program** (p. 8)
quotes James G. Blaine, in his eulogy of Garfield before the United
States Senate, as saying of him, "His Church was to him the gate of
heaven." Unfortunately for this statement, Blaine does not later represent Garfield as believing that heaven is so small a place as to need
no more than one gate. Mr. Blaine said:

"The religious element in Garfield's character was deep and
earnest. In his early youth he espoused the faith of the Disciples, a sect of that great Baptist communion, which in different ecclesiastical establishments is so numerous and influential throughout all parts of the United States. But the broad-
ening tendency of his mind and his active spirit of inquiry were
early apparent, and carried him beyond the dogmas of sect and
the restraints of association. The liberal tendency which he an-
ticipated as the result of wider culture was fully realized. He
was emancipated from mere sectarian belief, and with eager
interest pushed his investigations in the direction of modern
progressive thought. He followed with quickening step in the
paths of exploration and speculation so fearlessly trodden by
Darwin, by Huxley, by Tyndall and by other living scientists of
the radical and advanced type. The lines of his friendship and
his confidence encircled men of every creed, and men of no
creed, and to the end of his life, on his ever lengthening list
of friends, were to be found the names of a pious Catholic
priest and of an honest, high-minded and generous-hearted
Freethinker." (**Eulogy of Garfield,** by James G. Blaine.)

Blaine, one of Garfield's intimate friends, has here stated the
truth. Starting out a religious sectarian, President Garfield ended a
religious liberal, holding all Churches in respect, but not holding

rigidly to the doctrines of any. It is not known that he ever withdrew from the Disciples Church, which, being congregational in government and doctrine, is not overzealous in hunting out heresy.

President Garfield was an uncompromising advocate of absolute separation of Church and State, and a firm believer in the justice of taxing the Churches. On June 22, 1874, he said in Congress:

"The divorce between Church and State ought to be absolute. It ought to be so absolute that no Church property anywhere, in any State, or in the nation, should be exempt from equal taxation; for if you exempt the property of any Church organization, to that extent you impose a tax upon the whole community."

President Garfield was shot by an assassin, Guiteau, who, after his arrest, said, "he had tried to destroy the President wholly and solely for the good of the country, and at the command of God," and "had been influenced only by high and patriotic motives." (Ridpath, **Life of James A. Garfield,** p. 530.) Garfield's patience under the 10 weeks of intense suffering which preceded his death aroused not only the sympathy but the admiration of all. His old mother, when informed of his death, remarked, "If he had to die, why didn't God take him without all the terrible suffering he endured?" This is one of the questions involving "the ways of God to man," which has often been asked, but never answered.

CHAPTER X

WILLIAM McKINLEY, THE METHODIST PRESIDENT
Born, January 29, 1843. Died, September 14, 1901. President, March 4, 1897—September 14, 1901.

Nothwithstanding the fact that three others have been claimed as Methodist Presidents, only William McKinley professed the faith and was a communicant in that Church. Johnson, Grant and Hayes were Methodists only in their wives' names. President McKinley came from a Methodist family, his father and mother, as well as his brothers and sisters, being members of that Church. The future President was converted as a youth, during a camp meeting at Poland, Ohio, the home of his family. When the Civil War began, he entered the Union Army, served with honor, and left the service with the rank of major. Upon returning to civil life, he became a lawyer and settled in Canton, Ohio, where he married Miss Ida Saxton, daughter of a Canton banker, and also a Methodist.

At all times Mr. and Mrs. McKinley were constant in their devotion to the Church of their choice. When the question of the future of the Philippine Islands arose, there was great difference of opinion among U.S. statesmen. President McKinley, like a true Methodist, carried the problem to God, in prayer, and in an address to his fellow Methodists used this language:

"I walked the floor of the White House night after night, and I am not ashamed to tell you, gentlemen, that I went down on my knees and prayed Almighty God for guidance more than one night. And one night late it came to me in this way— I don't know how it was, but it came—There was nothing left for us to do but to take them all, and to educate the Filipinos, and uplift and Christianize them, and by God's grace to do the very best we could for them as our fellowmen for whom Christ died. And then I went to bed, and went to sleep and slept soundly."

When a man talks in this manner we know he is truly religious.

In the White House, however, no pretense was made of carrying into practice the Discipline of the Methodist Church. Wine was served at state dinners as before. For this practice, some of the brethren favored calling President and Mrs. McKinley before the Church for rebuke.

The Vice President during Roosevelt's second term was Charles W. Fairbanks, also a Methodist. Mr. Fairbanks sought the nomination for President in 1904. When it became known that at a dinner given to his friends cocktails were served, the might of the Methodist Church was hurled against him. President McKinley was more fortunate in escaping the result of what his Church considered moral turpitude.

The Methodist Church not only makes it an offense to manufacture or sell liquor, or serve it in the home, but also forbids members of the Church to rent property to dealers in liquor. It was charged that a store in a block in Canton owned by Mrs. McKinley was rented for saloon purposes. Yet while the Methodist Church stood for temperance and prohibition it kept at all times one eye turned politically on the Republican party in the North and on the Democratic party in the South.

In the last year of the 19th Century, however, the Methodists were not so strong nor so well organized as they are today. They did not then have a "Board," North and South, nor did they have lobby headquarters within the shadow of the capitol, "strategically" situated, as they stated when they built it, to dictate to Congressmen and hold them in line. They had to be circumspect until they were strong enough to be masters. In 1899 it would not do to offend the party, so the New York **Christian Advocate**, the leading church paper in the North, whose editor, the Rev. J. M. Buckley, was notorious as a Republican politician, patched the trouble up for the McKinleys. He asserted that the Canton building had been leased to third parties, who sub-rented it; hence, President and Mrs. McKinley were not responsible for the existence of the saloon.

This explanation, however, did not satisfy the **New York Voice**, the organ of the third party Prohibitionists, who never ceased to oppose President McKinley, nor to denounce him as a traitor to the cause of temperance and a violator of the Discipline of his Church.

Once, they accused President McKinley wrongfully. There was at that time in Washington a "Reform Bureau," headed by the Rev. Wilbur F. Crafts, one of the professional "reformers," of whom then, as now, there were many. This man circulated a story that while President McKinley was consulting with prominent members of Congress in the "President's room" of the Capitol, bottles of wine were brought in, and all present indulged in the tempting beverage. It was a false charge, as the bottles contained mineral water.

While McKinley did not take the highest rank among our statesmen, he was an admirable man personally, loved by all, and his assassination by the degenerate Czolgosz was a shock to the nation, and to the world.

CHAPTER XI

THEODORE ROOSEVELT, DUTCH REFORMED CHURCH, BUT NOT VERY RELIGIOUS

Born, October 27, 1858. Died, January 6, 1919. President, September 14, 1901—March 4, 1909.

President Roosevelt's parents were members of the Dutch Reformed Church. They maintained the old custom of family prayer, which the father conducted in the morning and the mother in the evening. Theodore Roosevelt's mother was Southern-born, and sympathized with the South during the rebellion, while his father favored the Northern cause. Theodore, who, at this time, was an active little lad, often shocked his mother by praying vociferously for the success of the Union armies. He attended Sunday School regularly, and, as a young man, taught a class in a mission Sunday School himself. As Mrs. Roosevelt informs us, he was a member and communicant of the Dutch Reformed Church, but he was never zealous in his religion. His writings and speeches are singularly free from references to God, Heaven, immortality, and other sentiments of which a religious writer generally makes much. Gamaliel Bradford, in **Harper's Magazine**, February, 1931, says:

> "I cannot find God insistent or palpable anywhere in the life or writings of Theodore Roosevelt. . . Whole books have been written about Roosevelt's religion.* To me they simply prove that he did not have any. He had a profound sense of conduct in this world, or morals."

This sentiment is in accordance with Roosevelt's own views, which he expressed as follows: "I know not how philosophy may define religion; but from Micah to James it has been defined as service to one's fellowman rendered by following the great rule of justice and mercy, of wisdom and righteousness."

But this, from the standpoint of the orthodox Church to which he belonged, is not religion, but morality; which, as taught by all orthodox Churches, is not, by itself, sufficient for salvation. While President Roosevelt had read Micah and James, he payed no attention to Paul, upon whose teachings Protestant orthodoxy is built.

Regarding the future, Bishop, in his **Life of Theodore Roosevelt**, quotes him as saying: "It is idle to complain or rail at the inevitable; serene and high of heart we must face our fate and go down into the darkness." This philosophy resembles that of an ancient Stoic, or it might be the condition of those whom Paul described as "without God or without hope in the world." Certainly such sentiments are not in accord with the creed of the Church to which he belonged, except that they might be interpreted as Calvinistic. Theodore Roosevelt probably clung to the Church in which he was born, like thousands of others, regardless of their later opinions. Too, membership in any Church "squares" a politician with political-ecclesiastical forces and prevents them from barking at his heels.

One of Roosevelt's official acts while he was President gave great

---

*One book of the character to which Mr. Bradford refers is by the Rev. Christian F. Reisner.

offense to the Churches and the ministers. He ordered the inscription
"In God we trust" taken off the coins. This pious sentiment had not
appeared on our coins until 1864, when it was introduced by Salmon
P. Chase, then Secretary of the Treasury. There was no law authorizing
it. But so great was the uproar at its removal, that Congress immediately restored the inscription.

In one respect, however, we might believe President Roosevelt to
have been religious, and an old type of religionist, at that. This view
gains support from the statements he made concerning Thomas Paine,
in his **Life of Gouverneur Morris** (1888), written when he was not
quite 30.

Poor Paine! He was obliged to suffer the unwarranted abuse of four
generations of Americans! Historians either ignored him altogether, or
referred to him as a drunkard or a reprobate. Ministers exhausted the
vocabulary of the English language in telling of his wickedness, what
harm he had done in the world, and how he died recanting, surrounded
by a legion of devils. Of course, all this is as fabulous as the story of
Washington, the cherry tree and the little hatchet, yet for 80 years,
in spite of the fact that evidence of its falsehood was available, this
myth was accepted by the religious community as gospel truth. Only
10 years after Paine's death, William Cobbett, the English writer, chased
out of New York City the originator of this lie, who was threatened with
charges of fraud and forgery.

However, these vilifiers of Paine overreached themselves. Thoughtful persons became interested in seeking to learn the truth about this
man, who had been painted as the incarnation of all evil, the em-
bodiment of his Satanic majesty on earth. It began to appear that
this thunderous abuse of Paine might be traced to representatives of the interests he had attacked in his writings. And the
horror that was expressed at his writings by those who had never
read them! In England, houses were searched for his books. Should
the constable find any, he used them for a bon-fire in the public square.
The constable of Bolton, after searching the place, reported to his
superiors that he had found "no reason, no rights of man nor no common sense in town."

Of the last of the historians worthy of notice who have spoken
disparagingly of Thomas Paine, we must mention John Bach McMasters.
In his **History of the People of the United States**, published in 1883,
he revamps all the old, exploded myths told of Paine. He gives as his
authority the **Life of Thomas Paine**, by James Cheetham, which, in
addition to being malignant, is no more truthful than Weem's **Life of
Washington**. Cheetham was Paine's mortal enemy, and vented his
malice by writing a mendacious biography of his foe, after Paine's
death.

An historian of the standing of Professor McMasters should have
known that Cheetham was found guilty and fined in a New York court
for statements, made in this biography, which reflected on a third
person. Dr. J. W. Francis, who knew both Paine and Cheetham, says:

> "Cheetham, who with settled malignity wrote the life of
> Paine, felt little desire to extenuate any of the faults of Paine's
> character. I have a suspicion that sinister motives of a po-
> litical nature were not overlooked by the biographer." (**Old
> New York**, p. 142.)

Dr. Francis shows that Cheetham, in a like manner, libeled Aaron
Burr, Alexander Hamilton and DeWitt Clinton. Yet, for 80 years so
great was the antagonism of our forefathers toward the very name
of Paine that one's moral standing and social position were in danger
if one uttered a word in his defense.

Professor John Fiske, as a critic of Paine, was of a different type than Professor McMasters. His works have been of geat value in promoting the rationalistic spirit in the United States, but when he speaks of Paine, while not showing the malignity and bad temper of certain other writers, he proves himself to have had only a superficial knowledge of Paine and his writings.

In 1892, G. P. Putnam's Sons published the first authentic **Life of Thomas Paine**, by Moncure D. Conway, who had spent years in the preparation of this book. All former biographies had been merely eulogies by his friends or denunciations by his enemies.

While Conway was the minister of a Unitarian church in Cincinnati, in 1860, he startled the country by preaching a sermon in which he refuted the fashionable falsehoods told about Paine. In writing this biography, Conway was careful to seek information from original sources, in England, France and America. The house of Putnam advanced $5,000 to aid his research.

While Robert G. Ingersoll, in 1877, had challenged the Presbyterian weekly, the **New York Observer**, with an offer of $1,000 if it was successful in proving the common sermon and tract stories told for years about Paine, and the editor admitted he could not do so, Dr. Conway, by irrefutable evidence, exposed them all, and proved all of them to be false. Here was opened a new era in the estimate of Thomas Paine. All writers, even religious ones, dealing with him since 1892 have modified their statements and opinions.

In 1896, in Washington, D.C., I heard read, before a meeting of the Daughters of the American Revolution, a paper eulogizing Thomas Paine. This would have been impossible 10 years earlier. Now Paine is given just treatment in all reputable histories, of which might be cited as examples, Tyler's **Literature of the Revolution**, and Woodrow Wilson's **History of the American People**. These works are antidotes to the slanderous books of McMasters and Roosevelt.

It is now conceded that an intelligent understanding of the great events of the last quarter of the 18th Century is impossible without a knowledge of the life and writings of Thomas Paine. To repeat the old slanders of our forefathers today is only evidence of ignorance or malignity. Roosevelt's book was published in 1888, four years before Dr. Conway provided the world with the facts regarding Paine. Yet, had Roosevelt had any authentic knowledge of Paine, he would never have written the following passage:

> "When, however, his [Morris'] foes were of sufficient importance to warrant his paying attention to them individually, Morris proved abundantly able to take care of himself, and to deal heavier blows than he received. This was shown in the controversy which convulsed Congress over the conduct of Silas Deane, the original envoy to France. Deane did not behave very well, but at first he was more sinned against than sinning, and Morris took up his cause warmly. Thomas Paine, the famous author of **Common Sense**, who was Secretary of the Committee of Foreign Affairs, attacked Deane and his defenders, as well as the court of France, with peculiar venom, using as weapons the secrets he became acquainted with through his official position, and which he was in honor bound not to divulge. For this, Morris had him removed from his Secretaryship, and in the debate handled him extremely roughly, characterizing him with contemptuous severity as 'a mere adventurer from England ignorant even of grammar,' and ridiculing his pretensions of importance. Paine was an adept in the art of invective; but he came out second best in this encounter, and never forgot

or forgave his antagonist." (**Life of Gouverneur Morris**, pp. 93-94.)

The following comment of Roosevelt is even less excusable: "One man had a very narrow escape. This was Thomas Paine, the Englishman, who had at one time rendered such striking service to the cause of American independence, while the rest of his life had been as ignoble as it was varied. He had been elected to the Convention, and having sided with the Gironde, was thrown into prison by the Jacobins. He at once asked Morris to demand him as an American citizen; a title to which he of course had no claim. Morris refused to interfere too actively, judging rightly that Paine would be saved by his own insignificance and would serve his own interest best by keeping still. So the filthy little Atheist had to stay in prison, 'where he amused himself with publishing a pamphlet against Jesus Christ.' "

Without intending any sarcasm, I shall here quote what Roosevelt himself said, in **The History of Literature**: "The great historian, if the facts will permit him, will put before us the men and women as they actually lived, so that we shall recognize them for what they were—living beings."

The first quotation contains two misstatements of fact. First, when Roosevelt accuses Paine of "using as weapons the secrets he became acquainted with through his official position, and which he was in honor bound not to divulge." The truth was that Paine was not required by his oath to keep secret anything except "**that which he shall be directed to keep secret.**" The information he gave to the public was not information he received through his official position, but information he obtained independently of it.

It would have been enlightening had Roosevelt read Paine's eleventh **Crisis**, or been in possession of the information later published in chapters nine and 10 of Dr. Conway's **Life of Paine**, published four years later. There he would have learned that Silas Deane not only made false pretenses, but that he had joined with the French minister in Philadelphia, M. Gerard, in demanding payment for supplies from France (which were to be a free gift) shipped to America in three vessels, two of which never arrived, but were captured by the British. Gerard had tried to purchase the service of Paine's pen, but failed to obtain it. Deane afterwards returned to England, where he was born, and became the friend of Benedict Arnold. His loyalty and honesty have always been called in question, and even Roosevelt does not wholly vouch for them. The hostility to Paine was due to there being a party in Congress that favored Deane, at the head of which was Gouverneur Morris.

This brings us to Roosevelt's second misstatement, that "Morris had him [Paine] discharged from his Secretaryship." He was not discharged by Morris, nor by anyone else. Congress, at Morris' instigation, made three attempts to discharge him, but failed. Then Paine, in disgust because Congress would not listen to his side of the question, resigned; but he did appeal to the people and set the facts before them, after which he was appointed clerk of the Pennsylvania Assembly.

The second quotation from Roosevelt's book is more grossly mendacious than is the first. While admitting Paine's "striking services to the cause of American independence," Roosevelt again displays his want of knowledge, and his inherited and acquired prejudice, when he says of Paine, "the rest of his life had been as ignoble as it was varied." No reputable historian of the present day would have written such a thing. When, in speaking of Paine's American citizenship, Roosevelt says that it was "a title to which, of course, he had no claim," he is guilty of another gross error. Paine was made an American citizen by the same law that made citizens of all foreigners who resided in this country at the close of the Revolution. Morris professed to have claimed Paine's release as an American citizen, but denied that on this ground his release could be effected. Here Mr. Roosevelt places his hero in an unenviable position by making him tell a falsehood at one time or the other, either when he said he claimed Paine as a citizen of the United States, or when he said that this claim was not valid. Paine's citizenship in France was merely honorary, like the French citizenship of Washington, Hamilton, and other prominent Americans.

All this becomes apparent when James Monroe, Morris' successor, did claim Paine as an American, and secured his immediate release. This fact is of itself a sufficient answer to Roosevelt, even were there no other. For his intrigues with England while representing America in France, Morris was obliged to escape from the country through Switzerland, and had he been found he, too, would have gone to prison, and neither his American citizenship, nor his office as American ambassador would have saved him.

All these facts are fully set forth in Conway's **Life of Paine**, chapters 29-35.

Sir Leslie Stephen, the English author, in his **History of English Thought in the 18th Century**, spoke disparagingly of Paine, repeating the old slanders of Cheetham and Oldys, the only books dealing with Paine's life at that time in the British Museum. Stephen's attention was called to his errors, and he apologized in the following words: "The account I gave of Paine, was, I have no doubt, erroneous. My only excuse, if it be an excuse, was the old one, 'pure ignorance.' " In August, 1893, Sir Leslie made amends by writing an article for **The Fortnightly Review**, in which he did justice to Paine.

But Roosevelt would never apologize nor even acknowledge his errors regarding the man who was, as much as any other, responsible for the existence of the U.S. government. Once he acknowledged the receipt of a letter calling his attention to them. It is said on another occasion that he admitted his mistake in private and expressed regret for making it; but when a delegation of people of prominence called upon him at the White House to interview him on the subject, he refused to receive them.

As a means of understanding the psychology of President Roosevelt, so far as it prevented him from acknowledging this mistake, as well as others, we will not quote one of his enemies, but one of his warmest friends, David E. Barry, who, in **Forty Years in Washington** (pp. 282-283), says:

"There was one weak spot in Mr. Roosevelt's character, not perhaps the only one, but it stood out prominently in all its ugliness against the background of his impeccable shield of honesty, courage, and high-minded lofty intelligence. Once he had convinced himself or allowed others to convince him that a man had acted an unworthy or discreditable part, he would at once withdraw his support and friendship from that man, often without giving him an adequate opportunity to explain and justify his conduct. The President's stubbornness and obstinacy in these cases were the cause of chagrin to his friends and supporters, who simply could not understand this peculiar weakness of the President's mind."

CHAPTER XII

THE BELIEFS OF OUR "PROSPERITY" PRESIDENTS

WARREN GAMALIEL HARDING
**Born, November 2, 1865. Died, August 2, 1923. President,
March 4, 1921—August 2, 1923.**

Warren Gamaliel Harding, the 29th President of the United States,
was born on a farm in Morrow County, Ohio. As a youth he worked on
farms and on the construction force of the Ohio Central Railroad.
He attended Central College, at Iberia, Ohio, where his scholastic record
was excellent. His experience as editor of the college paper gave him
a love for newspaper work, which impelled him to learn the printing
trade. He also acquired knowledge of press work. With this equipment
he became a reporter and afterwards an editorial writer on the Marion
(Ohio) **Daily Star**. In 1884 he purchased this journal and in time
made it one of the best and most influential newspapers in the State
of Ohio. He was a good editor, an excellent businessman, and was
connected with many corporations.

Harding entered Republican politics, as a member of the Ohio
State Senate (1900-1904), from which time his rise in the political
world was rapid. From 1904 until 1906 he was lieutenant-governor of
the State, but in 1910 he was, owing to internal party dissentions, defeated in his race for the governorship. In 1914 he was elected to
the U.S. Senate. In the Senate, Harding was a member of many important committees and took a prominent part in the debate on the
Versailles treaty. He was a strong advocate of the United States' entering the war, but at its close opposed our entrance into the League
of Nations.

On June 8, 1920, he was nominated for the Presidency, by the Republican party in convention at Chicago, and was elected by a larger
plurality than had ever before been received by a candidate. He did
not, however, live to complete his term. In July, 1932, he made a journey
to Alaska, the first President ever to visit that American possession.
He also stopped at Vancouver, B.C., thus becoming the first President
to visit Canada during his term of office.

While Harding was traveling in Oregon, the news flashed across
the country that he was ill with ptomaine poisoning. He died suddenly,
in San Francisco, on August 2, 1923. President Harding was a member of the Baptist Church, which he once said was the most liberal
Church in the world.

CALVIN COOLIDGE
**Born, July 4, 1872. Died, January 5, 1933. President,
August 2, 1923—March 4, 1929.**

President Coolidge was the sixth President of the United States to
take office through the death of a predecessor. Of these six, only he and
Theodore Roosevelt were elected to terms in their own right.

Calvin Coolidge was born at Plymouth, Vt., on July 4, 1872. In 1895,
he was graduated from Amherst College, and in 1897 he entered the
practice of law, at Northampton, Mass., where he also entered politics, becoming a member of the city council, in 1899. Later, he was city
solicitor, 1900-1901; clerk of court, 1904; member of the Massachusetts
house of representatives, 1907-1908; mayor of Northampton, 1910-1911;

member of the State senate, 1912-1915; and lieutenant–governor, 1916-1918; governor of Massachusetts, 1919–1920. Coolidge first brought himself to national attention by the vigorous manner in which he dealt with the Boston police strike, which occurred during his term as governor.

At the Republican national convention, in 1920, Coolidge was nominated for the Vice Presidency, as the running-mate of Warren G. Harding. On the death of President Harding, August 2, 1923, he succeeded to the Presidency. Prior to this time, Coolidge was not a member of any Church, but after he became President, he joined the Congregationalist denomination.

HERBERT CLARK HOOVER

Born, August 10, 1874. President, March 4, 1929—March 4, 1933.

Herbert Clark Hoover was born at West Branch, Iowa, of pre-Revolutionary Quaker ancestry. He was the first President of the United States to be born West of the Mississippi River. Herbert's mother died when he was a child, and he was taken by his maternal uncle, John Menthorn, of Newburg, Oregon, where Mr. Menthorn established a Quaker academy, which young Hoover attended.

In Salem, the capital of the State, he became acquainted with a civil engineer, who urged him to prepare himself for the profession. Young Hoover followed this advice, and entered Stanford University, from which he was graduated in 1895. His subsequent career as a promotor and exploiter of mining properties was highly successful, and he spent many years abroad.

When the World War began, in 1914, Hoover was in Europe. At the request of Walter Hines Page, U.S. ambassador to England, he organized and directed the American Relief Commission which assisted 200,000 "stranded" American tourists to return to the United States. In this capacity, Hoover exhibited great executive and financial ability. On August 10, 1917, he was appointed Food Commissioner, and later

In 1920, Hoover, who had been a Democrat and an advocate of the League of Nations, announced himself a Republican and a candidate for the Presidency. He failed to obtain the nomination, but President Harding appointed him Secretary of Commerce, to which office he was reappointed by President Coolidge In 1928, he received the Republican nomination for President of the United States.

The Democratic party had nominated Governor Alfred E. Smith, a member of the Roman Catholic Church. While the campaign was very bitter, both sides disclaimed any intention of bringing forward the religious question. Yet it, together with Prohibition, which was opposed by Smith, was a leading issue.

Hoover was elected by the second largest popular vote ever received by a candidate, 21,409,215 to 15,042,366. His electoral vote was 444, to 87 for Smith, and he carried all but eight states. For the first time in 50 years the "solid South" was broken, for, chiefly because of the religious question, North Carolina, Virginia, Florida, Tennessee and Texas swung into the Republican column.

President Hoover occasionally attended the Friends' Church, though his public utterances contain nothing to indicate the ardently religious man.

RESUME

To determine an individual's religious affiliation is often difficult, because the Churches themselves are not united in a uniform test of membership. The Roman Catholic Church regards as members all those who have ever been baptized. Some Protestant denominations consider as members only those who have made a profession of faith and are communicants. Other Churches claim all who are regular attendants and supporters.

Throughout this work I have given no religious label to a President unless I have been convinced by the evidence that he professed the faith and was a communicant in the Church to which he has been assigned.

Of the 32 Presidents of the United States, the following were communicants in orthodox Christian denominations: Andrew Jackson, James Knox Polk, James Buchanan, Grover Cleveland, Benjamin Harrison and Woodrow Wilson, Presbyterian; William McKinley, Methodist; Theodore Roosevelt, Dutch Reformed; Warren G. Harding, Baptist; Franklin Pierce and Franklin Delano Roosevelt, Episcopal; Calvin Coolidge, Congregationalist. Of these, Jackson, Polk, Pierce, Buchanan and Coolidge were not church members at the time of their election. Cleveland's religious status at the time of his election is also obscure.

The following six Presidents were members of unorthodox religious bodies: John Adams, John Quincy Adams, Millard Fillmore and William Howard Taft, Unitarian; James Abram Garfield, Disciple of Christ; Herbert Clark Hoover, Quaker.

Four Presidents, William Henry Harrison, Andrew Johnson, Ulysses Simpson Grant and Rutherford Birchard Hayes, were not members of any religious society, orthodox or heterodox.

Of six Presidents, James Madison, James Monroe, Martin Van Buren, John Tyler, Zachary Taylor and Chester Alan Arthur, there is no evidence that they were communicants, or even members, though most of them attended church occasionally.

One President, Thomas Jefferson, was, according to his own written works, a deistic Freethinker, who rejected revelation and held that no religion was of superior merit to another. While George Washington and Abraham Lincoln never made a statement of their opinions, circumstantial evidence indicates that they held the same views as did Jefferson.

It will be observed that in the days when orthodox religious opinion held the most complete sway over the minds of the people of the United States, fewer Presidents were of orthodox profession than in recent years, when there is a movement away from old-time rigid doctrines.

The orthodox Churches do not press their theological doctrines as they did in the past. For this reason, many who were formerly repelled now join that they may benefit through the social and business influence of the Church.

Most Churches are today openly active politically, asking favors of the government in the form of laws, special privileges and exemptions. At one time this was considered very improper and was strongly denounced. Today, it is accepted as a condition of politics that the "church vote" is an important element in the fortunes of politicians. In some localities even applicants for positions as school teachers are asked to what Church they belong.

Once religion was a serious conviction. No one thought of joining a Church without having had a "religious experience." While there are many sincerely religious persons today, yet there are many others to whom the Church is merely a social convention, a political expediency, or a commercial commodity.

APPENDIX I

Washington's last sickness and death, as told by the Rev. Mason L. Weems:

It has been said that a man's death is generally a copy of his life. It was Washington's case exactly. In his last illness he behaved with the firmness of a soldier, and the resignation of a Christian. Feeling that the hour of his departure out of this world was at hand, he desired that everybody would quit the room. They all went out; and, according to his wish, left him—with his God. Feeling that the silver cord of life is loosing, and that his spirit is ready to quit her old companion, the body, he extends himself on his bed—closed his eyes for the last time with his own hands—folds his arms decently on his breast, then breathing out "Father of mercies, take me to thyself"—he fell asleep. (Weems's **Life of Washington**, pp. 215, 217.)

In this fictitious account, Weems portrays Washington as no more than a Deist.

The same, as told by Tobias Lear, Washington's private secretary, who was present from the first to the last:[*]

Mt. Vernon, Saturday, December 14, 1799—This day being marked by an event, which will be memorable in the history of America, and perhaps of the world, I shall give a particular statement of it, to which I was an eye witness.

On Thursday, December 12, the General rode out to his farms about ten o'clock, and did not return home till past three. Soon after he went out, the weather became very bad, rain, hail, snow falling alternately, with a cold wind. When he came in, I carried some letters for him to frank, intending to send them to the post office in the evening. He franked the letters, but said the weather was too bad to send a servant to the office that evening. I observed to him, that I was afraid he had got wet. He said, No, his great coat had kept him dry. But his neck appeared to be wet, and the snow was hanging upon his hair. He came to dinner (which had been waiting for him) without changing his dress. In the evening he appeared as well as usual.

A heavy fall of snow took place on Friday, which prevented the General from riding out as usual. He had taken cold, undoubtedly from being so much exposed the day before, and complained of a sore throat. He, however, went out in the afternoon into the ground between the house and the river to mark some trees which were to be cut down in the improvements of that spot. He had a hoarseness which increased in the evening; but he made light of it.

In the evening the papers were brought from the post office, and he sat in the parlor with Mrs. Washington and myself reading them, till about nine o'clock, when Mrs. Washington went up into Mrs. Lewis' room, who was confined, and left the General and myself reading the papers. He was very cheerful, and when he met with anything interesting or entertaining, he read it aloud as well as his hoarseness would permit. He requested me to read to him the debates of the Virginia Assembly, on the election of a Senator and Governor; and on hearing Mr. Madison's observations respecting Mr. Monroe, he appeared much

*From Appendix 6, Sparks's **Life of Washington**, pp. 531-536.

affected, and spoke with some degree of asperity on the subject, which I endeavored to moderate, as I always did on such occasions. On his retiring, I observed to him, that he had better take something to remove his cold. He answered, "No, you know I never take anything for a cold. Let it go as it came."

Between two and three o'clock, on Saturday morning, he awoke Mrs. Washington, and told her that he was very unwell, and had had an ague. She observed, that he could hardly speak, and breathed with difficulty, and would have got up to call a servant. But he would not permit her, lest she should take a cold. As soon as the day appeared, the woman (Caroline) went into the room to make a fire, and Mrs. Washington sent her immediately to call me. I got up, put on my clothes as quickly as possible, and went to his chamber. Mrs. Washington was then up, and related to me his being ill, as before stated. I found the General breathing with difficulty, and hardly able to utter a word intelligibly. He desired Mr. Rawlins (one of the overseers) might be sent for to bleed him before the Doctor could arrive. I despatched a servant instantly for Rawlins, and another for Dr. Craik, and returned again to the General's chamber, where I found him in the same situation as I had left him.

A mixture of molasses, vinegar, and butter was prepared to try its effects in the throat; but he could not swallow a drop. Whenever he attempted it, he appeared to be distressed, convulsed, and almost suffocated. Rawlins came in after sunrise and prepared to bleed him. When the arm was ready, the General, observing that Rawlins appeared to be agitated, said, as well as he could speak, "Don't be afraid." And when the incision was made, he observed, "The orifice is not large enough." However, the blood ran very freely. Mrs. Washington, not knowing whether bleeding was proper or not in the General's situation, begged that much might not be taken from him, lest it should be injurious, and desired me to stop it; but, when I was about to untie the string, the General put up his hand to prevent it, and as soon as he could speak, he said, "More, more." Mrs. Washington being still very uneasy, lest too much blood should be taken, it was stopped after taking about a half a pint. Find that no relief was obtained from bleeding, and that nothing would go down the throat, I proposed bathing it externally with **sal volatile**, which was done, and in the operation, which was with the hand, and in the gentlest manner, he observed, "It is very sore." A piece of flannel dipped in **sal volatile** was put around his neck, and his feet bathed in warm water, but without affording any relief.

In the meantime before Dr. Craik arrived, Mrs. Washington desired me to send for Dr. Brown, of Port Tobacco, whom Dr. Craik had recommended to be called, if any case should ever occur, that was seriously alarming. I despatched a messenger immediately for Dr. Brown between eight and nine o'clock. Dr. Craik came in soon after, and upon examining the General, he put a blister of cantharides on the throat, took more blood from him, and had a gargle of vinegar and sage tea prepared; and ordered some vinegar and hot water for him to inhale the steam of it, which he did; but in attempting to use the gargle he was almost suffocated. When the gargle came from his throat, some phlegm followed, and he attempted to cough, which the Doctor encouraged him to do as much as possible; but he could only attempt it. About eleven o'clock, Dr. Craik requested that Dr. Dick might be sent for, as he feared Dr. Brown would not come in time. A messenger was accordingly despatched for him. About this time the General was bled again. No effect, however was produced by it, and he remained in the same state, unable to swallow anything.

Dr. Dick came about three o'clock, and Dr. Brown arrived soon after. Upon Dr. Dick's seeing the General and consulting a few minutes with Dr. Craik, he was bled again. The blood came very slow, was thick, and did not produce any symptoms of fainting. Dr. Brown came into the chamber soon after, and upon feeling the General's pulse, the physicians went out together. Dr. Craik returned soon after. The General could now swallow a little. Calomel and tartar emetic were administered, but without any effect.

About half past four o'clock he desired me to call Mrs. Washington to his bedside, when he requested her to go down into his room, and take from his desk two wills, which she should find there, and bring them to him, which she did. Upon looking at them he gave her one, which he observed was useless, as being superseded by the other, and desired her to burn it, which she did, and took the other and put it in her closet.

After this was done, I returned to his bedside and took his hand. He said to me, "I find I am going. My breath cannot last long. I believed from the first, that the disorder would prove fatal. Do you arrange and record all my late military letters and papers. Arrange my accounts and settle my books, as you know more about them than any one else, and let Mr. Rawlins finish recording my other letters, which he has begun." I told him this should be done. He then asked, if I recollected anything which it was essential for him to do, as he had but a short time to continue with us. I told him, that I could recollect nothing, but that I hoped he was not so near his end. He observed, smiling, that he certainly was, and that, as it was the debt which we must all pay, he looked to the event with perfect resignation.

In the course of the afternoon he appeared to be in great pain and distress, from the difficulty of breathing, and frequently changed his posture in bed. On these occasions I lay upon the bed and endeavored to raise him, and turned him with as much ease as possible. He appeared penetrated with gratitude for my attentions, and often said, "I am afraid I fatigue you too much"; and upon my assuring him, that I could feel nothing but a wish to give him ease, he replied, "Well, it is a debt we must pay to each other, and I hope, when you want aid of this kind, you will find it." He asked when Mr. Lewis and Washington Custis would return. (They were then in New Kent.) I told him about the 20th of the month.

About five o'clock Dr. Craik came again into the room, and, upon going to the bedside the General said to him, "Doctor, I die hard but I am not afraid to go. I believed, from my first attack, that I should not survive it. My breath cannot last long." The Doctor pressed his hand, but could not utter a word. He retired from the bedside, and sat by the fire absorbed in grief.

Between five and six o'clock Dr. Dick and Dr. Brown came into the room, and with Dr. Craik went to the bed, when Dr. Craik asked him if he could sit up in bed. He held out his hand and I raised him up. He then said to his physicians, "I feel myself going; I thank you for your attentions; but I pray you to take no more trouble about me. Let me go off quietly. I cannot last long." They found that all which had been done was without effect. He lay down again, and all retired except Dr. Craik. He continued in the same situation, uneasy and restless, but without complaining; frequently asking what hour it was. When I helped to move him at this time, he did not speak, but looked at me with strong expressions of gratitude.

About eight o'clock the physicians came again into the room, and applied blisters and cataplasms of wheat bran to his legs and feet, after which they went out, except Dr. Craik, without a ray of hope. I went out about this time, and wrote a line to Mr. Law and Mr. Peter, requesting them to come with their wives (Mrs. Washington's granddaughters) as soon as possible to Mt. Vernon.

About ten o'clock he made several attempts to speak to me before he could effect it. At last he said, "I am just going. Have me decently buried, and do not let my body be put into the vault in less than three days after I am dead." I bowed assent, for I could not speak. He then looked at me again and said, "Do you understand me?" I replied, "Yes." "Tis well," said he.

About ten minutes before he expired (which was between ten and eleven o'clock) his breathing became easier. He lay quietly, he withdrew his hand from mine and felt his own pulse. I saw his countenance change. I spoke to Dr. Craik, who sat by the fire. He came to the bedside. The General's hand fell from his wrist. I took it in mine and pressed it to my bosom. Dr. Craik put his hands over his eyes, and he expired without a struggle or a sigh.

While we were fixed in silent grief, Mrs. Washington, who was sitting at the foot of the bed, asked with a firm and collected voice, "Is he gone?" I could not speak, but held up my hand as a signal, that he was no more. " 'Tis well," said she, in the same voice, "all is over now; I shall soon follow him; I have no more trials to pass through."

Occurrences not noted in the preceding narrative.

The General's servant, Christopher, was in the room during the day; and in the afternoon the General directed him to sit down, as he had been standing almost the whole day. He did so. About eight o'clock in the morning he (the General) expressed a desire to get up. His clothes were put on, and he was led to a chair by the fire. He found no relief from that position, and lay down again about ten o'clock. About five in the afternoon, he was helped up again, and, after sitting about half an hour, he desired to be undressed and put in bed, which was done.

During his whole illness he spoke but seldom, and with great difficulty and distress; and in so low and broken a voice as at times hardly to be understood. His patience, fortitude, and resignation never forsook him for a moment. In all his distress he uttered not a sigh nor a complaint; always endeavoring, from a sense of duty as it appeared, to take what was offered him, and to do as was desired by his physicians.

At the time of his decease, Dr. Craik and myself were in the situation before mentioned. Mrs. Washington was sitting near the foot of the bed. Christopher was standing near the bedside. Caroline, Molly, and Charlotte were in the room, standing near the door. Mrs. Forbes, the housekeeper, was frequently in the room during the day and evening.

As soon as Dr. Craik could speak, after the distressing scene was closed, he desired one of the servants to ask the gentlemen below to come up stairs. When they came to the bedside, I kissed the cold hand, which I had held in my bosom, laid it down, and went to the other end of the room, where I was for some time lost in profound grief, until aroused by Christopher, desiring me to take care of the General's keys, and other things, which were taken out of his pockets, and which Mrs. Washington directed him to give to me. I wrapped them in the General's handkerchief, and took them to my room. About twelve o'clock the corpse was brought down stairs, and laid out in the large room.

(This was copied by Dr. Sparks from Mr. Lear's original manuscript. The following certificate, in the handwriting of Dr. Craik, is appended to the foregoing portion of Mr. Lear's narrative:

"**Sunday, December 15.** The foregoing statement, so far as I can recollect, is correct."   "Jas. Craik.")

NOTE: The Rev. Mason Locke Weems was born in Maryland in either 1759 or 1760. As to the exact date there is an uncertainty. He entered the Episcopal ministry, but there is a doubt whether he was ever ordained. Bishop Meade, however, thinks he was. As a minister he would have probably never have been known except that on the title page of his **Life of Washington** he advertised himself as "Formerly Rector of Mt. Vernon Parish." There was no such parish, though Weems sometimes officiated at Pohick Church, but after Washington ceased to attend it. In the **Diaries**, vol. three, p. 174, dated Saturday, March 3, 1787, Washington records, "The Rev. Mr. Weems, and young Dr. Craik who came here yesterday in the afternoon, left about noon for Port Tobacco." This seems to be the only mention Washington makes of him.

Mr. Weems was not long a minister. He left the pulpit and became a traveling book agent, owing, it is said, to his having too large a family to be supported by preaching. He had the reputation of knowing the United States South of Pennsylvania better than any other man. As a book agent he was very successful, selling among other books over 3,000 copies of a high-priced Bible. He also sold Paine's **Age of Reason.** He was a musician, and never missed a chance to play the fiddle at dances. He never lost an opportunity of making a speech, and would, during his travels, preach whenever invited. Weems died in Beauford, S.C., in 1825.

APPENDIX II

RELIGIOUS OPINIONS AND HABITS OF WASHINGTON.

(From Sparks's **Washington**, pp. 518-525.)

Such persons as have attentively perused Washington's writings may think any remarks on this subject superfluous. In certain quarters, nevertheless, there have been discussions tending to throw doubts over the religious belief of Washington; whether from ignorance of his character and writings, or from causes less creditable, it is needless to inquire. (1.) A formal attempt to confute insinuations of this kind, would be allowing them a weight, which they cannot claim, till supported by positive testimony, or till it is shown by at least a shadow of proof, that they have some foundation other than conjecture and inference. This has not been done, and nothing is hazarded in saying that it never will be done. (2.)

A hundred years have elapsed since the childhood of Washington; and so little is known of his early life, from written materials, that we cannot speak with confidence respecting his first religious impressions. It has always been the prevalent tradition, however, in the neighborhood of his birthplace, that he was educated under influences, that could not fail to fix in his mind the principles of the Christian religion, and a sacred regard for the precepts it inculcates. This is in part confirmed by his manuscripts, containing articles and extracts copied out by himself in his boyhood, which prove that his thoughts at that time had a religious tendency. One of these copies, being a series of verses **On Christmas Day**, begins thus:

"Assist me, Muse divine, to sing the morn,
On which the Saviour of mankind was born."

A boy of 13 would scarcely employ himself in transcribing pieces of this description, whose mind had not already received a decided bias from instructions of pious parents or teachers. (3.)

It should be observed, also, that in his first military campaigns he was careful to have religious service regularly performed in camp. Even in the midst of the active scenes at the Great Meadows this was the daily practice. During the French war, when the government of Virginia neglected to provide chaplains for the army, he remonstrated against such an impropriety, and urged his request till they were appointed. In the general orders he reproved and forbad the vicious habits and profane swearing of the soldiers.

The following is an extract from these orders. "Colonel Washington has observed, that the men of his regiment are very profane and reprobate. He takes this opportunity to inform them of his great displeasure at such practices, and assures them, that, if they do not leave them off, they shall be severely punished. The officers are desired, if they hear any man swear, or make use of an oath or execration, to order the offender 25 lashes immediately, without a court-martial. For the second offense, he shall be more severely punished." Similar orders were repeated, when the occasion required; and they afford a convincing proof of the high religious motives by which he was actuated in his command. (4.)

After the French war, while in retirement at Mt. Vernon, he took a lively interest in church affairs, regularly attending public worship, and

165

being at different times a vestryman in two parishes. (5.) The House of Burgesses, of which he was a member, passed an order (May 24, 1774), in reference to the act of Parliament for shutting up the port of Boston, that "the first day of June should be set apart as a day of fasting, humiliation and prayer, devoutly to implore the divine interposition for averting the heavy calamity, which threatened destruction to their civil rights, and the evils of civil war." On the day appointed, he writes in his **Diary**, "Went to church, and **fasted all day**," thus conforming not only to the spirit, but to the strict letter of the event. This **Diary** was kept for many years with much particularity. A Sunday rarely occurs, in which it is not recorded that he went to church. If there was an omission, it was caused by the weather, bad roads, the nearest church, as stated in the note, being seven miles from his residence. While attending the first Congress, he adhered to the same practice. (6.)

For a full knowledge of his religious opinions and habits during the Revolution and afterwards, and of the importance he attached to the principles and observances of religion, the reader is referred to his published letters, addresses and other writings. After an attentive perusal of them, no doubt can be left in any candid mind. To say that he was not a Christian, or at least that he did not believe himself to be a Christian, would be to impeach his sincerity and honesty. Of all men in the world, Washington was certainly the last, whom any one would charge with indifference or indirectness; and, if he was so scrupulous in avoiding even a shadow of these faults in every known act of his life, however unimportant, is it likely, is it credible, that in a matter of the highest and most serious importance, he should practise through a long series of years, a deliberate deception upon his friends and the public? (7.)

I shall here insert a letter on this subject, written to me by a lady who lived 20 years in Washington's family, and who was his adopted daughter, and the granddaughter of Mrs. Washington. The testimony it affords, and the hints it contains respecting the domestic habits of Washington, are interesting and valuable.

"Woodlawn, 26 February, 1833.

"SIR,

"I received your favor of the 20th instant last evening, and hasten to give you the information, which you desire.

"Truo Parish is the one in which Mt. Vernon, Pohick Church and Woodlawn are situated. Fairfax Parish is now Alexandria. Before the Federal District was ceded to Congress, Alexandria was in Fairfax County. General Washington had a pew in Pohick Church, and one in Christ Church at Alexandria. He was very instrumental in establishing Pohick Church, and I believe subscribed largely. His pew was near the pulpit. I have a perfect recollection of being there, before his election to the Presidency, with him and my grandmother. It was a beautiful church, and had a large, respectable, and wealthy congregation, who were regular attendants.

"He attended the church at Alexandria, when the weather and roads permitted a ride of 10 miles. In New York and Philadelphia he never omitted attendance at church in the morning, unless detained by indisposition. The afternoon was spent in his own room at home; the evening with his family, and without company. Sometimes an old and intimate friend called to see us for an hour or two; but visitors and visiting were prohibited for the day. No one in church attended to the services with more reverential respect. (8.)

"My grandmother, who was eminently pious, never deviated from her early habits. She always knelt. The General, as was then the

custom, stood during the devotional service. (9.) On communion Sundays, he left the church with me, after the blessing and returned home
and we sent the carriage back for my grandmother. (10.)

"It was his custom to retire to his library at nine or 10 o'clock
where he remained an hour before he went to his chamber. He always
rose before the sun, and remained in his library until called to breakfast. I never **witnessed** his private devotions. I never **inquired** about
them. I should have thought it the greatest heresy to doubt his belief
in Christianity. His life, his writings, prove that he was a
Christian. (11.) He was not one of those who act or pray, 'that they
be seen of men.' He communed with his God in secret.

"My mother resided two years at Mt. Vernon, after her marriage
with John Parke Custis, the only son of Mrs. Washington. I have heard
her say, that General Washington always received the sacrament with
my grandmother before the Revolution. When my aunt, Miss Custis
died suddenly at Mt. Vernon, before they could realize the event, he
knelt by her and prayed most fervently, most affectingly, for her recovery. Of this I was assured by Judge Washington's mother and other
witnesses. (12.)

"He was a silent, thoughtful man. He spoke little generally; never
of himself. I never heard him relate a single act of his life during
the war. I have often seen him perfectly abstracted, his lips moving
but no sound was perceptible. (13.) I have sometimes made him laugh
most heartily from sympathy with my joyous and extravagant spirits
I was, probably, one of the last persons on earth to whom he would have
addressed serious conversation, particularly when he knew that I had
the most perfect model of female excellence ever with me as my moni-
tress, who acted the part of a tender and devoted parent, loving me
as only a mother can love, and never extenuating or approving in me
what she disapproved in others. She never omitted her private devotions, or her public duties; and she and her husband were so perfectly
united and happy, that he must have been a Christian. She had no
doubts, no fears for him. (14.)

"After 40 years of devoted affection and uninterrupted happiness
she resigned him without a murmur into the arms of his Saviour and
his God, with the assured hope of eternal felicity. Is it necessary that
any one should certify, 'General Washington avowed himself to **me** a
believer in Christianity?' (15.) As well may we question his patriotism
his heroic, disinterested devotion to his country. His mottoes were
'**Deeds, not Words**' and '**For God and my Country.**' (16.)

"With sentiments of esteem, I am, etc. . ."

It seems proper to subjoin to this letter what was told to me by
Mr. Robert Lewis, at Fredericksburg, in the year 1827. Being a nephew
of Washington, and his private secretary during the first part of his
Presidency, Mr. Lewis lived with him on terms of intimacy, and had
the best opportunity for observing his habits. Mr. Lewis said he had
accidentally witnessed his private devotions in his library both morning and evening; that on those occasions he had seen him in a kneeling posture with an open Bible before him, and that he believed such
to be his daily practice. Mr. Lewis is since dead but he was a gentleman esteemed for his private worth and respectability. (17.) I relate
the anecdote as he told it to me, understanding at the time that he
was willing it should be made public on his authority. He added that it
was the President's custom to go to his library in the morning at four
o'clock, and that, after his devotions, he usually spent his time till
breakfast writing letters.

The circumstance of his withdrawing himself from the communion
service, at a certain period of his life, has been remarked as singular.
This may be admitted, and regretted, both on account of his example,

and the value of his opinions as to the importance and practical tendency of this rite. It does not follow, however, that he was an unbeliever, unless the same charge is proved to rest against the numerous class of persons, who believe themselves to be sincere Christians,
but who have scruples in regard to the ordinance of communion. (18.)
Whatever his motives may have been, it does not appear that they
were ever explained. Nor, is it known, or to be presumed, that any
occasion offered. It is probable that, after he took command of the
army, finding his thoughts and attention necessarily engrossed by
business that devolved upon him, in which frequently little distinction
could be observed between Sunday and other days, he may have believed it improper to partake of an ordinance, which, according to the
ideas he entertained of it, imposed severe restrictions on his outward
conduct, and a sacred pledge to perform duties impractical in his situation. (19.) Such an impression would be natural to a serious mind;
and though it might be founded on erroneous views of the nature of
the ordinance, it would have had the less weight with a man of a delicate conscience and habitual reverence for religion. (20.)

There is proof, however, that, on one occasion at least during the
war, he partook of the communion; but this was a season when the
army was in camp, and the activity of business was in some degree
suspended. (21.) An anecdote contained in Dr. Hosack's **Life of Dewitt
Clinton**, and related in the words of the Reverend Samuel H. Cox, who
communicated it to the author, establishes this fact.

"I have received the following anecdote," says Dr. Cox, "from un-
questionable authority. It has never, I think, been given to the public;
but I received it from a venerable clergyman, who had it from the
lips of the Reverend Dr. Johnes himself. (21.) To all Christians, and to
all Americans, it cannot fail to be acceptable.

"While the American army, under the command of Washington,
lay encamped at Morristown, New Jersey, it occurred that the service
of the communion (then observed semi-annually only) was to be
administered in the Presbyterian church of that village. In the morning of the previous week, the General, after his accustomed inspection
of the camp, visited the house of the Rev. Dr. Johnes, then pastor of
the church, and after the usual preliminaries, thus accosted him:
'Doctor, I understand that the Lord's Supper is to be celebrated with
you next Sunday; I would learn if it accords with the canon of your
church to admit communicants of another denomination?' The Doctor
rejoined, 'Most certainly; ours is not a Presbyterian table, General, but
the Lord's table, and we hence give the Lord's invitation to all his
followers of whatever name.'

"The General replied, 'I am glad of it, that is as it ought to be;
but as I was not quite sure of the fact, I thought I would ascertain it
from yourself, as I propose to join with you on that occasion. Though a
member of the Church of England I have no exclusive partialities.' (22.)
The Doctor assured him of a cordial welcome, and the General was
found seated with the communicants the next Sabbath."

The situation in which Washington stood, while President of the
United States, made it necessary that he should use much circumspec-
tion in whatever came from him touching theological subjects. He
received addresses from many Christian congregations or societies, including every denomination in the country, complimentary to his character, and expressing gratitude for his long and eminent public services.
In his replies, it would have been equally discourteous and impolitic
to employ language indicating a decided preference for the peculiar
tenets or forms of any particular Church. (23.) He took a wiser course,
the only one, indeed, which with propriety could be taken. He approved the general objects, and commended the zeal, of all the re-

ligious congregations or societies by which he was addressed, spoke of
their beneficial effects in promoting the welfare of mankind, declared
his cordial wishes for their success, and often concluded with his prayers
for the future happiness of the individuals belonging to them, both
in this world and in the world to come. (24.) All the answers of this
kind breathe a Christian spirit, and they may justly be regarded as
implying the author's acknowledgement of the truth and authority of
the Christian religion.

After a long and minute examination of the writings of Washington, public and private, in print and manuscript, I can affirm, that
I have never seen a single hint, or expression, from which it could be
inferred, that he had any doubt of the Christian revelation, or that he
thought with indifference or unconcern of that subject. On the contrary, wherever he approaches it, and indeed whenever he alludes in
any manner to religion, it is done with seriousness and reverence.

The foregoing observations have been made, not by way of argument, but merely as a statement of facts; for I must end as I began,
by saying, that I conceive any attempt at argument in so plain a case
would be misapplied. (25.) If a man who spoke, wrote, and acted as a
Christian through a long life, who gave numerous proofs of his believing himself to be such, and who was never known to say, write or do a
thing contrary to his professions, if such a man is not to be ranked
among the believers of Christianity, it would be impossible to establish
the point by any train of reasoning. (26.) How far he examined the
grounds of his faith is uncertain, but probably as far as the large
portion of Christians, who do not make theology a special study; and we
have a right to presume, that a mind like his would not receive an
opinion without a special reason. He was educated in the Episcopal
Church, to which he always adhered; and my conviction is, that he
believed in the fundamental doctrines of Christianity as taught in that
Church, according to his understanding of them; but without a particle of intolerance, or disrespect for the faith and modes of worship
adopted by Christians of other denominations.

COMMENTS

(1.) This entire chapter by Mr. Sparks consists of one long special
plea. He begins by casting reflection upon any who have called into
question Washington's religious opinions. The impropriety of this attitude becomes apparent when one considers that men in a position
to know, Bishop White, the Rev. Dr. Abercrombie, the Rev. Dr. Wilson,
Thomas Jefferson, and Gouverneur Morris, either said they did not
know what Washington's religious opinions were, or expressed doubt
that he was orthodox. The fact that Mr. Sparks, in a foot-note in this
chapter, refers to the statement of Bishop White which is found in
our text, and yet writes as he does, indicates, to say the least, a want
of candor.

(2.) Mr. Sparks infers that those who denied that Washington's
belief was orthodox were speaking to his dishonor. Sparks certainly
knew that many other Revolutionary heroes were unbelievers. Sparks
himself wrote a life of Franklin. In it he admits that Franklin was
not orthodox, and he does not even mention "insinuations." He says
any charge of unorthodoxy against Washington must be supported
by "positive testimony." Yet he utterly fails to give us "positive testimony" that Washington was an evangelical Christian according to the
creed of the Church of England. All he does, to use his own words, is
to make use of "conjecture and inference." Sparks wrote, almost 100
years ago, a biography of Washington and published a collection of
his writings. If he knew how much has been learned about Washington
since his time, he would "turn over in his grave."

(3.) The religious teachings instilled into the mind of a child, and the sentiments written in his copy books are no indication of what he thought in mature life. Most unbelievers and unorthodox people have been reared in an orthodox atmosphere. Sparks himself, though a minister, departed from the religious teachings of his childhood.

(4.) That Washington gave conventional adherence to and showed respect for the religious observances of his time and did not combat them, we all know. Nearly all public men do this now, even though many are unbelievers. The late Franklin K. Lane, in his **Autobiography**, admits his unbelief, but says he never mentioned it while in politics.

Washington's Virginia soldiers in the French war were, as a rule, backwoodsmen, rough, hard drinkers and not subject to discipline. He no doubt thought prayer in camp might have a good influence over them. Yet, when it was proposed to open the Constitutional Convention, over which he presided, with prayer, the motion was lost. Only three or four of the delegates favored it, and it is not recorded that Washington was one of them.

As a means of promoting discipline among the rough men of the frontier, Washington issued an order against the use of profane language. Yet it is notorious that when he was angry, he would sometimes utter oaths himself. He issued an order against gambling, also in the interest of discipline, yet he took part in games of cards and dice for money. Disgusted with the drinking habits of his locality, he refused, when first a candidate for the House of Burgesses, to serve the electors with liquor. His opponent, who did serve liquor, was elected. At the next election, Washington served liquor, and won. He was far from being the straight-laced man whom Sparks portrays.

(5-6.) I have shown by his **Diaries** how "regularly" he attended public worship, and what the office of vestryman really meant.

(7.) The real fact is that the writings spoken of here throw no light upon the question, more than that Washington believed in God and recognized his providence. He practiced no deception in the attitude he took. Religiously he left all to their own views, respected the opinions of all, and minded his own business, as he knew that was the only way to keep the peace with the different Churches. Those who claim he was orthodox in his views are the ones who practically accuse him of deception.

(8.) Nellie Custis was the granddaughter of Mrs. Washington, her father being John Parke Custis, who died following the Battle of Yorktown. What she said in this letter does not pertain to Washington's religious belief; it only tells how he subscribed to churches, and attended them. If no churches were erected except with the money of believers, there would be fewer of them. That Washington acted like a gentleman in church, as elsewhere, is admitted. The point is, did he believe in religious doctrines and conform to religious practices? This is the test of the kind of Christian they say Washington was.

(9.) The difference between General and Mrs. Washington is here apparent. She was a practical Christian, who knelt in prayer, and took communion. The General did not kneel and did not take communion.

(10.) This is further proof that on communion Sundays Washington retired while his wife remained.

(11.) Miss Custis, Washington's adopted daughter, says she never witnessed his private devotions, which have been the source of many fables. She accounts it a heresy to doubt his belief in Christianity though she admits there is no evidence for it. She never saw Washington pray at home. Neither did he pray in Church.

(12.) Someone told someone else about Washington's religious beliefs. He never told about them himself, and those who talked about them could only repeat hearsay. Patsy Custis, the aunt Nellie speaks of, died at Mt. Vernon before Nellie was born. Patsy was an unhealthy child, subject to fits. Washington gave her the benefit of the best medical attention, taking her to the best physicians in distant places, but all to no purpose. Nellie says she "was assured by Judge Washington's mother and other witnesses" that Washington "knelt by her side and prayed most fervently and effectively for her recovery." On June 19, 1773, she fell from her chair at the table and died within two minutes. Washington hardly prayed for her recovery. No doubt he felt grieved, but the grief was tempered with a feeling of resignation at the death of one whom disease made miserable. Washington wrote to Burwell Bassett on the day of her death: "The sweet, innocent girl entered into a more happy and peaceful abode than any she has met with in the afflicted path she hitherto has trod."* (See **Diaries**, vol. 2, p. 115.)

(13.) Many thoughtful men talk inaudibly to themselves, their lips moving, but this practice is scarcely evidence of their being engaged in prayer.

(14.) Many husbands and wives have lived happily, though they differed religiously. This only proves that Washington and his wife were reasonable, considerate creatures.

(15.) At the time of Washington's death, Nellie Custis, by that time Mrs. Lewis, was still sick from the birth of her first child. She had no personal knowledge of what happened, although she lived in the house. Nothing is said in Lear's account of Mrs. Washington's resigning her husband "into the arms of his Saviour, and his God"; but she did say, "Is he gone? 'Tis well; all is now over; I shall soon follow him; I have no more trials to pass through."

(16.) A man's "patriotism, his heroic, disinterested devotion to his country," is not always to be measured by his religion.

(17.) Mr. Robert Lewis, a nephew of Washington, is said to have told Mr. Sparks that he "accidentally witnessed Washington's private devotions," saw him kneeling in his library with an open Bible before him. Of course, Mr. Lewis, like all the other witnesses was dead; we must take his statement second hand, as he never thought this occurrence important enough to sign a written statement concerning it. We never before heard of a man who was so fearful of having his "religion" discovered as was Washington. He had to "sneak" his prayers, and it required the services of a spy to catch him. Two or three times he was "accidentally" discovered. In a strong religious age, he was careful not to let it be publicly known that he was a Christian!

(18.) The only apparent significance of this passage is that Washington did not realize the importance of the communion, and cared little for the influence of his example. He was quite careful in setting an example in other things.

(19.) Throughout the Revolution Washington had plenty of opportunity to take the communion had he desired to do so. For almost three years his army was in camp, never fought a battle, and there were many Churches in the vicinity.

(20.) Dr. Sparks thinks Washington held erroneous views of the communion, and thinks he made a mistake in neglecting the ordinance. Yet, according to the same Dr. Sparks, when Washington did seriously consider it, he found a reason for not taking it!

(21.) The story of the Presbyterian communion is commented upon in the first chapter of this book.

---

*Woodrow Wilson, in his **George Washington**, says the death of Patsy Custis called forth all "the latent Christian faith" of Washington. The use of the word "latent" here is significant. (Page 147.)

(22.) According to this account, Washington called upon the Rev. Dr. Johnes. According to another, he wrote him a letter.

(23.) A great mystery is that in all of Washington's writings he never once hinted what his religious views were. Why should he hesitate to reveal them? Why, when the ministers of Philadelphia waited upon him in a body with an address, did he answer every question they put, except the one of religion? He was retiring from office for good and no one could be offended, if in fact they could have been offended at any other time. Why were the ministers so anxious to obtain this information, if Washington had the reputation of being sound in his belief? The truth was, that in that very orthodox age he was under suspicion.

(24.) The virtues of kindness, justice, toleration, and generosity are not exclusively Christian, and are practiced by non-believers, while many Christians honor them "more in the breach than in the observance." The liberality Dr. Sparks so eulogizes in Washington, was, at that time, almost exclusively exercised by Deists.

As we consider Dr. Sparks's labored efforts to make Washington a believer, we must remember that he was himself a heretic—a Unitarian, who rejected the divinity of Christ, the plenary inspiration of the Bible, and all that was then considered "sound doctrine." He might call Washington a Christian from his standpoint, but not from the standpoint of the Protestant Episcopal Church.

APPENDIX III

DR. HOLLAND AND THE "BATEMAN INTERVIEW."

Six decades ago, Dr. Josiah G. Holland was one of the best known writers in the United States. He had a diction any author might envy, and a wide circle of readers. He was editor of **Scribner's Monthly** from its inception until his death.

Early in 1866, Dr. Holland published his **Life of Abraham Lincoln.** His reputation as a writer was enough to assure for it a big circulation. But it was hurriedly written, and, like all the other biographies of the great statesman published at the time, was inaccurate. In it he made the statement that Lincoln had always been religious. He was the first and only responsible writer to make this assertion. Prior to the publication of Holland's book, it was not claimed that Lincoln was religious, but thousands afterwards believed it on the word of Dr. Holland.

I have told of the controversy aroused, in 1872, by the publication of Lamon's **Life of Lincoln,** which presented the evidence proving that, at least in Illinois, Lincoln was known as a skeptic. In the face of the evidence, Dr. Holland, in his magazine, was obliged to admit his error. He then joined hands with the Rev. J. A. Reed, pastor of the First Presbyterian Church, of Springfield, Illinois, in an attempt to prove that, while Lincoln was an "Infidel" in Illinois, he was converted in Washington. In this manner he tried to save his book and himself.

The "Bateman Interview" (see chapter on Lincoln) was the report Dr. Holland made of a conversation he alleged he had held with Newton Bateman, superintendent of public instruction in Illinois, in which Mr. Bateman had quoted Lincoln as believing in Christ. As Dr. Holland has been responsible for much misunderstanding and misrepresentation upon this subject, the "Interview" merits a rigid examination. Dr. Holland visited in Springfield, in 1865, to obtain, from Lncoln's old friends, data for his biography. Among others, he called on William H. Herndon, Lincoln's former law-partner, who received him kindly and gave him all the aid in his power. Dr. Holland admits this in his preface. Speaking of this visit, Mr. Herndon said:

> "Holland came into my office, in 1865, and asked me this question: 'What about Mr. Lincoln's Christianity?' To this I replied, 'The less said about it the better.' Holland then said to me, 'Oh, never mind, I'll fix that,' and went over to Bateman and had it fixed."

When Dr. Holland's book reached Springfield, Herndon went to Bateman and confronted him with Lincoln's supposed statements. Mr. Herndon says: "Bateman was frightened, excited, conscience smitten when I approached him on the subject, and in after years he confessed to me that his notes in Holland's **Life of Lincoln were colored.**" He refused, however, at the time to either affirm or deny the accuracy of Holland's report of his conversation, only saying that he and Lincoln were "talking politics and not religion." Bateman did, however, permit Mr. Herndon to make public a letter he had written in 1867, which reads:

> "He [Lincoln] was applying the principles of moral and religious truth to the duties of the hour, the condition of the

173

country, and the conduct of public men—ministers of the gospel. I had no thought of orthodoxy, or heterodoxy, Unitarianism, Trinitarianism, or any other ism, during the entire conversation, and I don't suppose or believe he had."

All myths have some basis of fact, and we are led to believe from what Mr. Bateman here says that he and Mr. Lincoln were examining the poll books, and were surprised to find that so many ministers and church members were aligned on the side of slavery. Lincoln expressed great surprise, no doubt, but that he uttered the words which Dr. Holland puts in his mouth is impossible. He may have said that Christ teaches freedom, and that Christ is the Christian God, but he could scarcely have said, "Christ is God." How does it happen that he never said it on any other occasion?

If he did say it, how does it happen that he also said on the same occasion, "I am not a Christian"? More suspicious than anything else, is this sentiment which Dr. Holland has Lincoln express: "God knows I would be one." We know from the testimony of all of Lincoln's friends that the the very reason he was not a Christian was due to the fact that he did not believe Christ was God.

Another great inconsistency of which Dr. Holland was guilty, lay in his assertion that "Lincoln never exposed his religious life to those who had no sympathy with it. It is doubtful whether the clergymen of Springfield know anything of these experiences." Is it possible that clergymen, whose duty it is to save sinners, have no sympathy with a religious life? And while the clergy had no knowledge of Mr. Lincoln's religious experience, it was afterwards contended that Lincoln had been converted by two Springfield ministers, one a Presbyterian, and the other a Methodist!

The Bateman Interview may have some basis of truth. That it was partly untrue Mr. Bateman himself admitted, so we must dismiss it as poor evidence. The law holds that what is false in part is false in all.

In this connection it is well, in justice to Mr. Bateman, to remember that he was at the time an office-holder and a politician, and did not want to take part in the very bitter controversy which followed the discussion of the religious beliefs of Abraham Lincoln. The clergy and the church people were bitterly insistent that Lincoln was thoroughly orthodox. They maintained that Bateman's interview with Dr. Holland occurred as it was reported. Bateman did not relish, nor do most men relish, being torn by theological beak and claw, as were Messrs. Herndon and Lamon.

APPENDIX IV

Testimony of W. H. Herndon, Lincoln's law-partner for 22 years, concerning his religious belief.

William H. Herndon was the law-partner of Abraham Lincoln from 1843 until the President's death in 1865. He was born at Greensburg, Ky., on December 28, 1818, and died on his farm near Springfield, Ill., on March 18, 1891.

Herndon was one of the pioneers of the anti-slavery movement, one of the founders of the Republican party in Illinois, and was a presidential elector from the Springfield district in the campaign of 1856. He was appointed Bank Commissioner by three Illinois governors, Bissell, Yates and Ogelsby, was Mayor of Springfield, and held high positions in the service of education. He was the friend and correspondent of Charles Sumner, William Lloyd Garrison and Theodore Parker. He was honored and respected by his fellow-townsmen all his life.

The Rev. J. A. Reed, minister of the First Presbyterian Church of Springfield, was angered because Herndon answered him so conclusively on the question of Lincoln's religious belief. Reed therefore circulated the basest slanders about Herndon, charging that he was a drunkard, an unreliable man, that he was insane and a pauper. Mutual friends saved the cleric from arrest for libel, but the **Daily Monitor** editorially refuted his slanders in these words:

"Mr. Herndon is not a pauper, he is not a drunkard; whisky did not ruin him, and, in a word, the whole thing is a lie. Mr. Herndon lives on his farm near this city. He is a great admirer of nature, loves flowers, and spends his whole time on his farm, except when doing his trading, or coming into the city to see his children or grandchildren. He doesn't drink, he doesn't chew tobacco, he doesn't gamble, he is honorable and truthful, and he is highly respected by his fellow-citizens. He is a great reader, a great thinker, loves his neighbors and his neighbors love him. He has a great, big, kind heart for his fellow-man in distress, and, while never worth 'considerable property,' he has always had enough for his generous purposes. Just why this thing should be allowed we are at a loss to know, and have waited to see if some of those who profess so much of the Christ-like in their composition would not have enough of the man-like to be men, and not allow a good and true man like Mr. Herndon to be thus infamously maligned and belied by those whose works in the salvation of men would have more effect if more akin to Christ in practice."

It has been asserted by some of Mr. Herndon's enemies that he caused it to be circulated that Lincoln was an unbeliever because the latter never appointed him to an office. Mr. Herndon himself answers this:

"I will say that during this last interview Mr. Lincoln, for the first time, brought up the subject of an office under his administration. He asked me if I wanted an appointment at his hands, and, if so, what I wanted. I answered that I had no desire for a Federal office, that I was then holding the office of Bank Commissioner of Illinois under appointment of Gov. Bis-

175

sell, and if he would request my retention in office by Yates, the
incoming Governor, I should be satisfied. He made the necessary recommendation, and Gov. Yates complied." (**Life of Lincoln,** by Herndon and Weik, vol. 2, p. 194, footnote.)

Mr. Herndon took a great interest in scientific, historical and philo-
osophical subjects, and was often called upon to lecture upon them.
Shortly before his death he published his **Life of Lincoln,** written in
collaboration with Jesse W. Weik. This is now universally considered to
be the best history of Lincoln, the man. Mr. Herndon had collected a
vast amount of data pertaining to Lincoln, and all who have written
concerning the great President have made use of his collection of
Lincolniana. Horace White, who reported the Lincoln-Douglas debates,
said: "As a portraiture of the man Lincoln—and this is what we look
for above all things in a biography—I venture to think that Mr. Herndon's work will never be surpassed." This estimate is confirmed by the
reviews of the press.

The **Chicago Tribune** said: "All these loving adherents of Lincoln
will hail Herndon's **Lincoln** with unmixed, unbounded joy." The **Chicago
Times** said: "Herndon's **Life** is the best yet written." The **Inter Ocean,**
of the same city, said: "Herndon knew more of Lincoln's inner life
than any living man." The **Chicago Herald** said: "It enables one to approach more closely to the great President." The **Chicago Evening
Journal** said: "It presents a truthful and living picture of the greatest
of Americans." **The Nation,** in referring to it, said: "The sincerity and
honesty of the biographer appear on every page." The **New York Sun**
said: "The marks of unflinching veracity are patent in every line." The
Washington Capital said that it places "Lincoln before the world as he
really was." The Cincinnati **Gazette** said: "He describes the life of his
friend Lincoln just as he saw it." The **Morning Call,** of San Francisco,
said that it "contains the only true history of the lamented President."
The St. Louis Republic said: "It will do more to shape the judgment of
posterity on Lincoln's character than all that has been written or
will be written."

Some parts of the testimony of Mr. Herndon which follows have
been published. Other parts are to be found in private letters to Mr.
Remsburg, who received from Mr. Herndon permission to use them as
he saw fit. The following letter appeared, in 1870, in the **Index,** a journal published in Toledo, Ohio, and edited by Francis E. Abbott:

"Mr. Abbott:

"Some time since I promised you that I would send you a letter in
relation to Mr. Lincoln's religion. I do so now. Before entering on that
question, one or two preliminary remarks will help us to understand
why he disagreed with the Christian world in its principles as well as
in its theology. In the first place, Mr. Lincoln's mind was a purely logical
mind; secondly, Mr. Lincoln's was a purely practical mind. He had no
fancy or imagination, and not much emotion. He was a realist as opposed to an idealist. As a rule, it is true that a purely logical mind has
not much hope, if it ever has faith, in the unseen and unknown. Mr.
Lincoln had not much hope and no faith in the unseen and unknown.
Mr. Lincoln had not much hope and no faith in things that lie outside
of the domain of demonstration; he was so constituted, so organized
that he could believe nothing unless his senses or logic could reach it.
I have often read to him a law point, a decision, or something I fancied.
He could not understand it until he took the book out of my hand,
and read the thing for himself. He was terribly, vexatiously skeptical.
He could scarcely understand anything, unless he had time and place
fixed in his mind.

"I became acquainted with Mr. Lincoln in 1834, and I think I knew
him well to the day of his death. His mind, when a boy in Kentucky,

showed a certain gloom, an unsocial nature, a peculiar abstractness, a bold and daring skepticism. In Indiana, from 1817 to 1830, it manifested the same qualities or attributes as in Kentucky; it only intensified, developed itself, along those lines in Indiana. He came to Illinois in 1830, and, after some little roving, settled in New Salem, now in Menard County and State of Illinois. This village lies about 20 miles northwest of this city. It was here that Mr. Lincoln became acquainted with a class of men the world never saw the like of before or since. They were large men—large in body and large in mind; hard to whip and never to be fooled. They were a bold, daring, and reckless sort of men; they were men of their own minds—believed what was demonstrable; were men of great common sense. With these men Mr. Lincoln was thrown; with them he lived, and with them he moved and almost had his being. They were skeptics all—scoffers some. These scoffers were good men, and their scoffs were protests against theology—loud protests against the follies of Christianity. They had never heard of Theism and the newer and better religious thoughts of this age. Hence, being natural skeptics, and being bold, brave men, they uttered their thoughts freely. They declared that Jesus was an illegitimate child. They were on all occasions, when an opportunity offered, debating the various questions of Christianity among themselves. They took their stand on common sense and on their own souls; and though their arguments were rude and rough, no man could overthrow their homely logic. They riddled all divines, and not unfrequently made them skeptics, unbelievers as bad as themselves. They were a jovial, healthful, generous, social, true, and manly set of people.

"It was here and among these people that Mr. Lincoln was thrown. About the year 1834 he chanced to come across Volney's **Ruins** and some of Paine's theological works. He at once seized hold of them, and assimilated them into his own being. Volney and Paine became a part of Lincoln from 1834 to the end of his life.

"In 1835 he wrote out a small work on Infidelity, and intended to have it published. This book was an attack upon the whole grounds of Christianity, and especially was it an attack upon the idea that Jesus was the Christ, the true and only-begotten son of God, as the Christian world contends. Mr. Lincoln was at that time in New Salem, keeping store for Mr. Samuel Hill, a merchant and postmaster of that place. Lincoln and Hill were very friendly. Hill, I think, was a skeptic at this time. Lincoln, one day after the book was finished, read it to Mr. Hill, his good friend. Hill tried to persuade him not to make it public, not to publish it. Hill, at that time, saw in Lincoln a rising man, and wished him success. Lincoln refused to destroy it—said it should be published. Hill swore it should never see the light of day. He had an eye on Lincoln's popularity—his present and future success; and believing that if the book was published it would kill Lincoln forever, he snatched it from Lincoln's hand when Lincoln was not expecting it, and ran it into an old-fashioned tin plate stove, heated as hot as a furnace; and so Lincoln's book went up to the clouds in smoke. It is confessed by all who heard parts of it that it was at once able and eloquent; and, if I may judge it from Mr. Lincoln's subsequent ideas and opinions, often expressed to me and to others in my presence, it was able, strong, plain and fair. His argument was grounded on the internal mistakes of the Old and New Testaments, and on reason and on the experiences and observations of men. The criticisms from internal defects were sharp, strong, and manly.

"Mr. Lincoln moved to this city in 1837, and here became acquainted with various men of his own way of thinking. At that time they called themselves Freethinkers, or Freethinking men. I remember all these things distinctly; for I was with them, heard them and was one of them. Mr. Lincoln here found other works—Hume, Gibbon, and others—and drank them in. He made no secret of his views; no concealment of his religion. He boldly avowed himself an Infidel.

"When Mr. Lincoln was a candidate for our legislature, he was accused of being an Infidel and of having said that Jesus was an illegitimate child. He never denied his opinions nor flinched from his religious views. He was a true man, and yet it may be truthfully said that in 1837 his religion was low indeed. In his moments of gloom he would doubt, if he did not sometimes deny, God.

"Mr. Lincoln ran for Congress against the Rev. Peter Cartwright in the year 1846. In that contest he was accused of being an Infidel, if not an Atheist. He never denied the charge—would not—'would die first.' In the first place, because it could and would be proved on him; and in the second place, he was too true to his own convictions, to his own soul, to deny it.

"When Mr. Lincoln left this city for Washington, I knew he had undergone no change in his religious opinions or views. He held many of the Christian ideas in abhorrence, and among them this one, namely, that God would forgive the sinner for a violation of his laws. Lincoln maintained that God could not forgive; that Christianity was wrong in teaching forgiveness.

"From what I know of Mr. Lincoln, and from what I have heard and verily believe, I can say, first, that he did not believe in special creation, his idea being that all creation was an evolution under law; secondly, that he did not believe that the Bible was a special revelation from God, as the Christian world contends; thirdly, he did not believe in miracles as understood by Christians; fourthly, he believed in universal inspiration and miracles under law; fifthly, he did not believe that Jesus was the Christ, the son of God, as the Christian church contends; sixthly, he believed that all things, both matter and mind, were governed by laws, universal, absolute and eternal. All his speeches and remarks in Washington conclusively prove this. Law was to Lincoln everything, and special interferences, shams and delusions."

In 1874, Mr. Herndon delivered in Springfield a lecture on Lincoln's religion, in reply to the Rev. J. A. Reed, who had claimed that he was a believer. It was published in the **State Register**. I quote the following excerpts:

"It is a curious fact that when any man by his genius, good fortune, or otherwise rises to public notice or fame, it does not make much difference what life he led, that the whole world claims him as a Christian, to be forever held up to view as a hero and a saint during all the coming ages, just as if religion would die out of the soul of man unless the great dead be canonized as a model Christian. This is a species of hero or saint worship. Lincoln they are determined to enthrone among the saints, to be forever worshiped as such."

"I believe that Mr. Lincoln did not late in life become a firm believer in the Christian religion. What! Mr. Lincoln discard his logical faculties and reason with his heart? What! Mr. Lincoln believe that Jesus was the Christ of God, the true and only begotten son of him, as the Christian creed contends? What! Mr. Lincoln believe that the New Testament is of special divine authority, and fully inspired, as the Christian contends? What! Mr. Lincoln abandon his lifelong ideas of universal, eternal and absolute laws and contend that the New Testament is any more inspired than Homer's poems, Milton's **Paradise Lost**, than Shakespeare, than his own eloquent and inspired oration at Gettysburg? What! Mr. Lincoln believe that the great creator had connection through the form and instrumentality of a shadow with a Jewish girl? Blasphemy! These things must be believed and acknowledged in order to be a Christian."

"One word concerning this discussion about Mr. Lincoln's religious views. It is important in this: 1. It settles an historic fact. 2. It makes it possible to write a true history of a man free from the fear of fire and stake. 3. It assures the reading public that the life of Mr. Lincoln will be truly written. 4. It will be a warning forever to all untrue men, that the life they have lived will be held up to view. 5. It should convince the Christian pulpit and press that it is impossible in this day, at least in America, to daub up sin, and make a hero out of a fool, a knave, or a villain, which Mr. Lincoln was not. Some true spirit will drag the fraud and lie out to the light of day. 6. Its tendency will be to arrest and put a stop to romantic biographies. And now let it be written in history, and on Mr. Lincoln's tomb: 'He died an unbeliever.'"

In the **Liberal Age**, published in Milwaukee, Mr. Herndon, in 1883, contributed an article on "Lincoln's Religion." From it I quote the following excerpts:

"In 1837, Mr. Lincoln moved to the city of Springfield, and there came across many people of his own belief. They called themselves at that time Freethinkers. Some of these men were highly educated and polished gentlemen. Mr. Lincoln read in this city Hume, Gibbon, and other liberal books. He was in this city from 1837 to 1861, an Infidel—Freethinker—Liberal—Free Religionist—of the radical type.

"In his philosophy he was a realist, as opposed to an idealist; he was a sensationalist, as opposed to an intuitionalist; and was a materialist as opposed to a spiritualist.

"Some good men and women say Mr. Lincoln was a Christian because he was a moral man. They say he was a **rational** Christian, because he loved morality. Do not other people, who are not Christians, love morality? Morality is not **the** test of Christianity, by any means. If it is the test, then all moral men, Atheists, Agnostics, Infidels, Mohammedans, Buddhists, Mormons and the rest, are Christians. A **rational** Christian is an anomaly, an impossibility; because where reason is left free, it demands proofs—it relies upon experience, observation, logic, nature, laws. Why not call Mr. Lincoln a rational Buddhist, a rational Mohammedan, a rational Confucian, a rational Mormon, for all of these, if true to their faith, love morality?

"Did not Mr. Lincoln believe in prayer as a means of moving God? It is said to me by Christians, touching his religion: 'Did he not, in his parting speech in Springfield, in 1861, say, "I hope you, my friends, will pray that I may receive," etc?' and to which I say, yes. In his last Inaugural he said, 'Fondly do we hope, fervently do we pray.' These expressions are merely conventional. They do not prove that Mr. Lincoln believed that prayer is a means of moving God . . . He believed, as I understood him, that human prayer did the **prayer** good; that prayer was but a drum-beat—the taps of the spirit on the living human soul, arousing it to acts of repentance for bad deeds done, or to inspire it to a loftier and higher effort for a nobler and grander life.

"Did Mr. Lincoln, in his said Inaugural, say: 'Both read the same **Word of God**'? No, because that would be admitting revelation. He said: 'Both read the same **Bible**.' Did Mr. Lincoln say: 'Yet if God wills it (the war) continue till all the wealth piled up by the bondsman's 250 years of unrequited toil shall be sunk, and until every drop of blood drawn by the lash shall be paid with another drawn by the sword, **as was said by God** 3,000 years ago'? He did not; he was cautious and said: 'As was said 3,000 years ago.' Jove never nods."

A little later in the same year, Herndon wrote an article for the New York **Truth Seeker**, on "Abraham Lincoln's Religious Belief." The following excerpts are of interest:

"In 1842, I heard Mr. Lincoln deliver a speech before the Washingtonian Temperance Society, of this city. . . . He scored the Christians for the position they had taken. He said in that lecture this: 'If they [the Christians] believe, as they profess— that Omnipotence condescended to take on himself the form of sinful man,' etc. This was spoken with energy. He scornfully and contemptuously emphasized the words, **as they profess**. The rebuke was as much in the manner of utterance as in the substance of what was said. I heard the criticisms of some of the Christians that night. They said the speech was an outrage."

"It is my opinion that no man ever heard Mr. Lincoln pray, in the true evangelistic sense of that word. His philosophy is against all human prayer, as a means of reversing God's decrees."

"He has told me often that there was no freedom in the human will, and no punishment beyond this world. He denied God's higher law, and wrote on the margin of a newspaper to his friends in the Chicago convention in 1860, this: 'Lincoln agrees with Seward in his irrepressible conflict idea; but he is opposed to Seward's **higher law**.' This paper was handed to Judge Davis, Judge Logan, and other friends."

"Mr. Lincoln and a minister, whose name is kept in the dark, had a conversation about religion. It appears that Mr. Lincoln said that when his son—bone of his bone, and blood of his own heart—died, though a severe affliction, it did not arouse him to think of Christ; but when he saw the graves of so many soldiers—strangers to him . . . that sad sight aroused him to love Jesus. . . . It is a fine thing for the reputation of the 'Illinois Clergyman' that his name to the world is unknown. It is a most heartless thing, this supposed conversation of Lincoln with the Illinois clergyman. What! Lincoln feel more for the **graves** of strangers than for the death of his once living, loving, and lovable son, now dead, moldering to ashes in the silent tomb! The charge is barbarous. To make Lincoln a lover of Jesus, whom he once ridiculed, this minister makes him a savage."

"I wish to give an illustration of the uncertainty and unreliability of those loose things that float around in the newspapers of the day, and how liable things are to be inaccurate— so made even by the best of men. Mr. Lincoln, on the morning he started for Washington to take the oath of office, and be inaugurated President of this great republic, gave a short farewell address to his old friends. It was eloquent and touching. The speech is copied in Holland's **Life of Lincoln**, in Arnold's **Lincoln and Slavery**, and in Lamon's **Life of Lincoln**, and no two are exactly alike. If it is hard to get the exact truth on such occasions as this, how impossible to get at Mr. Lincoln's sayings which have been written out by men weeks and months after what he said have passed by! All these loose and foolish things that Mr. Lincoln is supposed to have said are like the cords of driftwood, floating on the bosom of the great Mississippi, down to the great gulf of—Forgetfulness. Let them go." In his **Life of Lincoln,** pp. 445-446, Mr. Herndon said: "No man had a stronger or firmer faith in Providence—God—than Mr. Lincoln, but the continued use by him late in life of the word **God** must not be interpreted to mean that he believed in a personal God. In 1854, he asked me to erase the word God from a speech I had written and read to him for criticism, because my language indicated a personal God, whereas he insisted that no such personality ever existed."

I shall conclude this Appendix by quoting from private letters from Herndon to Mr. Remsburg, and published for the first time in **Abraham Lincoln: Was He a Christian?** in 1893.

"I was the personal friend of Lincoln from 1834 to the day of his death. In 1843 we entered into a partnership which was never formally dissolved. When he became unpopular in this Congressional district because of his speeches on the Mexican War, I was faithful to him. When he espoused the anti-slavery cause and in the eyes of most men had hopelessly ruined his political prospects, I stood by him, and through the press defended his course. In those dark hours, by our unity of sentiment and by political ostracism, we were driven to a close and enduring friendship. You should take it for granted, then, that I knew Mr. Lincoln well. During all this time, from 1834 to 1862, when I last saw him, he never intimated to me, either directly or indirectly, that he had changed his religious opinions. Had he done so—had he let drop one word or look in that direction, I should have detected it.

"I had an excellent private library,* probably the best in the city for admired books. To this library Mr. Lincoln had, as a matter of course, full and free access at all times. I purchased such books as Locke, Kant, Fichte, Lewes; Sir William Hamilton's **Discussions on Philosophy;** Spencer's **First Principles, Social Statics,** etc.; Buckle's **History of Civilization,** and Lecky's **History of Rationalism.** I also possessed the works of Paine, Parker, Emerson and Strauss; Gregg's **Creed of Christendom, McNaught on Inspiration,** Volney's **Ruins,** Feuerbach's **Essence of Christianity,** and other works on Infidelity. Mr. Lincoln read some of these works. About the year 1843 he borrowed **The Vestiges of Creation** of Mr. James W. Keyes, of this city, and read it carefully. He subsequently read the sixth edition of this work, which I loaned him. Mr. Lincoln had always denied special creation, but from his want of education he did not know just what to believe. He adopted the progressive and development theory as taught more or less directly in that work. He despised speculation, especially in the metaphysical world. He was purely a practical man. He adopted Locke's notions as to his system of mental philosophy, with some modifications to suit his own views. He held that reason drew her inferences as to law, etc., from observations, experience and reflection on the facts and phenomena of Nature. He was a pure sensationalist, except as above. He was a materialist in his philosophy. He denied dualism, and at times immortality in any sense.

"Before I wrote my Abbott letter, I diligently searched through Lincoln's letters, speeches, state papers, etc., to find the word **immortality,** and I could not find it anywhere except in his letter to his father. The word **immortality** appears but once in his writings."

"If he had been asked the plain question, 'Do you **know** that a God

---

*A Springfield book seller is quoted as saying that Mr. Herndon was the largest book buyer in the city.

exists?' he would have said: 'I do **not know** that a God exists.' "

"At one moment of his life I know that he was an Atheist. I was preparing a speech on Kansas, and in it, like nearly all reformers, I invoked **God**. He made me wipe out that word and substitute the word **Maker**, affirming that said Maker was a principle of the universe. When he went to Washington he did the same to a friend there."

"Mr. Lincoln told me, over and over, that man has no freedom of the will, or, as he termed it, 'No man has a freedom of mind.' He was in one sense a fatalist, and so he died. He believed that he was under the thumb of Providence (which to him was but another name for fate). The longer he lived, the more firmly he believed it, and hence his oft invocation of God. But these invocations are no evidence to a rational mind that he adopted the blasphemy that God seduced his own daughter, begat a son on purpose to have mankind kill him, in order that he, God, might become reconciled to his own mistakes, according to the Christian view."

"Lincoln would wait patiently on the flow and logic of events. He believed that conditions make the man and not man the conditions. Under his own hand he says: 'I attempt no compliment to my own sagacity. I claim not to have controlled events, but confess plainly that events have controlled me.' He believed in the supreme reign of law. This law **fated** things, as he would express it. Now, how could a man be a Christian—could believe that Jesus Christ was God—could believe in the efficacy of prayer—and entertain such a belief?"

"He did not believe in the efficacy of prayer, although he used that conventional language. He said in Washington, 'God has his own purposes.' If God has his own purposes, then prayer will not change God's purposes."

"I have often said to you, and now repeat it, that Lincoln was a scientific materialist, i. e., that this was his tendency as opposed to the Spiritualistic idea. Lincoln always contended that general and universal laws ruled the Universe—always did—do now—and ever will. He was an Agnostic generally, sometimes an Atheist."

"That Mr. Lincoln was an Infidel from 1834 to 1861, I know, and that he remained one to the day of his death, I honestly believe. I always understood that he was an Infidel, sometimes bordering on Atheism. I never saw any change in the man, and the change could not have escaped my observation had it happened."

"Lincoln's task was a terrible one. When he took the oath of office his soul was bent on securing harmony among all the people of the North, and so he chose for his cabinet officers his opponents for the Presidential candidacy in order and as a means of creating a united North. He let all parties, professions, and callings have their way where their wishes did not cut across his own. He was apparently pliant and supple. He ruled men when men thought they were ruling him. He often said to me that the Christian religion was a dangerous element to deal with when aroused. He saw in the Kansas affairs—in the whole history of slavery, in fact—its rigor and encroachments, that Christianity was aroused. It must be controlled, and that in the right direction. Hence he bent to it, fed it, and kept it within bounds, well knowing that it would crush his administration to atoms unless appeased. His oft and oft invocations of God, his conversations with Christians, his apparent respect for Christianity, etc., were all means to an end. And yet sometimes he showed that he hated its nasal whines."

"A gentleman of veracity in Washington told me this story and vouched for its truthfulness: 'A tall saddle-faced man,' he said, 'came to Washington to pray with Lincoln, having declared this to be his intention at the hotel. About 10 o'clock a.m. the bloodless man, dressed in black, with white cravat, went to the White House, sent in his card, and was admitted. Lincoln glanced at the man and knew his motives in an instant. He said to him, angrily: "What, have you, too, come to torment me with your prayers?" The man was squelched and said, "No, Mr. Lincoln"—lied out and out. Lincoln spoiled those prayers.' "

"Mr. Lincoln was thought to be understood by the mob. But what a delusion! He was one of the most reticent men that ever lived. All of us—Stuart, Speed, Logan, Matheny, myself and others, had to guess at much of the man. He was a mystery to the world—a sphinx to most men. One peculiarity of Mr. Lincoln was his irritability when anyone tried to peep into his own mind's laboratory. Considering all this, what can be thought of the stories about what he is said to have confided to strangers in regard to his religion?"

"I see frequently quoted a supposed speech made by Mr. Lincoln to the colored people of Baltimore, on the presentation of a Bible to him. This supposed speech contains the following: 'All the good from the Saviour of the world is communicated to us through this book.' This idea is false and foolish. What becomes of nine-tenths of the life of Jesus of which we have no history—nine-tenths of the great facts of this grand man's life not recorded in this book? Mr. Lincoln was full and exact in his language. He never used the word Saviour, unless in a conventional sense; in fact, he never used the word at all. Again, he is made to say: 'But for this book, we could not know right from wrong.' The lowest organized life, I was about to say, knows right from wrong in its particular sphere. Every good dog that comes in possession of a bone, knows that the bone belongs to him, and he knows that it is wrong for another dog to rob him of it. He protests with bristling hair and glistening teeth against such dog robbery. It requires no revelation to teach him right from wrong in the dog world; yet it requires a special revelation from God to teach us right from wrong in the human world. According to this speech, the dog has the advantage. But Mr. Lincoln never uttered such nonsense."

"I do think that anyone who knew Mr. Lincoln—his history—his philosophy—his opinions—and still asserts that he was a Christian, is an unbounded falsifier. I hate to speak thus planly, but I cannot respect an untruthful man."

"Let me ask the Christian claimant a few questions. Do you mean to say, when you assert that Mr. Lincoln was a Christian, that he believed that Jesus was the Christ of God, as the evangelical world contends? If so, where did you get this information? Do you mean to say that Mr. Lincoln was a converted man and that he so declared? If so, where, when, and before whom did he declare or reveal it? Do you mean to say that Mr. Lincoln joined a Church? If so, what Church did he join, and when did he join it? Do you mean to say that Mr. Lincoln was a secret Christian, acting under the cloak of the devil to advance Christianity? If so, what is your authority? If you will tell me when it was that the Creator caught in his almighty arms, Abraham, and held him fast while he poured the oil of grace on his rebellious soul, then I will know when it was that he was converted from Infidel views to Christianity."

"The best evidence this side of Lincoln's own written statement that he was an Infidel, if not an Atheist, as claimed by some, is the fact that he never mentions the name of Jesus. If he was a Christian, it could be proved by his letters and speeches. That man is a poor defender of a principle, of a person, or a thing, who never mentions that principle, person or thing. I have never seen the name of Jesus mentioned by Mr. Lincoln."

"Mr. Lincoln never mentioned the name of Christ in his letters and speeches as a Christian. I have searched for such evidence, but could not find it. I have had others search, but they could not find it. This dead silence on the part of Mr. Lincoln is overwhelming proof that he was an unbeliever."

"While Lincoln frequently, in a conventional way, appeals to God, he never appeals to Christ nor mentions him. I know that he at first maintained that Jesus was a bastard, and later that he was the son of Joseph and not of God."

"Lincoln was not a Christian in any sense other than that he lived a good life and was a noble man. If a good life constitutes one a Christian, then Mill and a million other men who repudiated and denied Christianity were Christians, for they lived good and noble lives."

"If Mr. Lincoln changed his religious views, he owed it to me to warn me, as he above all other men caused me to become an unbeliever. He said nothing to me, intimated nothing to me, either directly or indirectly. He owed this debt to many young men whom he had led astray, if astray the Christian calls it. I know of two young men of promise, now dead and gone—gone into endless misery, according to the evangelical creed—caused by Lincoln's teachings. I know some of the living here, men in prominent positions of life, who were made unbelievers by him."

"One by one, these apocryphal stories go by the board. Courageous and remorseless criticism will wipe out all these things. There will not be a vestige of them in 50 years to laugh at or to weep at."

APPENDIX V

THANKSGIVING PROCLAMATIONS

Thanksgiving Day had its origin with the Pilgrim Fathers, who, in 1621, after the first harvest, met together to thank God for the blessings of the past year. Abraham Lincoln, in 1863, issued such a proclamation to please the religious element of the country, and repeated it in 1864. I have mentioned that Thomas Jefferson, in his eight years of office, declined to issue such a document, holding that he had no legal right to do so. Two letters have recently been unearthed, written by Presidents Jackson and Taylor, in which it appears that both of these chief executives made the same refusal, and gave their reasons for so doing. These letters were published in the **New York Times**, and are the property of Thomas F. Madagan, an autograph dealer of New York City.

President Jackson wrote:

"Washington, June 12th, 1832.

"Dr. Sir: I have the pleasure to acknowledge the receipt of your letter of the 10th inst. submitting to me an extract from the minutes of the session of the General Synod of the Reformed Church of North America, relative to the observance of a day for fasting, humiliation and prayer, at this time, which it is recommended that the President of the United States should appoint. Whilst I concur with the Synod in the efficacy of prayer, and in the hope that our country may be preserved from the attacks of pestilence, 'and that the judgments now abroad in the earth may be sanctified to the nations,' I am constrained to decline the designation of any period or mode as proper for the public manifestation of this reliance. I could not do otherwise without transcending the limits prescribed by the Constitution for the President, without feeling that I might in some degree disturb the security which religion now enjoys in this country, in its complete separation from the political concerns of the General Government.

"It is the province of the pulpits and the state tribunals to recommend the mode by which the people may best attest their reliance on the protecting arm of the Almighty in times of great public distress. Whether the apprehension that the cholera may visit our land furnishes a proper occasion for their solemn notice, I must therefore leave to their consideration.

"Your other letters were duly recd. I am awaiting further information from the Cherokees before I reply to them.

"I am, very respectfully,

"Yr. Servt.

"ANDREW JACKSON,

"The Revd. J. F. Schermerhorn."

President Taylor's letter:

"Washington, Nov. 5, 1849.

"Sir: Your communication of Oct. 6th in relation to a proclamation for a day of National Thanksgiving was duly received, and, with many others of the same import, has been considered with the attention which its importance demands.

While uniting cordially in the universal feeling of thankfulness to God for his manifold blessings, and especially for the abatement of pestilence which so lately walked in our midst, I have yet thought it most proper to leave the subject of a Thanksgiving Proclamation where custom in many parts of the country has so long consigned it, in the hands of the Governors of the several States. This decision has been strengthened by the consideration that this is the season usually set apart for that purpose, and that several of the Governors have already issued their annual proclamations accordingly.

"With respect, I remain,

"Yr. friend and Obt. Servt.

"Z. TAYLOR.

"Revd. Nicholas Murray,
"Mod. Genl. Assem. Pres. Church,
"Elizabethtown, N.J."

Since Lincoln started the custom during the Civil War, it has been generally continued.

Bibliography

Adams, Charles Francis (Editor). *The Works of John Adams*, 10 volumes. Boston, Little, Brown & Co., 1856.

Adams, John and Abigail. *Letters of John Adams and his Wife*. New York City, Hurd & Houghton, 1871.

Adams, John Quincy. *Diary of*, 1787-1788, *While a Law Student in the Office of Theophilus Parsons at Newburyport, Mass.* Boston, Little, Brown & Co.

Adams, John Quincy. *Poems*. Auburn, N.Y., Derby & Miller, 1850. *The Diary of John Quincy Adams.* Edited by Allen Nevins, New York City, Longmans, Green & Co.

Adams, John Quincy, and Charles Francis. *Life of John Adams.* Philadelphia, J. B. Lippincott, 1871.

Americana Encyclopedia. New York City, Scientific American Publishing Co.

Badeau, Adam. *Grant in Peace from Appomattox to Mt. McGregor.* Hartford, Conn., S. S. Scranton & Co., 1887.

Baker, Ray Stannard. *Woodrow Wilson, Life and Letters.* New York City, Doubleday, Page & Co., 1927.

Barry, David S. *Forty Years in Washington.* Little, Brown & Co., 1924.

Bennett, D. M. *A Truth Seeker Around the World.* New York City, The Truth Seeker Co., 1883. *Champions of the Church, Their Crimes and Persecutions.* New York City, 1876. *Report of Trial of.* New York City, 1879. D. M. Bennett.

Benton, Thomas Hart. *Thirty Years View: A History of the Workings of the American Government for Thirty Years.* Two volumes. New York City, D. Appleton & Co., 1856.

Beveridge, Albert J. *Abraham Lincoln 1809-1858.* Boston and New York, Houghton, Mifflin & Co., 1928. *The Life of John Marshall.* Four volumes. Boston and New York, Houghton, Mifflin & Co.

Blaine, James G. *Eulogy on James A. Garfield.* Washington, D.C., Government Printing Office. *Twenty Years of Congress.* Two volumes. Norwich, Conn., Henry Bill & Co., 1885.

Broun, Heywood, and Margaret Lynch. *Anthony Comstock, Roundsman of the Lord.* New York City, Albert & Charles Boni, 1927.

Browne, Francis Fisher. *The Every-Day Life of Abraham Lincoln.* Chicago, Brown & Howell Co., 1913.

Bundy, J. M. *The Life of James Abram Garfield.* New York, A. S. Barnes & Co., 1880.

Carpenter, Frank B. *Anecdotes and Personal Reminiscences of President Lincoln.* Published serially in the New York *Independent*, and afterwards in book form.

Chapman, Ervin, D. D. *Latest Light on Abraham Lincoln.* One volume. Chicago, Fleming H. Revell & Co., 1917.

Clark, Allen C. *Life and Letters of Dolly Madison.* Washington, D.C., W. F. Roberts Co., 1914.

Conway, Moncure Daniel. *Autobiography, Memories and Experiences.* Boston and New York, Houghton, Mifflin & Co., 1904. *Life of Thomas Paine.* London, Rationalist Press Association Reprint, 1909.

Cobb, Sanford H. *The Rise of Religious Liberty in America.* New York City, The Macmillan Co., 1902.

Curtis, William E. *Abraham Lincoln.* Philadelphia and London, J. B. Lippincott Co., 1902.

Decker, Carl, and Angus McSween. *Historic Arlington.* Washington, D.C., Decker & McSween Publishing Co., 1892.

Doherty, Edward. *Grover Fished on Sunday*. In *Liberty*, September 27, 1930.
Duffey, Herbert S. *William Howard Taft*. New York, Minton, Balch & Co., 1930.
Encyclopedia Britannica. 14th Edition, article, "Abraham Lincoln." 1930.
First World Convention, *Churches of Christ, Program of*. Washington, D.C., 1930.
Fiske, John. *The American Revolution*. Two volumes. Houghton, Mifflin & Co., 1919.
Ford, Paul Leicester. *The True George Washington*. Philadelphia, J. B. Lippincott, 1896.
Francis, Dr. J. W. *Old New York*. New York City, W. J. Widdleton, 1856.
Gay, Sidney Howard. *James Madison*. Boston, Houghton, Mifflin & Co., 1912.
Gilman, Daniel C. *James Monroe*. In American Statesman Series, Boston, Houghton, Mifflin & Co., 1911.
Goodell, William. *Slavery and Anti-Slavery*. Boston, 1852.
Goodrich, Frederick E. *The Life and Public Service of Grover Cleveland*. Meadville, Pa., Beach & Odell, 1888.
Griffis, William Elliott. *Millard Fillmore*. Ithaca, N.Y., Andrus & Church, 1915.
Gross, Anthony (Editor). *Lincoln's Own Stories*. Garden City, N.Y., Publishing Co.
Harper & Bros. *Encyclopedia of United States History*. 10 volumes. New York City, 1902.
Hawthorne, Nathaniel. *Life of Franklin Pierce*. Boston, Ticknor, Reed & Fields, 1852.
Herndon, W. H., and Jesse W. Weik. *Abraham Lincoln, The True Story of a Great Life*. Two volumes. New York City, D. Appleton & Co., 1892.
Hildreth, Richard. *History of the United States of America*. Three volumes. New York City, Harper & Bros., 1849.
Holland, J. G. *Life of Abraham Lincoln*. Springfield, Mass., Gordon Bill, 1866.
Hubbard, Elbert. *Little Journeys to the Homes of American Statesmen*. New York City and London, G. P. Putnam's Sons, 1898.
Hughes, Rupert. *George Washington, The Human Being and the Hero*. New York City, William Morrow & Co., 1926. *George Washington, the Rebel and the Patriot*. William Morrow & Co., 1927. *George Washington, The Savior of the States*. William Morrow & Co., 1930.
Hunt, Gaillard. *The Life of James Madison*. New York City, Doubleday, Page & Co., 1902.
Jefferson, Thomas. *Writings*. 10 volumes. New York City, G. P. Putnam's Sons, 1894. Four volumes, published in 1829.
King, General Charles. *The True U. S. Grant*. Philadelphia, J. B. Lippincott, 1915.
Lamon, Ward H. *Life of Abraham Lincoln*. Boston, 1872. *Recollections of Abraham Lincoln*. Washington, D.C., 1911.
Lincoln, Abraham. *Complete Works*. Edited by John C. Nicolay and John Hay. New York City, The Century Co., 1894.
Lynch, Denis Tilden. *An Epoch and a Man: Martin Van Buren and His Time*. New York City, Horace Liveright, 1929.
Madison, James. *Works*. Four volumes. Philadelphia, J. B. Lippincott, 1865.
Martin, Carlos. *Wendell Phillips*. New York City, Funk & Wagnalls, 1890.
McCabe, Joseph. *Biographical Dictionary of Modern Rationalists*. London, Watts & Co., 1920.
McCormac, Eugene Irving. *James K. Polk, A Political Biography*. Berkeley, Calif., University of California Press, 1922.
Metcalf, Henry Harrison. *Dedication of the Statue of Franklin Pierce*. Published by the State of New Hampshire, Concord, 1914.
Montgomery, H. *The Life of Major General Zachary Taylor, Twelfth President of the United States*. Auburn, N.Y., Derby & Miller, 1851. *Life of William Henry Harrison, Ninth President of the United States*. Philadelphia, The John C. Winston Co.

Moran, Thomas Francis. *American Presidents, Their Individualities and Their Contributions to American Progress*. New York City, Thomas Y. Crowell Co., 1928.

Morgan, George. *Life of James Monroe*. Boston.

Morgan, James. *Our Presidents*. New York City, The Macmillan Co., 1926.

Mosheim, John Lawrence. *An Ecclesiastical History from the Birth of Christ to the Beginning of the 18th Century*. London, Thomas Tegg & Son, 1838.

Munsey's Magazine. "Barbara Frietchie." January, 1902, volume 26, page 542.

Nicolay & Hay. *Life of Abraham Lincoln*. 10 volumes. New York City, The Century Co., 1909.

Nicholas, Prof. Roy F. *Private letter*. February 24, 1931.

Oldroyd, O. H. *The Lincoln Memorial Album*.

Parker, Theodore. *Historic Americans*. Boston, Horace B. Fuller, 1878.

Parton, James. *Life of Andrew Jackson*. Three volumes. New York City, Mason Bros., 1861. *Life of Thomas Jefferson*. Cambridge, Houghton, Mifflin & Co., The Riverside Press, 1880.

Paine, Thomas. *Age of Reason*. New York City, G. P. Putnam's Sons, 1890. *Works of*. Boston, J. P. Mendum, 1870.

Plunkett, Mrs. H. M. *Josiah Gilbert Holland*. New York City, Charles Scribner's Sons, 1894.

Poore, Ben Perley. *Reminiscences of 60 Years in the National Capital*. Two volumes. Philadelphia, Hubbard & Howard Co., 1886.

Putnam, George Haven. *Memories of a Publisher*. New York City, G. P. Putnam's Sons, 1915. *Memories of My Youth*. New York City, G. P. Putnam's Sons, 1914.

Putnam, Samuel P. *Four Hundred Years of Freethought*. New York City, The Truth Seeker Co., 1894.

Randall, Henry S. *The Life of Thomas Jefferson*. Three volumes, New York City, Derby & Jackson, 1858.

Rankin, Henry B. *Personal Recollections of Abraham Lincoln*. New York, City, G. P. Putnam's Sons, 1916.

Raymond, Henry J. *The Life and Public Services of Abraham Lincoln*. New York City, Derby & Miller, 1865.

Read, Opie. *I Remember*. New York City, Richard R. Smith, 1930.

Remsburg, J. E. *Six Historic Americans*. New York City, The Truth Seeker Co., 1906.

Rice, Allen Thorndike (Editor). *Reminiscences of Abraham Lincoln*, New York City.

Ridpath, John Clark. *Life and Work of James A. Garfield*. New York City, Phillips & Hunt, 1881.

Roosevelt, Theodore. *An Autobiography*. New York City, Scribner's, 1929. *Gouverneur Morris*. Boston, Houghton, Mifflin & Co., 1888.

Sandburg, Carl. *Abraham Lincoln, the Prairie Years*. Two volumes. New York City, Harcourt, Brace & Co., 1927.

Scribner's Monthly. Volumes 4 and 5.

Simpson, Bishop Matthew. *Funeral Address over Abraham Lincoln*. Christian Advocate, New York City, February 11, 1904.

Smith, Theodore Clark. *The Life and Letters of James Abram Garfield*. Two volumes. New Haven, Yale University Press, 1925.

Sparks, Jared. *Life of George Washington*. Boston, Tappan & Dennet, 1843.

Sprague, William B. *Annals of the American Pulpit*. New York City, Robert Carter & Bros., 1859.

Stryker, Lloyd Paul. *Andrew Johnson, A Study in Courage*. New York City, The Macmillan Co., 1929.

Thompson, Richard W. *Recollections of 16 Presidents from Washington to Lincoln*. Indianapolis, Bowen, Merrill Co., 1894.

Tyler, Lyon G. *The Letters and Times of the Tylers*. Richmond, Whittet & Shepperson, 1884.

Van Buren, Martin. *Autobiography*. Edited by John C. Fitzpatrick. Washington, Government Printing Office, 1920.

Villard, Oswald Garrison. *John Brown, A Biography 50 Years After.* Boston, Houghton, Mifflin & Co., 1910.

Ward, Julius H. *The Life and Letters of Bishop White.* New York City, Dodd, Mead & Co., 1892.

Washburn, Charles G. *Theodore Roosevelt, the Logic of His Career.* Boston, Houghton, Mifflin & Co., 1916.

Washington, George. *George Washington's Diaries.* Edited by John C. Fitzpatrick. Four volumes. Cambridge, Houghton, Mifflin & Co., 1925. *Writings.* Edited by Jared Sparks. 10 volumes. Harper & Bros., 1847. *Writings.* Edited by Worthington C. Ford. 14 volumes. New York City, G. P. Putnam's Sons, 1893.

Watson, John F. *Annals of Philadelphia.* Two volumes. Edition of 1850.

Weik, Jesse W. *The Real Lincoln, A Portrait.* Boston and New York City, Houghton, Mifflin & Co., 1922.

White, Andrew Dickson. *A History of the Warfare Between Science and Theology in Christendom.* New York City, D. Appleton & Co., 1894.

White, William Allen. *Woodrow Wilson, the Man, His Times and His Task.*

Williams, Charles Richard. *Diary and Letters of Rutherford B. Hayes.* The Ohio State Archeological and Historical Society, 1926. *Life of Rutherford B. Hayes.* Two volumes. Boston, Houghton, Mifflin & Co., 1914.

Winston, Robert W. *Andrew Johnson, Plebeian and Patriot.* New York City, Henry Holt & Co., 1928.

Wise, Henry A. *Seven Decades of the Union.* Philadelphia, J. B. Lippincott, 1872.

Wise, John A. *Recollections of 13 Presidents.* New York City, Doubleday, Page & Co., 1905.

Wood, Frederick S. *Roosevelt as We Knew Him.* Boston and New York City, The John C. Winston Co., 1927.

Woodward, W. E. *George Washington, The Man and the Image.* New York City, Horace Liveright, 1926. *Meet General Grant.* New York City, Horace Liveright, 1928.